LIBERALISM'S CROOKED CIRCLE

Liberalism's Crooked Circle

LETTERS TO ADAM MICHNIK

BY IRA KATZNELSON

PRINCETON UNIVERSITY PRESS, PRINCETON, NEW JERSEY

Published by Princeton University Press, 41 William Street,
Princeton, New Jersey 08540
In the United Kingdom: Princeton University Press,
Chichester, West Sussex

Library of Congress Cataloging-in-Publication Data

Katznelson, Ira
Liberalism's crooked circle : letters to Adam Michnik / Ira Katznelson
p. cm.
Includes bibliographical references and index.
ISBN 0-691-03438-9 (alk. paper).
1. Liberalism.   2. Socialism.   3. Pluralism (Social sciences)
4. Post-communism.   I. Michnik, Adam.   II. Title.
JC574.K37   1996
320.5'1—dc20   95-43184

This book has been composed in Baskerville

Princeton University Press books are printed on
acid-free paper and meet the guidelines for
permanence and durability of the Committee on
Production Guidelines for Book Longevity of
the Council on Library Resources

Printed in the United States of America by
Princeton Academic Press

10   9   8   7   6   5   4   3   2   1

*For the New School for Social Research
and the values of its
Graduate Faculty of Political and
Social Science*

CONTENTS

PREFACE AND ACKNOWLEDGMENTS

As a fourth-year undergraduate, I enrolled in a tutorial with the Columbia University historian Richard Hofstadter. In the privacy of his Hamilton Hall office, he read aloud my clumsy prose about the Chicago race riot of 1919. With an ironic smile, he would remove his reading glasses to gently exhort: "Surely there must be a more felicitous way to make this point." On occasion, he would talk about the choices authors face in discovering their voice and identifying an audience. He taught me to prize the craft of writing history and social science as an aspect of public life and political responsibility.[1]

Ever since, I have been a pushover for books about the experience of authorship. *The Writing Life* by Annie Dillard recently caught my attention on the shelves of the New York Society Library. Conveying what it is like to invent words and set them down, Dillard discusses getting stuck; the situation when an author is well along in writing a book, "knows what comes next, and yet cannot go on; when every morning for a week or month you enter its room and turn your back on it." I had been turning my back on this book for more than half a year when I read her shrewd assessment that "the trouble is either of two things. Either the structure has forked, so the narrative, or the logic has developed a hairline fracture that will shortly split it up the middle—or you are approaching a fatal mistake." I read on. "What you had planned will not do. If you pursue your present

---

[1] For a brief on behalf of scholarship with a public face focusing on literary criticism and modeled on the example of Lionel Trilling, the author's teacher, see Morris Dickstein, *Double Agent: The Critic and Society* (New York: Oxford University Press, 1992). There is an uncanny similarity in the address Vaclav Havel delivered at Victoria University in New Zealand in March 1995, published as "The Responsibility of Intellectuals," *New York Review of Books*, June 22, 1995.

course, the book will explode or collapse, and you do not know about it yet, quite."[2]

My problem hovered between fracture and fatality. I was trying to perform a task for which I am not equipped, the analysis of change in East and Central Europe (where, for the past decade, I have found myself a frequent traveler and an unexpected participant in certain aspects of scholarly and political life) as I was pursuing a different, if closely related, project motivated by anxieties about developments at home. I thought it urgent to find a fresh way to reflect on the capacities and frailties of Western liberalism at a moment marked not only by Bolshevism's fabulous unanticipated crash and the end of the Cold War, but by a disturbing triumphalism, intellectual weakness and political fragmentation on the left, and a displacement of political struggle to university settings. With the defeat of liberalism's leading adversary, a battle for the soul of liberalism began. Regrettably, prescriptions that advance the least appealing parts of Western liberalism's patrimony—complacency about unwarranted inequalities, silence about key dimensions of private power, contentment with a narrow reading of Western values and civilization, uneasiness with moral and cultural heterogeneity, and a reduction in the scope of politics and the public sphere—have been crowding out more desirable possibilities. In this circumstance, the intellectual and political weakness of the left has been appalling. Bereft of ideas and voters, unsure of its relationship to the liberal or socialist traditions, and divided into movement and interest group subspecialties, the foibles and frailties of the left in the United States and most of Europe have created a political space assertively filled by libertarian, authoritarian populist, nakedly racist, and more traditional elitist versions of the right wing. A tremendous ethical and political opportunity to redefine and reorient the liberal tradition is being squandered.

My attempt to achieve the goal of making sense of changes on the ground in East and Central Europe, I came to realize,

[2] Annie Dillard, *The Writing Life* (New York: Harper and Row, 1989), p. 9.

was paralyzing my endeavor to engage in the fight for the kind of liberalism we should wish to have. The events of late 1989, moreover, were so very novel when I first considered composing this book, and optimism about transitions to democracy so pronounced, that the text I began to write quickly became unbalanced by a lack of perspective. As I walked down Wenceslas Square four months after the velvet revolution, the hub of the modern city and the focal point of the mass events that had brought down the Communist regime, I remembered how I had left Prague only fifteen months earlier with a taste of fear. I had taken complicated precautions with my notes, including the transliteration of key names and addresses into Hebrew. Then, any contact with foreigners had been suspect and closely regulated by the state (in 1988, only some 200 of Prague's 1,500 taxi drivers had been licensed to pick up foreigners from hotels or have contact with them at the airport). As in Poland or Hungary, the other countries to which I had traveled, there had been no mistaking the dividing line between authorities and intellectuals. But in Czechoslovakia there was no social movement to lend support and no possibility of negotiation with the regime; only recurring scholarly unemployment and, as something of a constant, the secret police.

Now, in the festive center of post-Communist Czechoslovakia, the transformation of the grand public space of Wenceslas Square was astonishing. A geography of apprehension had been transformed into a geography of hope. The mood was "like the feeling in a football game when the momentum changes, when helplessness gives way to confidence, and what looked like sure defeat opens up to the possibility of victory."[3] There had been an explosion of color and a fusion of markets and public theater. Posters on the environment (the dangers of Freon), neutrality, and the elections were juxtaposed with pictures of Havel up and down the promenade, with the largest at the base of the statue of King Wenceslas. Just below was a

---

[3] Wallace Stegner, *Where the Bluebird Sings to the Lemonade Springs: Living and Writing in the West* (New York: Random House, 1992), p. xxiii.

xii PREFACE AND ACKNOWLEDGMENTS

table with a petition demanding the equalization of resources for all political parties during the elections. A few yards down the square, a round area with flowers was filled with tens of yellow and orange lit candles surrounding a large picture of Jan Palach, the young man who had immolated himself two decades earlier in protest against the destruction of the Prague Spring, flanked by photographs of Thomas Masaryk, the great figure of interwar Czechoslovakia, and President Eduard Benes, who had governed at the time of the 1948 Communist coup. Teenagers were hawking newspapers on the street. A bookshop attracted a large, jostling crowd to an outdoor table displaying the works of such authors as James Fenimore Cooper and dissident writers like Ivan Klima and Pavel Kohout.

The questions I had begun to ask in this remarkable, but inevitably short-lived, setting of liberation concerned the transformation of dissidents and their movements into governing elites; the challenges they faced from nonliberal forces in their attempts to create liberal democratic societies where such had not existed for at least four decades (and, in some post-Communist countries, never at all); the constitutional and moral questions entailed in making a framework for new regimes; and the creation of categories for a democratic politics at a moment of radical transformation. In such circumstances, I wanted to ask, what is "right" and "left"? These remain pressing issues, but in seeking to craft empirically grounded answers, I was forced to confront not only my lack of specialized knowledge about East and Central Europe but my inability to discern and adequately understand differences in style, language, and the utilization of key political concepts. I simply lacked a way to know when small variations masked large distinctions and when even considerable deviations overlaid fundamental similarities.[4] I knew even less about the region's vital reforms in the areas of finance, privatization, trade, and the price system. Fur-

---

[4] An illuminating discussion of the problem of the East-West contrast and of problems of translation can be found in Perry Anderson, "The Antinomies of Antonio Gramsci," *New Left Review* 100 (November 1976–January 1977).

ther, there was little I as a sometime traveler could add to the rich descriptions of Timothy Garton Ash, the cool analytical coverage of Neal Ascherson, the deeply personal reflections of Eva Hoffman, or the synoptic sweep and embedded interpretations of my colleagues Robert Heilbroner, Jeffrey Goldfarb, and Andrew Arato.[5]

The manner in which I have inquired about liberalism and its prospects after 1989 nonetheless remains deeply inscribed by my experiences in East Europe, by my understanding of the character and implications of dissident political thought, and by my sense that the opportunities to reshape and deepen the liberal tradition opened by the velvet revolutions have yet to be seized. If 1989 is to prove genuinely revolutionary not only for having put Bolshevism to rest but for liberalism itself,[6] I believe we need to focus on the issues of equality and pluralism and their relationship to the liberal tradition. By pursuing these

[5] Timothy Garton Ash, *The Polish Revolution: Solidarity* (New York: Scribner, 1984); Timothy Garton Ash, *The Uses of Adversity: Essays on the Fate of Central Europe* (New York: Random House, 1989); Timothy Garton Ash, *The Magic Lantern: The Revolution of '89 Witnessed in Warsaw, Budapest, Berlin, and Prague* (New York: Random House, 1990); Neal Ascherson, *The Polish August: The Self-Limiting Revolution* (New York: Viking Press, 1982); Neal Ascherson, *The Struggles for Poland* (New York: Random House, 1987); Eva Hoffman, *Lost in Translation: A Life in a New Language* (New York: E.P. Dutton, 1989); Eva Hoffman, *Exit into History: A Journey through the New Eastern Europe* (New York: Viking, 1993); Robert Heilbroner, *21st Century Capitalism* (New York: Norton 1993); Jeffrey Goldfarb, *Beyond Glasnost: The Post-Totalitarian Mind* (Chicago: University of Chicago Press, 1989); Jeffrey Goldfarb, *After the Fall: The Pursuit of Democracy in Central Europe* (New York: Basic Books, 1992); Andrew Arato, *From Neo-Marxism to Democratic Theory: Essays on the Critical Theory of Soviet-Type Societies* (Armonk, New York: M.E. Sharpe, 1993).

At a critical moment, I was reminded of the possibilities of producing an anodyne travel document when I read the report of John Kenneth Galbraith's trip to Poland and Yugoslavia in 1959, when he was at the peak of his powers. John Kenneth Galbraith, "Heresy Revisited: An Economist's Notebook in Warsaw and Belgrade," *Encounter* 64 (January 1959): 45–53. I also was chastened by Tzvetan Todorov's account of the reports of famous nineteenth-century French travelers to Bulgaria who managed to produce both idyllic and dark reports tinged with remarkable misunderstandings, and by a fine history of European travel by Americans. Tzvetan Todorov, "Bulgaria in France," in Todorov, *The Morals of History* (Minneapolis: University of Minnesota Press, 1995); William W. Stowe, *Going Abroad: European Travel in Nineteenth-Century American Culture* (Princeton: Princeton University Press, 1994).

[6] For a variant of this formulation, see Bruce Ackerman, *The Future of Liberal Revolution* (New Haven: Yale University Press, 1992).

questions, I want to contribute to much-needed debate about the equivocal relationship connecting liberalism and socialism and the uncertain aptitude of both for appreciating and managing deep differences in ethics and group identities.

I think we still have much to learn from the manner in which the democratic opposition to Communism grappled with these puzzles while embracing political liberalism emphatically as a coherent doctrine, as a set of institutions, and as an ethical imperative. In particular, we have much to gain by attending to the opposition's accommodation to more than one type of property relation; to the time horizons of its practical reason; to the way it sought to secure and politicize the zone of the private; and to its keen opposition to unitary thought and practice.[7] I believe these impulses must be central to the purpose of vivifying liberalism at a time when the liberal tradition lacks effective competitors but yet, on its own, is insensible and insufficient, hence in critical respects lacking and vulnerable. I write about these matters as a partisan of the democratic left to ask whether, and how, a toughened critical impulse can be nourished inside liberal ideas, values, and institutions. These, of course, remain pressing issues in East Europe, but they are equally vital where liberalism seems most assured, in the West.

On a recent visit with the sociologist who lives in my former house in Chicago, I asked about the rhythmic Caribbean music deliciously filling the living room. A protest song from the Ukraine, I was told, about a prisoner confined for opposition activities who pined for her lover. The cassette had been brought to the American Midwest by a Ukrainian graduate student who helped look after my friend's son.

Ukrainian reggae! So little seems fixed these days: not our boundaries or institutions; our interests or identities; certainly not our theories or ideologies. At a time no less uncertain, in the year he published *Howard's End*, E. M. Forster observed that

---

[7] Here I draw on Jeffrey Isaac, "The Meanings of 1989," ms., 1993.

1941 is not a good year in which to sum up anything. Our judgments, to put it mildly, are not at their prime. We are all of us upon the Leaning Tower, as [Virginia Woolf] called even those of us who date from the nineteenth century, when the earth was still horizontal and the buildings perpendicular. We cannot judge the landscape properly as we look down, for everything is tilted. Isolated objects are not so puzzling; a tree, a wave, a hat, a jewel, an old gentleman's bald head look as they always did. But the relation between objects—that we cannot estimate, and that is why the verdict must be left to another generation.[8]

I have written *Liberalism's Crooked Circle* upon our own Leaning Tower under similar circumstances of uncertainty.[9] This attempt to contribute to political discussion, however, is not a pursuit of objectivity in political or intellectual life; it is, rather, a search for appealing vantage points with which to deal with the permanent shattering of univocity and certitude.

Liberalism's Crooked Circle, however, is firmly rooted in two sets of personal and intellectual engagements: in my experience of the ambition and milieu of my undergraduate teachers at Columbia; and in a quite remarkable decade-long conversation conducted in a network of seminars on democracy superintended by the Graduate Faculty of the New School for Social Research.

My tutorial with Hofstadter had an impact more considerable than the usual set of supervisions, for it provided a window

[8] E. M. Forster, "Virginia Woolf," *Two Cheers for Democracy* (New York: Harcourt, Brace and World, 1951), p. 251.

[9] In thinking about uncertainty, transitions, and change, I have been influenced a good deal by Geoffrey Barraclough's Charles Beard Lectures, delivered at Ruskin College, Oxford, in 1963 and published as *An Introduction to Contemporary History* (New York: Basic Books, 1964). Barraclough stressed two new features of contemporary history: first, that it truly is a world history that cannot be contained within traditional analysis and research, and, second, that the factors that have led to the demise of the world in which Bismarck lived and died do not necessarily provide guideposts to an understanding of the origins or character of the world created in its wake after two world wars, economic crises, massive scientific and technical change, and shifts from individualism to mass democracy, among other central hallmarks.

xvi PREFACE AND ACKNOWLEDGMENTS

into a remarkable effort in which he along with such close colleagues as Lionel Trilling and C. Wright Mills had sought to make liberalism adequate to their time. Disillusioned with marxism, Hofstadter and Trilling were dedicated to a distinctly modern humanism that sought to thicken liberalism by emphasizing pluralism and an ironic, tragic sensibility. Committed both to civility and to the project of the liberal university, they were perplexed and offended by many of the ideas and passions of the New Left, for which Wright Mills was an important founding figure. A part of Trilling's world, Mills had been especially close to Hofstader with whom he shared the comity of mutual regard. My enterprise in this book is quite similar to the project of that generation which tried to bring a sense of complexity into liberalism, in part by bringing it more directly into contact with the sensibilities of European political culture; *Liberalism's Crooked Circle* is located in the intellectual and political space that defined the tensions characterizing the relationship between Hofstadter and Trilling's robust liberalism and the critical New Left impulse of Mills. Like Mills, I find the liberalism of the 1950s to be limited and inadequate, but like its creators I should like to enrich the liberal tradition. I trust the effort would secure Hofstader's characteristic wry smile.

In late 1984, the New School's president Jonathan Fanton, Jeffrey Goldfarb, and Adrian DeWind, a lawyer active in human rights activities and a New School trustee, flew to Warsaw to present an honorary degree to Adam Michnik for his human rights work.[10] This semipublic event attracted some of Poland's leading intellectuals (as well as interest from the state police), who urged the New School to contribute to the region's "Flying University" activities. At the turn of the century, members of Warsaw's leftist intelligentsia had created an institution with this name to signify that it had no fixed place; to secure itself against the Russian secret police, their portable university had to "fly" from location to location. In the fall of 1977, a group of

[10] I discuss Michnik's background and the occasion for the presentation of this award in the introduction.

scholars active in KOR (the Workers' Defence Committee founded in 1976 to support imprisoned workers in the factories of Radom and Ursus)[11] resurrected this idea: "For the freedom to learn," KOR's *Information Bulletin* stated,

> In November of this year a group of scholars took the initiative of organizing a series of lecture courses to be held outside official scholarly organizations. These lectures . . . will address problems that are falsified or disregarded in university studies. Meetings are to take place in private apartments in Warsaw and in other university cities. The planned courses will include: "On the History of People's Poland"—Adam Michnik; "On Economic History and the History of Economic Thought in Contemporary Poland"— Tadeusz Kowalik; "Contemporary Political Ideologies"— Jerzy Jedlicki; "An Overview of Great Discussions of the Postwar Period"—Jan Strzelicki; . . .[12]

The New School soon became a partner to this ongoing pattern of unofficial intellectual life. By 1986, a network of seminars on democracy and democratic theory was meeting under the cochairmanship of Michnik (with the sociologist Jerzy

[11] KOR dissolved in 1981 in deference to Solidarity, the trade union and movement it had helped to spawn.

[12] Jan Jozef Lipski, *KOR; A History of the Workers' Defense Committee in Poland, 1976–1981* (Berkeley: University of California Press, 1985), p. 208. "To its credit," he writes, "KOR agreed immediately that the Flying University was one of the most important social initiatives, and that it had to be supported because of its importance for the national culture. We must also give credit to the intelligence of those in charge of the Security Service that they decided quickly (after several months) that in a totalitarian system such an undertaking constituted a particularly dangerous threat. In order to liquidate this institution, the secret political police, acting on the correct assumption that the stifling of national culture and higher education was crucial to its future good, resorted to particularly brutal methods" (p. 209). On February 11, 1978, the police used tear gas to break up a lecture by Adam Michnik. The next day he was attacked and beaten by police in the street. Immediately thereafter, a declaration signed by fifty-eight scholars announced the founding of the Society for Scientific Courses (p. 211). To that date, Michnik was best known for his 1976 book *Church Left Dialogue* (recently edited, translated, and introduced by David Ost as *The Church and the Left* [Chicago: University of Chicago Press, 1993]), and for a remarkably prescient essay, "A New Evolutionism," also written in 1976, which sought to identify a path to change grounded in civil society that avoided a direct confrontation with state power.

Szacki) in Warsaw, and the chairmanship of Goldfarb in New York; in 1987, the philosopher Gyorgy Bence successfully convened a parallel seminar in Budapest. Participants in the three cities shared readings (each seminar's first session considered Hannah Arendt's *Origins of Totalitarianism*).[13] They also exchanged papers and summaries through the use of couriers. The New School soon initiated scholarly exchanges that sent American colleagues to East Europe and, where possible, brought leading figures from the region to New York; and its journal *Social Research* began to publish special issues devoted to East European social science. Under the brilliant leadership of Elzbieta Matynia, what came to be called the East and Central Europe Program also started an effort to provide scholarly materials to various underground seminars and to a number of research libraries, and it provided grants to younger scholars who, for reasons of political commitment, were unable to find official posts or leave their home countries to work abroad. Today, the democracy seminar network extends to sixteen cities, and the New School has become a significant force for renewing higher education and democratic political life in the region.[14]

Bence perfectly captured the character of the original democracy seminars this way:

> From the professional point of view, the American core is dominated by political theory, but in a special version,

[13] Hannah Arendt, *The Origins of Totalitarianism* (New York: Harcourt, Brace and Company, 1951). Szacki, in an act of solidarity, took up the seminar's organizational work after Michnik was again arrested. After his release, they cochaired the seminar.

[14] In a largely forgotten episode, the New School once before participated in a far-flung, antitotalitarian network of seminars and discussion groups attached to opposition intellectuals. In 1929, a number of antifascist Italian intellectuals in exile in Paris founded Giustizia e Liberta, with close ties to dissidents inside Italy, including Noberto Bobbio, many of whom were arrested by Mussolini's regime. Giustizi e Liberta had branches in the United States, including, under President Alvin Johnson's patronage, one at the New School. A good many of the network's discussions focused on the prospective character of postfascist Italy, including regional issues and the ties between socialism and liberalism. For a discussion, see Nadia Urbinati, "Introduction," in Carlo Rosselli, *Liberal Socialism* (Princeton: Princeton University Press, 1994), pp. xxvii–xxxi.

characteristic of this group. They do not handle political theory in an abstract manner as if they were dealing with philosophy, like a good part of mainstream political theorists do, but neither do they base themselves merely on modern, mainly Western, experience, as another part of political science does. Their approach is characterized by a wide, comparative perspective, and considerable historical depth. Their political stand is special, as well. First of all, they are politically committed scholars. On the American political spectrum, they are somewhat between left liberalism and radicalism, but they have never been dogmatic Marxists or communists. In a European terminology, they would belong to the non-dogmatic Left. . . . I do not know the work of the Warsaw branch well enough to dare label them in any way. . . . I cannot suppress the suspicion that, if we had to place them on a right-left continuum, a large part of the group would fall somewhere left of the centre.[15]

My largest debt in writing this book is owed to the teachers, friends, colleagues, and institutions already named who created venues for rigorous and realistic discussion of issues that matter in this shared intellectual and political climate and who have sought to craft a broadly common politics marked by the sensibilities and commitments sketched by Bence. Of those I have mentioned, the most outstanding notes of obligation are held by Jonathan Fanton, whose vision and energy not only renewed the New School but tethered the institution to its traditional values of free inquiry and human rights; to Jeffrey Goldfarb, whose exemplary energy and sense of responsibility gave shape to the Democracy Seminar project; and to Elzbieta Matynia, who, even to the moment this manuscript was due at the press, took time to maintain her mentorship, discover new materials, and correct my mistakes. Within the ambit of the extended discussion circle of the New School, I also owe warm thanks to Jan Urban and Alena Hromádková of Prague, Rumyana Kolarova of Sofia, and Kostek Gebert of Warsaw for their tutelage, to Robert Gates for his intellectual and administrative partnership, and to Agnes Heller and the late Ferenc Feher for their intellectual fire and for teaching me that with respect to some subjects one can only write about silences. Jiri Musil and Ivan Szelenyi proved notable walkers and talkers in Prague and Budapest (not to speak of New York). Irene Runge, a rediscovered New York nursery school friend whose refugee Communist parents took her to Germany from New York in 1951, guided me in East Berlin and introduced me to its small Jewish community in the last years of the DDR. In 1979, in better days for Dubrovnik, Steven Lukes first introduced me to the names and personas of key oppositional figures in Czechoslovakia, Poland, and Hungary and to the role he and fellow Oxford scholars had begun to play in the region's underground seminars. Later, he opened doors in Prague at a difficult time.

I am grateful, too, to Krzysztof Michalski and his colleagues at the Institute for the Human Sciences in Vienna. I have been afforded a second vantage point into developments in East Europe by serving on the institute's "Expert Committee" (with colleagues far more expert than I) on the social costs of the post-Communist transformations. There, I have profited especially from excursions to Bratislava in the company of Claus Offe. Walter Lippincott of Princeton University Press encouraged this book from the beginning. Thomas Bender, James Morone, and Sayres Rudy read the penultimate version and provided me with enormously helpful editorial commentary.

Above all, I thank Adam Michnik for so graciously permitting me to incorporate him in this project.

Columbia University
September 1995

LIBERALISM'S CROOKED CIRCLE

INTRODUCTION: THE CLUB OF THE CROOKED CIRCLE

The Talmud cautions us to be wary when a witness offers too many reasons. I hope I have not transgressed this rule. For I have written this book in the light and shadow cast by 1989 to make sense of two Prague stories, to respond to a challenge put to me a dozen years ago by Allan Bloom, and to estimate elements of a public philosophy for the democratic left in the exigent spirit of the "Letter to the New Left" C. Wright Mills composed in 1960.[1]

I

In the opening vignette of Jiri Weil's last novel,[2] two SS men in occupied Prague are ordered to take Mendelssohn's statue from the roof of the Academy of Music. Unsure which is the right one, they resolve to remove the figure with the largest nose. They identify Wagner.

On Sunday, March 18, 1990, a crowd of well over a thousand at the Obecni Dum's Smetana auditorium rose and applauded with solemn dignity as President Vaclav Havel made his way down center aisle. He climbed the stairs to a platform arranged in a single row of chairs underneath a large suspended logo of Charter 77, the most significant Czech dissident organization during the long repression initiated in 1968 by the Soviet

---

[1] The letter was published originally in the *New Left Review* 5 (September/October 1960), then reprinted in the United States under the title "On the New Left," *Studies on the Left* 2 (#1, 1961).

[2] Jiri Weil, *Mendelssohn Is on the Roof* (New York: Penguin Books, 1991). The novel was first published in Czech in 1960.

invasion that quashed the Prague Spring.[3] Across the stage sat the movement's spokespeople, some thirty in number, whose political tendencies ranged from Dubcek-era reform Communism to advocacy of Thatcherite market policies. At considerable personal risk, they had represented democratic and liberal aspirations when these seemed utopian. Havel opened the meeting just four months after the "velvet revolution" of November 1989. His subdued talk began: "In prison and outside, I dreamt of the day Charter 77 could meet in a public hall and not be disturbed by the police." He spoke gently of the egalitarian imperatives of common justice and the conditions of decency. Just when he turned to the moral advantages of a politics oriented to the self-organization of civil society rather than the state, Havel was interrupted by an aide. Apologetically, the leader of the country's new (doomed) binational democracy excused himself to attend to presidential affairs.

As he withdrew and the mood of celebration turned to elegy, I wondered how this anti-king would learn to inhabit the Castle and what a posttotalitarian liberal politics might look like. If totalitarianism is dead, I considered further, is Mendelssohn secure at last on the academy's roof?

Shortly after I left the University of Chicago in 1982, Allan Bloom, who soon became famous for his jeremiad on *The Closing of the American Mind*,[4] invited me back to speak in a series on religion and politics. Bloom was contemptuous of liberalism,

---

[3] The Charter, signed originally by 241 individuals, was created as an appeal to and a monitor of the 1976 Helsinki Accords, which Czechoslovakia had ratified. This number grew to approximately 1,300 signatories in 1987. For a useful treatment, see Gordon Skilling, *Charter 77 and Human Rights in Czechoslovakia* (London: Allen and Unwin, 1981).

[4] Allan Bloom, *The Closing of the American Mind* (New York: Simon and Schuster, 1987). Bloom was a neighbor and a friend when I taught at the University of Chicago. If Michnik is my principal interlocutor, Bloom's challenges make him an implicit second. Like Michnik, he has questioned the character of my radicalism; but unlike Michnik, who has done so from the very best impulses of liberalism, Bloom, who was a student of Leo Strauss and regarded in the academic world for his erudite translations of Plato and Rousseau and for his contributions to the history of political thought, essentially took a premodern stance, preferring the ancients to the moderns. Looking over my shoulder as I talk to Michnik, Bloom remains a demanding challenger

ethical and group pluralism, and the left; that is, of the values I hold dear. His warm but aggressive letter requested that I talk as "a man who is a Jew, a radical, and an American."

I took up the challenge by understanding his "American" to mean an adherent of the best in the liberal tradition, "radical" to refer to my putative socialism, and "Jew" not only to my ethnicity and religion but to my unwillingness to think these superstitious or provincial. I asked whether socialism and liberalism can coexist and whether a multicultural liberalism can be crafted without abjuring demanding common standards of value and purpose. These persist as my central questions. I also explained my skepticism about liberalism's capacities for social justice and genuine pluralism as a product of my experiences as a Jew, a radical, and an American.[5] This remains my orienting stance.

Liberalism's and the left's fate and capacities likewise were vital concerns of Wright Mills in 1948, the year of Czechoslovakia's Communist coup d'etat of February 25. He characterized America's left as "powerless, distracted, and confused." Then, "confronted with the main drift and the program of the right,"[6] the left was disoriented by the start of the Cold War; by an incapacity to make up its mind about the status of marxism and the Bolshevik experiment; by an increasingly assertive assault on the policy legacies of the New Deal (especially the rights of labor); by an ambivalence about the significance of race as compared to class; by a bewildering inability to place the mass murder of the Jews within any of its categories; and by a willful and widespread right-wing demagogy that sought to tarnish and marginalize the left by reducing its complex heterogeneity to

who stands for an important aspect of the right-wing reaction to liberalism currently successful in the United States.

[5] I deal with the American Jewish experience in Ira Katznelson, "Between Separation and Disappearance: Jews on the Margins of American Liberalism," in Pierre Birnbaum and Ira Katznelson, eds., *Paths of Emancipation: Jews, States, and Citizenship* (Princeton: Princeton University Press, 1995).

[6] C. Wright Mills, *The New Men of Power: America's Labor Leaders* (New York: Harcourt, Brace and Company, 1948), p. 250.

an appendage of Stalinism. Soon, pressures for conformity proved overwhelming; even a once iconoclastic intelligentsia turned mainstream.[7]

Today, at the end of a half-century of bipolarity, nuclear standoff, and fierce ideological confrontation, the main drift and program of the right are again at least temporarily ascendant. The New Deal coalition is in tatters, the labor movement is comatose, and race still scars deeply. Further, the end of the Communist era has affected even the staunchly anti-Bolshevik left by delegitimating all kinds of socialism and by exposing to renewed examination the ways in which a significant minority of Western left-wing intellectuals once accommodated to the empire and the domestic depredations of the Soviet Union.[8]

I write, in short, at a time of deep difficulty and disillusionment for the left. In East Europe, its impulses have been kidnapped by opportunist elites of the old regime, or, worse, by authoritarian, xenophobic, ultranationalist fanatics. In the West, the left either has grown fat with power or, more commonly, is withering in opposition. Its social base—in the electorate, in unions, and in social movements—has been contract-

---

[7] See, for evidence and self-conscious reflections on this shift in light of the fascist experience and the Soviet challenge—joined at the hip by the linkage concept of totalitarianism—the symposium on "Our Country and Our Culture," *Partisan Review* (May–June 1952). The notable contributors included Norman Mailer, Leslie Fiedler, Reinhold Niebhur, David Riesman, and Philip Rahv.

[8] For a telling account of the delegitimation of the left, see Neal Ascherson, "Bring on the Hypnotist," *London Review of Books*, March 12, 1992. Ascherson was reviewing a collection of essays that mainly had appeared in *New Left Review.* Robin Blackburn, ed., *After the Fall: The Failure of Communism and the Future of Socialism* (London: Verso Books, 1991). For a retrospective on the ties between the Western left and the Soviet Union, see Tony Judt, *Past Imperfect: French Intellectuals, 1944–1956* (Berkeley: University of California Press, 1992). Judt has extended this critique to the orientation of French intellectuals on the left to East Europe during the Communist and post-Communist moments in his "Misjudgments of Paris," *Times Literary Supplement*, May 15, 1992. The two Communist-sponsored peace conferences held in New York in March and April 1949 were local instances of such accommodation. The first of these, held at the Waldorf-Astoria in March, was attended by Aleksander Fadeyev, secretary general of the Soviet Writers' Union, Dimitri Shostakovich, Howard Fast, Aaron Copeland, and Lillian Hellman; its American sponsors included Paul Robeson and Leonard Bernstein. An unfriendly report can be found in Dwight McDonald, "The Waldorf Conference," *Politics* (Winter 1949).

ing. Perversely, at a time when marxism has been discredited, its political sociology appears vindicated by the virtual elimination of the blue collar, cloth cap, male, working class underpinning of the social democratic unions, labor movement, and electoral left of the postwar period. These circumstances should be disheartening not only to partisans because the left's weakness forecloses meaningful political choice, flattens political debate, and leaves unattended vast human needs and distortions of power.

When Wright Mills addressed his "Letter to the New Left" in 1960, his essay's independence both from the burdens of Soviet-style socialism and from the incubus of self-congratulatory liberalism helped inspire a new generation of critical insurgency.[9] A combination marked by the fatuous philistinism of everyday politics, the integration of the working class into the postwar consensus, the decline of Western imperialism after the demoralization of Suez, and the 1956 crisis of Communism opened a space, Mills estimated, for new progressive political thought and activism. Just a year before his "Letter," Mills had discerned the beginning of "a post-modern period," in which "our basic definitions of society and of self are being overtaken by new realities," and he had written of the "struggle to grasp the outline of the new epoch we suppose ourselves to be entering." He recommended jettisoning our old language and categories of analysis:

I mean that when we try to orient ourselves—if we do try— we find that too many of our old expectations and images

[9] Mills had caused quite a stir in American academic circles the previous dozen years for scorning the aseptic and obfuscating qualities of American social science and for excoriating its instrumental opportunism, routinized ethos, and remoteness from significant practical and moral issues. He also had made his mark by composing hardheaded, in-your-face assessments of the American labor movement and white-collar work, by insisting that the United States was ruled by interlocking political, economic, and military elites, and by celebrating the Cuban revolution. A fine discussion of Mills, his "moral optic," and his influence can be found in James Miller, *Democracy Is in the Streets: From Port Huron to the Siege of Chicago* (New York: Simon and Schuster, 1987), chap. 4. Also see two intellectual biographies: John Eldridge, *C. Wright Mills* (London: Tavistock Publications, 1983), and the more substantial volume, Irving Louis Horowitz, *C. Wright Mills: An American Utopian* (New York: Free Press, 1983).

are, after all, tied down historically: that too many of our standard categories of thought and of feeling as often disorient us as help to explain what is happening around us; that too many of our explanations are derived from the great transition from the Medieval to the Modern Age; and that when they are generalized for use today, they become unwieldy, irrelevant, not convincing. I also mean that our major orientations—liberalism and socialism—have virtually collapsed as adequate explanations of the world and of ourselves.[10]

But soon his text turned to an important puzzle. Marxism had "so often become a dreary rhetoric of bureaucratic defense and abuse," and liberalism "a trivial and irrelevant way of masking social reality." Yet, he observed, liberalism and socialism are the only major political traditions we possess to guide the quest for the cherished values of freedom and reason. He called, urgently, for a "contemporary political re-statement of liberal and socialist goals" to "include as central the idea of a society in which all men would become men of substantive reason, whose independent reasoning would have structural consequences for their societies, its history, and thus for their own life fates." Echoing the most basic of liberal images and aspirations, he defined freedom as, "first of all, the chance to formulate the available choices, to argue over them—and then, the opportunity to choose. That is why freedom cannot exist without an enlarged role of reason in human affairs."[11]

Mills continued to prod the renewal of an engaged, critical politics inside the liberal tradition in his "Letter." His fierce

[10] C. Wright Mills, *The Sociological Imagination* (New York: Oxford Univesity Press, 1969), p. 166.

[11] Ibid., pp. 173, 174. In recognizing the indispensability of these resources in spite of their shortcomings, Mills stopped short of the kind of utopianism that later characterized some aspects of the antipolitics stance of the East European opposition, particularly its idea that left and right, socialism and capitalism, are outmoded categories. This muzziness, Neal Ascherson has observed, had the effect of mystifying both the sources and the conceptions of power. Neal Ascherson, "On East Europe," *London Review of Books*, March 8, 1990.

assault on "NATO intellectuals" for an unvexed contentment uncomfortably similar to the Soviet Union's official line of "big optimism" and his polemic against the "smug conservatives, tired liberals and disillusioned radicals" for their "bi-partisan banality" and "sickness of complacency" had an electrifying effect on many of us coming of age at the time, and they continue to ring true. As a key figure on the English left put it in his eulogy, Mills taught us "that social analysis could be probing, tough-minded, critical, relevant, and scholarly, that ideas need not be handled as undertakers handle bodies, with care but without passion, that commitment need not be dogmatic, and that radicalism need not be a substitute for hard thinking."[12] Mills told those of us who were young, politically active intellectuals that we were important, that we constituted an international community of agents for change, that we could learn to deploy our workmanship to tell truth to power and "to imagine social science as a sort of public intelligence apparatus, concerned with public issues and private troubles and with the structural trends of our time underlying them both"; that is, "to act the value of reason."[13]

Mills as a sociologist was devoted to the explication of specific situations and historical configurations; he would have acknowledged that we face the end of one epoch and the start of another radically different from the transition he perceived in the early postwar decades. Mills was obsessed with the mind-numbing consequences of the Cold War; but we are more free from antitotalitarian anxieties than at any time in more than a half-century. Yet, the temper of Mills's mood and the timbre of his insistent voice challenge us to specify better liberalism's designs, purposes, ambitions, and limitations.

Liberalism, however, is not a self-evident term, especially for Americans. It has become the name we give to the political position favoring active government in pursuit of a reduction in inequality. But this usage as the opposite of conservatism

[12] Ralph Miliband, "C. Wright Mills," *New Left Review* 15 (May–June 1962): 15.
[13] Mills, *The Sociological Imagination*, p. 181.

narrows and reduces the term to a situational and partisan definition. By liberalism, Mills certainly meant the orienting set of principles, practices, and rights first fashioned in early modern Europe as a brief for religious toleration and equal respect, as a prophylactic against predatory rule by providing for citizenship buttressed by rights and by law, and as a guide to the construction of constitutional political regimes respectful of human autonomy based on reason and choice. Liberalism has appreciated the state as a remarkable instrument for taming violence and reducing the costs of human interaction, but it also has understood that because states concentrate coercion they constitute a potential tool for disaster. In this broader usage, liberalism is the opposite of illiberalism.[14] Like Mills, I want to ask whether in a world of capitalism and states a radical liberalism is possible, what it might look like, and how it might orient the tasks of political judgment and decision at a moment when the political landscape has been transformed beyond recognition. But like Weil and Havel, I am certain there are no grounds for excessive comfort about liberalism's security and capacities; and, as in my response to Bloom, I still wonder whether liberalism's limitations are inherent.

II

With his permission, I have conjured the conceit of a semiphilosophical correspondence with Adam Michnik to probe these themes.[15] More relaxed in style and structure than a scholarly essay, yet more systematic than journalism, the vintage practice

[14] There is an interesting, if quirky, discussion of liberalism as the opposite both of conservatism and illiberalism in Leo Strauss, *Liberalism Ancient and Modern* (New York: Basic Books, 1968), pp. v–ix.

[15] "The essays . . . are semiphilosophical sermons in which I was trying to point out a number of unpleasant and insoluble dilemmas that loom up every time we attempt to be perfectly consistent when we think about our culture, our politics, and our religious life. More often than not we want to have the best from incompatible worlds and, as a result, we get nothing; when we instead pawn our mental resources on one side, we cannot buy them out again and we are trapped in a kind of dogmatic immobility." Leszek Kolakowski, *Modernity on Endless Trial* (Chicago: University of Chicago Press, 1990), p. vii.

of open letters is especially appropriate as a provisional form of discourse whose shifts of voice abide unstable compounds of analysis and experience, assertion and doubt. It is a way to share anxieties and ideas. But not for these reasons alone am I writing my homily in this genre. I came to realize I had been searching for a way to inquire about liberalism and the left in the United States while hearing my words read back to me, as it were, by a valued interlocutor.

I met Michnik, arguably East Europe's emblematic democratic intellectual, in May 1987, in Warsaw's gaudy Hotel Victoria, with plainclothes police seated on bogus leather chairs nearby. With characteristic nervous energy, he introduced himself as "once a little Jew, but now a big Pole." Neither "historian" nor "dissident" fully captures his qualities or outlook.[16] Committed to linguistic clarity and to finding permissible limits of compromise, his social and intellectual activism has aspired, above all, to create pluralism and self-determination from below, even in very difficult conditions. His resonant readings of Polish history have aimed at a usable past for liberal, democratic, and socialist ends.

Michnik became an admired, even venerated, figure in Poland not only because of his ideas and intellectual integrity, but because of his willingness, and capacity, to act. Labeled by the government press as a "ringleader of student unrest at Warsaw University," Michnik was sent to prison in March 1968 (for the first time), serving until September 1969, then forced to abandon his studies and become a welder at the Rosa Luxemburg Light Bulb Factory. He became an activist in KOR, a szamisdat writer, and famous for saving some policemen in Otwock in May 1981 by calming a seething crowd after an incident of police brutality.[17]

---

[16] Elzbieta Matynia, "A Michnik Reader," unpublished manuscript, New School for Social Research, 1988. Matynia has kindly translated relevant autobiographical passages in Adam Michnik, Jozef Tischner, and Jacek Zakowski, *Miedzy: Panem a Plebanem* (Krakow: Znak, 1995).

[17] Matynia wrote in 1988 that Michnik had become a folk hero, seen as "a man who can do no wrong in the most difficult circumstances, and—what's probably more

In 1961, when just a fifteen-year-old secondary-school student, Michnik joined the Club of the Crooked Circle (Klub
Krzywego Kola), a Warsaw discussion society. The son of successful Communist parents, he was a child of privilege; a Jew in
post-Hitler Poland, he belonged to a precarious remnant
group. Likewise, the club he entered was perched in a zone
delineating possibility and ambiguity, accompanied by a whiff
of danger.

The Club of the Crooked Circle comprised a group of skeptical intellectuals in a polity that valued conformity. Its fellowship
had a leftist commitment to egalitarianism, but unlike Poland's
ruling class its commitments were democratic in value and in
practice. Philosophically liberal—but also socialist, Catholic,
and nationalist, depending on the individual—the club's members and those of such successor institutions as Solidarity in Poland and Charter 77 in Czechoslovakia were devoted to the development of a diverse political culture and a multifarious civil
society. Between 1956 and 1962, the club's membership included such outstanding scholars as sociologist Stanislaw Ossowski, social philosopher Maria Ossowska, and economist Edward Lipinski. A harbinger of KOR, the Club of the Crooked
Circle probably was the first recurring gathering of dissidents in
the region entirely independent of the ruling Communist
Party.[18] They engaged in what has proven to be a very long-term

---

interesting—in the moments of greatest success as well. There is a popular conviction
about him that he is a strong, pure, incorruptible, indomitable, superhuman force for
resistance." Matynia, "A Michnik Reader," 1988, p. 3. Even if we discount for hyperbole,
it is clear that today Michnik, who now edits Poland's leading newspaper, *Gazeta
Wyborcza*, no longer is such a universal hero. After his break with Walesa and his continuing pursuit of compromise during and after the Roundtable discussions that produced the transition to post-Communism under the banner "For amnesty . . . against
amnesia," and his crafting of human relations with such old enemies as Jaruzelski and
even Kiszczak, Michnik has emerged as a more contentious, controversial, figure. For a
serious critique, see John Michael, "The Intellectual in Uncivil Society: Michnik, Poland, and Commmunity," *Telos* 88 (Summer 1991); for an unserious one, see Radek
Sikorski, "Adam's Curse," *The American Spectator* (April/May 1994); and for a wry characterization of Michnik and other former dissidents like Gyorgy Konrad and Janos Kis
as "Great White Gods," see Eva Hoffman, *Exit into History* (New York: Penguin Books,
1994).

[18] Jan Jozef Lipski, *KOR: A History of the Workers' Defense Committee in Poland, 1976–*

struggle to achieve a decent politics and society enfolded within the premises of the liberal political tradition.[19] To this end, they devoted their discussions primarily to two topics in the hope of discovering adequate guides to a principled politics: the relationship between socialism and liberalism, and the recovery of Poland's traduced and hidden traditions of ethical pluralism and group diversity.

Their subject, and mine, might be described as liberalism's crooked circle. The club's members—democrats in a totalitarian environment; disproportionately Jewish in a deeply Catholic milieu—were not innocents. They understood that a simple faith in human decency and progress bordered on the gullible. They tackled these inquiries in the nonutopian spirit of what the late political theorist Judith Shklar called a liberalism of fear;[20] a liberalism that stares hard at cruelty, suffering, coercion, and tyrannical abuses of public power. Institutions, rights, and the law, in this view, are judged not only by the ways they protect conscience, reduce inequality, or promote autonomous human development. These they valued for their capacity to allow people of vastly different ascriptive characteristics, social standing, and ethical values to live together without sanctioned harm, free to pursue a contentious public politics while being bound by rules of fairness and inclusion, guaranteed by the

---

1981 (Berkeley: University of California Press, 1985), pp. 9–11. Of course, there have been a number of very significant, self-conscious discussion circles of this kind joining politically committed members of the intelligentsia. Two very much like the Club of the Crooked Circle in the manner in which they tackled the character and prospects of liberalism were the Rainbow Circle (called that because their members represented a range of liberal opinion and met in London's Rainbow pub) of New Liberals in the 1890s who founded *The Progressive Review* and the more metapolitical Circolo di Cultura, founded in Italy in 1921 by Gaetano Salvemini, in which the liberal socialist Carlo Rosselli played a key role (and which heard from such outside speakers as England's R. H. Tawney).

[19] "I had the opportunity," writes Andrzej Tymowski in reference to an early version of this text, "to ask Adam Michnik in October 1994 if he agreed that the members of the Crooked Circle Club were liberals; he replied, 'Yes, of course.'" Andrzej Tymowski, "The Unwanted Revolution: From Moral Economy to Liberal Society in Poland," ms., 1995, p. 29.

[20] Judith Shklar, "The Liberalism of Fear," in Nancy L. Rosenblum, ed., *Liberalism and the Moral Life* (Cambridge: Harvard University Press, 1989).

trump cards of rights that cannot be taken away. The club's members knew that the circumference of liberalism's circle never runs smooth. They understood that liberal tolerance requires difficult judgments about tolerated differences. They recognized that all liberal regimes are built on foundations of state violence and coercion; that these tools in the basements of the state can be used to topple the upper floors of open societies; that, at best, they remain in place as hidden instruments of rule.

Even if we now know that Communism's end may have been entailed in its beginning,[21] no one who read Jonathan Schell's introduction to Michnik's prison writings would have scoffed at Schell's prognosis that "the disappearance of the [Soviet domination of the region] is about as unlikely as any event could be in our world."[22] In a compelling rumination about changes in the East, written six years later, the Polish poet Adam Zagajewski observed from his exile in Paris that "Totalitarianism seemed indestructible, eternal. Why, even Hannah Arendt suspected it was capable of changing human nature, or turning people into slaves. . . . And now? A totalitarian system bites the dust every week."[23] Even after the recent backlash against former dissidents who, in office, imposed the rigors of privatization and the creation of markets in capital, land, and labor, members of yesterday's pitifully beleaguered opposition movements either remain in power, as in the case of President Havel, or are active contenders for popular support.[24] The collapse of Communism has encroached even on the Soviet Union, and the familiar postwar system of international relations has come

---

[21] Zygmunt Bauman, "The End Was in the Beginning," *Times Literary Supplement*, December 22–28, 1989.

[22] Jonathan Schell, "Introduction," in Adam Michnik, *Letters from Prison and Other Essays* (Berkeley: University of California Press, 1985), p. xxii.

[23] Adam Zagajewski, "History's Children," *New Republic*, December 2, 1991, p. 30. For a discussion of the antitotalitarian ethic in Zagajewski's work, see Neal Ascherson, "How to Leave a House of Slavery," *New York Review of Books*, August 15, 1991.

[24] For an account, however, of the substantial difficulties the opposition intelligentsia has experienced in power, see Petr Pithart, "Intellectuals in Politics: Double Dissent in the Past, Double Disappointments Today," *Social Research* 60 (Winter 1993).

to an end. In this century, only the emergence of total war during World War I, the Holocaust, and the rapid collapse of Western imperialism (including the internal colonialism of American segregation) after World War II rival this set of occurrences as largely unforeseen moral and geopolitical developments of the highest significance.

Before 1989, East Europe's nonliberal "otherness" helped shed light on ideas and circumstances in the West through contrast. Since the rout of Bolshevism, this dissimilarity has been both eroding and enlarging. As the post-Communist countries grapple with transitions to liberal citizenship and liberal markets—the institutional underpinnings of Western liberalism—they and we have come to share a common agenda: not whether it is desirable to have a liberal politics, economics, and social order, but how to judge and choose among contending kinds of liberalism. Concurrently, the specific circumstances of the region have produced highly distinctive configurations of politics, society, and policy whose differences with those of the West must not be underestimated. This mix of similarity and disparity makes an engagement with East Europe so absorbing for a consideration of the fate and character of politics enfolded within liberal values and practices.

Of course, the stunning transformation in East Europe in the past decade does not mark the first time revolutionary situations abroad have required Americans to take stock of their own politics and society. As the historian David Brion Davis recently observed, when Americans confront such dramatic changes in other countries, they are forced to compare the tense relationship between their own stated ideals and more disappointing realities on the ground. Foreign revolutions, he writes, have provided models that "confirmed or challenged the ideological balance Americans have tried to maintain between an existing social order and dreams of a better world."[25]

---

[25] David Brion Davis, *Revolutions: Reflections on American Equality and Foreign Liberations* (Cambridge: Harvard University Press, 1990), p. 29. For a collection of essays grappling with how Europeans, in turn, have sought to learn from America, see Karen

The epic of 1989 changed the standing of liberalism qualitatively, if provisionally, moving its status elsewhere closer to its condition in America, where the liberal tradition has designated the country's enveloping assumptions and institutions since the eighteenth century; some observers, including, notably, Lionel Trilling and Louis Hartz, have thought America to be so suffused with liberal values as to lose all capacity for political differentiation and critical perspective.[26] Once an embattled ideology—against religious intolerance, prescientific ways of knowing, feudalism and its legacies, and various kinds of nonliberal political regimes and visions—liberalism today has become a meta-ideology.[27] As a hegemonic, though fragile, basis of moral and instrumental political reason, it underpins even the current practices and professed beliefs of the former Communists of Eastern Europe and the former fascists of Southern Europe. These actors now show at least public regard for the central doctrinal and institutional orientations of liberalism, including law, constitutionalism, toleration, competitive politics, and free political representation, expression, and assembly; as well as for the separations essential to liberalism that divide the state from civil society and sovereignty from property. To be sure, nonliberal polities and practices persist in the world, but currently no other legitimate systematic alternative exists.[28]

Ordahl Kupperman, ed., *America in European Consciousness, 1493–1750* (Chapel Hill: University of North Carolina Press, 1995).

[26] Lionel Trilling, *The Liberal Imagination: Essays on Literature and Society* (New York: Harcourt, Brace, and World, 1950); Louis Hartz, *The Liberal Tradition in America* (New York: Harcourt Brace, 1955). Also see Sacvan Bercovitch, *The Rites of Assent: Transformations in the Symbolic Construction of America* (Boston: Routledge, 1993).

[27] Richard Bellamy, "Liberalism," in Roger Eatwell and Anthony Wright, eds., *Contemporary Political Ideologies* (London: Pinter Publishers, 1993), p. 23.

[28] In this, but certainly not in his vision of an end to history, Fukuyama was right to observe a few months before the fall of Communism that "The triumph of the West, of the Western *idea*, is evident first of all in the total exhaustion of viable systematic alternatives to Western liberalism." Francis Fukuyama, "The End of History," *The National Interest* (Summer 1989): 3. One need not inflate his originality (it is virtually nil) or subscribe to his complacency or to his inability to see the tensions and vulnerabilities inherent inside liberalism to give credence to the relative security of liberalism today as

Where they prevail, liberal institutions are under less threat than at any moment in this century; where they do not, they still find considerable support at a moment when liberalism has become the primary constitutive grammar of political thought in what Perry Anderson calls the globe's single time zone of the imaginary. At present, all political parties in Europe and North America have effectively become liberal (making Liberal parties obsolete as serious electoral forces). At least for now, assertive totalitarianism as a ruling force has been consigned to history.[29] Just these developments, of course, make the quest for a more capable, textured liberalism more pressing, for not only is there no longer an ancien régime alternative to liberalism, neither does there exist a credible radiant future of the kind Communism promised. Yet, as we know from the American experience, it is precisely when such options are foreclosed that liberalism runs the greatest risk of narrowing its spectrum for choice and naturalizing the background conditions of inequality.

Liberalism's current welcome hegemony, in short, invites a certain complacency about liberalism's effectuality and prospects and may actually heighten the tendency to one-dimensional political thought. The triumphalist mood has been cut short, of course, by the mostly unexpected emergence of violence based on allegiances of nation, blood, and kin, a form of venom poisoning most countries of the late Warsaw Pact and former Yugoslavia, and secondarily by the electoral signals that the region's former Communists cannot be counted out for good.[30] But there are other, immanent reasons for apprehen-

---

compared to any time since the outbreak of World War I. For two appreciative but skeptical readings of Fukuyama, see Paul Hirst, "Endism," *London Review of Books*, November 23, 1989; and Stephen Holmes, "The Scowl of Minerva," *The New Republic*, March 23, 1992. Also see Timothy Burns, *After History? Francis Fukuyama and His Critics* (London: Littlefield Adams, 1994); and Francis Fukuyama, "In the Zone of Peace: Some Fallacies of Fashionable Pessimism," *Times Literary Supplement*, November 26, 1993.

[29] Perry Anderson, "Nation-States and National Identity," *London Review of Books*, May 9, 1991, p. 6.

[30] When Timothy Garton Ash surveyed the first nine months of East European

sion about liberalism's future: its thin doctrine makes it vulnerable to less austere convictions; reciprocally, its own commitments have made it compatible with ugly exclusions and deep
inequalities.

If it is absurd to envision a normatively appealing politics not
grounded in liberalism's political premises, we must guard
against a haughty, self-enclosed liberalism. For the past four
centuries, after all, the applicability of liberalism's promise has
been contained by what until very recently was thought to be
the lack of requisite character by the vast majority of humanity,
including Europe's women, non-Christians, and the unproper-
tied, and virtually all the world's population with dark skins;
and by its silences about state power and inequalities of condition fostered routinely by the operation of capitalist economies.
If we are not just to "improve" liberalism but also to secure it as
the best available, albeit deeply flawed, political instrument on
offer, we had better also address these characteristic limitations. More than ever, in short, we need the kind of "philo-

---

politics and society after Communism's demise, he wrote about emergent internal tensions in the postrevolutionary situation but had virtually nothing to say about issues of
national, ethnic, or religious bases of difference. Timothy Garton Ash, "Eastern Europe: Apres le Deluge," *New York Review of Books*, August 16, 1990; also see his "Poland
after Solidarity," *New York Review of Books*, June 13, 1991, for an account of the breakup
of Solidarity with similar silences. Michnik, by contrast, did underscore the dangers of
nationalist populism. "The greatest danger to democracy today," he wrote, "is no longer
communism, either as a political movement or as an ideology. The threat grows instead
from a combination of chauvinism, xenophobia, populism, and authoritarianism. . . .
When considering the fate of Eastern and Central Europe, I often ask myself whether
chauvinism will once again gain the upper hand. Whether the victors will be those in
Berlin and Dresden who screamed *Polen raus*, or wrote those words on walls, in November and December of last year; those in Bulgaria who deny Muslims the right to their
own names; those in Transylvania who deny Hungarians the right to their own schools;
those in Poland who promote anti-Semitism and a country without Jews. These people
could be victorious." Adam Michnik, "The Two Faces of Europe," *New York Review of
Books*, July 19, 1990, p. 7. A short time later, Vaclav Havel presented a much more
benign portrait of the transition and issues of democratic governance in "The New Year
in Prague," *New York Review of Books*, March 7, 1991. By 1992, however, he wrote of
"Paradise Lost," *New York Review of Books*, April 9, 1992; he was soon issuing increasingly
forlorn calls for civility, as in "The Culture of Everything," *New York Review of Books*, May
28, 1992.

sophically sound and sociologically realistic"[31] political theory and institutional creativity entwined in history, philosophy, strategy, and policy that the Club of the Crooked Circle and Michnik in particular have sought to advance.

III

The political scientist David Apter once remarked that when he was raised in New York in the 1930s he was well aware that the United States had a two-party system, only he thought they were the Stalinists and Trotskyists. My American adolescence came two decades later. In the Brooklyn neighborhood of Midwood, in Flatbush, the political spectrum also was composed of different kinds of "Left," but by the 1950s, after the New Deal and McCarthyism, the adults in this resolutely middle-class area of second- and third-generation settlement, nearly to a person, were liberal Democrats with residual socialist proclivities, including labor Zionist inclinations. I was taught in a "modern orthodox" day school with the kind of *Haskalah* Dual Curriculum so richly described in Cynthia Ozick's *The Cannibal Galaxy*, one that fused the sacred and secular ("lordly civilization enmeshed with lordly civilization, King David's heel caught in Victor Hugo's lyre, the metaphysicians Maimonides and Pascal, Bialik and Keats, Gemara hooked to the fires of algebra").[32]

From there, I journeyed to Columbia University in the early 1960s. In something of a familiar pattern, my sensibilities shifted from being those of a borderline socialist Young Democrat to those of a less vaguely socialist member of the New Left. From graduate student days in England's Cambridge University working on the entry of black newcomers to the liberal political regimes of the American North and Britain to my current preoccupations with post–New Deal American politics, my scholar-

[31] John A. Hall, *Liberalism: Politics, Ideology, and Market* (London: Paladin Books, 1988), p. 4.
[32] Cynthia Ozick, *The Cannibal Galaxy* (London: Penguin Books, 1983), p. 57.

ship has continued to have an affinity with the themes and persuasions of the left, if at a distance from some of its strongest enthusiasms.

All this, and none of it, prepared me for East Europe in the 1980s. There my family roots are situated, at one immense, fortuitous remove. In my local culture this region was, and is, associated with catastrophe. It belongs to the mourned past. On the eve of my 1988 trip to the region, my mother wanted to know, "What do you do when you are there?"; implicitly asking, "Must you really go?" To the extent, moreover, that I had associated the region with current events, I had considered it something of an anomalous annoyance. Often, in the heat of political discussion, I had found myself confronted by the skeptical objection, "But what about East Europe and the Soviet Union?" Though the question was serious, most of the time it was deployed mischievously as a debater's ploy, and it felt unfair. After all, like most other Americans on the left to whom it was directed, I thought "actually existing socialism" a sour caricature of our aspirations and an outstanding impediment to their realization.

Why did I go? The question falls into two geographic parts. Germany, including both halves of Berlin, was one of the places to which I had begun to travel after I joined the Graduate Faculty in 1983. I knew at the time, of course, that the New School, which had been founded in 1919 as a school for adults by such Progressive Era intellectuals as John Dewey, Charles Beard, and Thorstein Veblen, had created a University in Exile for refugees from Nazism in 1933, and that the institution where I had agreed to work as dean was inscribed by the tragic history and deep learning of the German Jewish intelligentsia. Before I took up my post I simply had not considered whether the job would require trips to Germany (a country I had never planned to see and whose consumer goods I boycotted). I soon learned that my new post did demand such visits: to raise funds (an extended form of reparations); to help organize and speak at a fiftieth-anniversary celebration for the Graduate Faculty at the

State Library in West Berlin; and to contact scholars whose research in such fields as philosophy and sociology has close affinities with work under way at the New School.

Just before the anniversary convocation in Berlin, a parallel ceremony in New York conferred honorary degrees on such venturesome advocates of human rights as Martin Luther King's aide the Reverend C. T. Vivian, the Maryknoll Sisters, Jaime Castillo Velasco, the former Chilean minister of justice, South Africa's Helen Suzman, Soviet dissident Lev Kopalev, and Poland's Adam Michnik. Confined to a prison cell, Michnik could not attend. Those of us who could, however, will never forget the charged silence in Greenwich Village's First Presbyterian Church when the poet and Nobel Laureate Czeslaw Milosz accepted the degree for the absent Michnik. Milosz read out Michnik's letter to General Kiszczak, then minister of internal affairs, explaining why he had rejected the general's offer of exile. Michnik spurned what he called the exchange of the Cote d'Azur for a "moral suicide," and he observed, "I have no idea whether I will yet live to see the victory of truth over lies and of Solidarity over this present antiworker dictatorship. The point is, General, that for me, the value of our struggle lies not in its chances of victory but rather in the value of the cause. Let my little gesture of denial be a small contribution to the sense of honor and dignity in this country that is being made more miserable every day. For you, traders in other people's freedom, let it be a slap in the face."[33]

Michnik indeed did live to see the collapse of the Jaruzelski regime and, unexpectedly, far more: the termination of the Bolshevik experiment everywhere, even in Moscow. He was among the first to recognize, as most did not, that the revolutions of 1989 signified more than a rout of liberalism's adversaries or a deep crisis for the socialist tradition and project. For

---

[33] The text of the full letter has been reprinted in Michnik, *Letters from Prison*, pp. 64–70. When Michnik had been indicted on an earlier occasion, in 1977, he was in France but returned from the West to answer charges that he was working to harm the republic in collaboration with foreign bodies like Radio Free Europe.

Michnik, Communism's downfall also helped reveal significant predicaments inside Western liberalism and its far too abstract portrait of civil society as composed of individuals living outside community, meaning, and belief.[34] It also quickly demonstrated the limits of a liberalism oriented to the creation of free space in the niches of totalitarianism as a guide to the challenges once addressed by the Club of the Crooked Circle: the possibility of a liberal socialism (an oxymoron to many liberals and socialists alike) and of a plural liberalism able to accommodate deep ethical and group differences inside a common polity.

My letters to Michnik are geared to explore how the braids of liberalism, socialism, and pluralism might be plaited. I ask if liberalism can learn to grapple with the inequalities and imprisoning attributes generated by the routine operation of capitalist markets;[35] how liberalism can find buffers to deflect attacks on its cherished values of reasoned reflection, wide-ranging opinion, and choice by autonomous agents; and whether liberalism can transcend its penchant for abstract individuals to grasp the emotions and passions of people embedded in history, memory, culture, and commitment at a moment when the fear of difference and appeals against intruders, the traditional stock in trade of what Umberto Eco calls "Ur-Fascism," have reared their ugly heads.[36] These discussions are anchored by two of Michnik's texts, "Conversation in the Citadel" and *The Church and the Left*.[37]

In 1982, behind bars, Michnik agreed to present a series of

[34] In the West, this insight first belonged, I believe, to George Steiner. For a discussion, see Peter Sherwood, "The Errata of History," *Times Literary Supplement*, March 20, 1992.

[35] Charles E. Lindblom, "The Market as Prison," *The Journal of Politics* 44 (May 1982).

[36] Umberto Eco, "Ur-Fascism," *New York Review of Books*, June 22, 1995.

[37] Adam Michnik, "Conversation in the Citadel," in Michnik, *Letters from Prison; The Church and the Left* (Chicago: University of Chicago Press, 1991). The second text originally was intended to be published in the émigré periodical *Aneks*, edited in Paris by Aleksander Smolar, as part of a larger conversation about relationships between the opposition intelligentsia and the Catholic church. It appeared in Polish as *Kosciol, lewicka, dialog* (Paris: Instytut Literacki, 1977).

lectures to his fellow inmates, planning to speak about the "nocturnal disputes and heartfelt quarrels" of jailed street demonstrators eight decades earlier who had been arrested after a church service devoted to the cause of a free Poland. When he was moved to solitary confinement, he transmuted these talks into the essay "Conversation in the Citadel," taking as its subject the character of Poland's ideological and political lineage dating from the early years of this century and as its goal the identification of traditions of value in Polish political culture.

Michnik concluded "Citadel" with six guidelines drawn from this heritage. "We need," he wrote, "self-determination," "a politics of activism," "the Catholic Church," "national solidarity," "socialism," and "freedom."[38] His identification of socialism as a normative goal and instrumental tool from the isolation of a Communist jail rang a bell of surprise. Michnik has let me know he would write no longer as a socialist but as a "radical democrat." Nonetheless, the issue he identified remains pressing. Whether labeled as liberal socialist, social liberal, or social democratic, only a socialism that does not challenge liberalism's constitutional imperatives and only a liberalism capable of rectifying capitalist inequality can ground a normatively appealing politics that addresses both the significance of universal citizenship and how experiences of citizenship are marked and scarred by the class system.[39]

---

[38] Michnik, *Letters from Prison*, pp. 326–29.

[39] In 1981, a year before "Citadel," Michnik wrote "A Response to Critics" as an afterword to his *The Church and the Left*. He commented there on the book's terminology: "I also used the term 'democratic socialism' in my book. Today I use those words carefully and with great reluctance. Not because I have changed my ideological orientation, but because in Polish life today these words are virtually meaningless." Nonetheless, Michnik defended his socialist values against his critics, including Father Jozef Tischner. Replying to Tischner's claim that Michnik's concept of democratic socialism amounts to "a square circle," Michnik wrote, "In my understanding, the adjective 'democratic' is the complete opposite of all forms of political despotism, including all forms of dictatorship that go under the name of socialist. 'Socialism,' meanwhile, is for me the continual movement toward the self-determination of labor, a movement for the liberation of labor, a movement based on the ideas of freedom and tolerance, human rights and national rights, a just distribution of the national income and an equal start in life for all. My definition is completely arbitrary and does not have much in common with

Taking up Michnik's challenge, I try to show in my first letter, "La lutte continue," what a self-limiting socialism nestled within a liberal political framework might look like, and, in turn, what changes to liberalism's conceptions socialists should seek to secure. I write in the intellectual and political space located between the strong socialism of Harold Laski[40] and the strong liberalism of Ralf Dahrendorf. In texts that self-consciously borrowed titles and ambitions from Edmund Burke's *Reflections on the Revolution in France*,[41] both sought to construct public philosophies to advance powerful normative visions. Laski strained unsuccessfully to stay within liberal political confines, as his attempt to find value in Stalinism signifies. Dahrendorf's liberalism, though too subtle to conjure a return to any simple individualism, turned its back on ideology in favor of a pragmatic and problem-oriented politics so thoroughly that he downplayed the deeply inscribed inequalities of capitalism with which not only socialism but any serious liberalism must reckon. For him, the very genus of right and left concerned with divisions of class is obfuscating and obsolete. Laski's and Dahrendorf's positions were not merely unattractive options; they remain (unsymmetrical) moral disasters.

From the start, liberal doctrine has valued religious toleration, at least for Christians, but liberalism's (and the Enlightenment's) views about deep diversity, minority status, gender, nationalism and nationality, as well as vastly different ethical systems and ways of life often have been perplexing and prob-

---

the Leninist notion of the 'dictatorship of the proletariat.' The dominant position of the industrial proletariat was supposed to hinge on its actual place in the system of production and the social structure. It did not entail the limitation of the political rights of any other group of people. I do not see a square circle here." Michnik, *The Church and the Left*, pp. 234, 238–39.

[40] The ghost of Laski hovers over this book; not only for his flawed effort to join liberalism and socialism, but also because of his early work advocating a strong pluralism and because of the importance of being Jewish for his thought and politics.

[41] Harold Laski, *Reflections on the Revolution of Our Time* (New York: Viking Press, 1943); Ralf Dahrendorf, *Reflections on the Revolutions in Europe* (New York: Times Books, 1990). Dahrendorf's text is written as an open letter to an imaginary "gentleman in Warsaw."

lematical. My second letter, "The Storehouse of Power and Un-reason," takes up these questions. "Liberalism," Steven Lukes has argued, "is about fairness between conflicting moral and religious positions, but it is also about filtering out those that are incompatible with a liberal order and taming those that re-main."[42] We need to understand better what such a formulation implies for the breadth of the zone of compatibility and for how views outside the ambit of liberalism can, or should, be tamed; that is, for the scope of liberalism's toleration and the contours of its dogmatism.

Here I draw on Michnik's *The Church and the Left*. Written in 1975–76 to consider the relationship of the "secular left" to religion, this text pursued the strategic aim of building an effec-tive opposition grounded deeply in Polish culture and its imbri-cation of religiosity and power. Michnik did battle with secular anticlericalism ("Whoever in today's Poland fights against the Church in the name of human freedom is either an ignoramus, an idiot, or a knight of totalitarian reaction disguised in liberal phraseology");[43] and he challenged the left to rethink its reflex-ive hostility to the questions, practices, and insights of premod-ern religiosity and, by implication, to reconsider liberal and so-cialist legacies of limited pluralism. His history and sociology was brushed by ethics and religion. He feared that unless the liberal and democratic socialist left identified a significant place for the Church, the Church, in turn, finding no location in the liberal imaginary, would reinforce its antiliberal, funda-mentalist elements. Michnik further understood that the differ-ences between liberalism and the Church were too established to be overcome by goodwill, but he thought it possible to dis-cover ideas and institutions that would permit both to persist without undue compromise. He struggled to find a middle path between an all-embracing Church and a secular mirror-image that could find no place for the Church.

---

[42] Steven Lukes, *Moral Conflict and Politics* (Oxford: Clarendon Press, 1991), p. 18, n. 39.

[43] Michnik, *The Church and the Left*, p. 145.

His goal was the discovery of doctrines and institutions with the capacity to appreciate and succor "the pluralistic unity of our culture."[44] Michnik not only put himself at odds with efforts by the Church to impose its views of morality through the state; he seriously engaged the fears of the Church by showing an understanding that "from a doctrinal view, the Church cannot accept liberal ideas."[45] Though sketchy, unsystematic, and ambiguous (and written for a historically grounded context very different from our own), *The Church and the Left* provides important tools with which to interrogate the liberal tradition's insecure and limited pluralism.

What follows are letters from an American, a radical, and a Jew to a Pole, a radical, and a Jew. They constitute an attempt to construct mirrors in which we can see each other's political ideas and circumstances; not just the flat mirrors that reproduce faithfully and literally or mirrors that enlarge, contract, or distort; but mirrors like the metaphysical Metamirs Primo Levi describes in his 1985 short story, "The Mirror Maker." These instruments, when applied to the forehead of another, reveal "your image as it is seen by the person who stands before you."[46] By writing, I am asking Michnik to look into my Metamir, to see how his, and his region's, ideas and circumstances are seen; and in this way, to look at how I view my, and our, situation.

I am searching for what might be called a liberalism of adjectives. In his discussion of the simplifying tendencies of totalitarian language, Zagajewski reminds us that "what color is to painting, the adjective is to language." Too often, liberalism has constructed sentences about universal citizens without regard for their class or communal or gender situations, their moral

---

[44] Ibid., p. 147. Michnick's text also highlighted his antiauthoritarian strain. In responding to his critics, he wrote, "I have always been intrigued by the type of person, well-known from Polish literature, who professes Christian values but distrusts their official Church guardians, who holds socialist dreams of freedom and justice but distrusts those political parties claiming to bring such ideals to life. Without such people, twentieth-century Polish culture would be barren and gloomy" (p. 243).

[45] Ibid., p. 143.

[46] Primo Levi, "The Mirror Maker," in *The Mirror Maker: Stories and Essays* (New York: Schocken Books, 1989), p. 49.

beliefs, or their differential integration with the state. Liberalism has elaborated a strong and compelling language of nouns—liberty, citizenship, contract, standards, rights—and a vocabulary of verbs devoted to acts of choice. But it is adjectives that appreciate hybrids, syncretic variety, and shadings of difference; by preserving "the vivifying taste" of distinctiveness they enhance the assets and adroitness of a politics required to take both justice and pluralism seriously.[47]

I think Michnik will discover that he and I remain children of 1968.

---

[47] Zagajewski, "History's Children," pp. 30–31. For its part, socialism has had its own set of nouns concerning equality and justice but has especially been drawn to such verbs as arise, awake, change, empower, liberate, and smash.

One: "La lutte continue"

Winter 1995

Dear Adam,

I decided to write late last summer after returning to Cambridge across beautiful meadows connecting the city with the adjacent village of Granchester. There, in The Orchard, a century-old tea garden that once was the haunt of Keynes and Wittgenstein, Russell and Virginia Woolf, I read your "Conversation in the Citadel,"[1] thought about the impact of the wreckage of Soviet-style socialism on the left, and considered the two framed items you have seen hanging over the sink of my kitchen in New York: the famous May 1968 Paris placard lettered *"la lutte continue"* and the front page of *Gazeta Wyborcza*,[2] which you inscribed at the newspaper's first Warsaw offices in March 1990 when its title still proudly carried the red logo of Solidarity. As I recalled your 1988 affirmation of loyalty "to the whole antiauthoritarian project" of 1968, I considered whether these icons of political preference complement or clash.[3]

If *Gazeta's* politics essentially are liberal and democratic, the politics of May '68 were democratic and socialist. If *Gazeta* is a tangible product of the self-limiting revolutions you and other members of the East European opposition sought to achieve within the confines of the possible, "la lutte continue" was the emblem of what my long-time colleague Aristide Zolberg has called "moments of madness": times "when human beings living in societies believe that 'all is possible' ... when politics bursts its bounds to invade all of life."[4] And if Solidarity was rooted in Poland's collective identities of nation, church, and

---

[1] Adam Michnik, "Conversation in the Citadel," in Michnik, *Letters from Prison and Other Essays* (Berkeley: University of California Press, 1985).

[2] The paper today is Poland's, indeed Europe's, largest circulation nontabloid newspaper. Michnik remains its editor.

[3] *Kontakt* (Paris) 74–75 (July–August 1988): 54; cited in David Ost, "Introduction," in Adam Michnik, *The Church and the Left* (Chicago: University of Chicago Press, 1990), p. 5.

[4] Aristide Zolberg, "Moments of Madness," *Politics and Society* 2 (Winter 1972): 183.

class, we now can see how May '68's call for freedom was marked in key aspects by an "exaggerated individualism" and by an orientation to received norms reminiscent of the heretical North African Adamites of the second and third centuries who lived as if they had rescued Adam's state of innocence.[5]

Gazeta, and your politics, also can trace their lineage to 1968, but to March when First Secretary Wladyslaw Gomulka played the anti-Semitic card by inventing a Jewish "fifth column," unmistakably revealing a totalitarian and megalomaniacal nationalist fist inside his reform socialist glove. This ugly 1968 was dark and brooding, troubling for what it divulged about the silent complicity of much of the population, the inadequacy of the Church's response, and the renting of the intelligentsia, many of whose members took the road to exile (a course I know your parents encouraged but you rejected, feeling yourself to be more a Pole and more dedicated to the Polish struggle for freedom now that you had been labeled a Jew). Yet March 1968, by putting an end to the illusion of Communist reform (a phantasm put to rest even more decisively in August by the Soviet invasion of Czechoslovakia) and by invoking a total alienation between democratic impulses and the existing regime, renewed the covenants of Poland's nontotalitarian liberal socialist and pluralist traditions and opened pathways toward what later became the politics of KOR and then of Solidarity.[6]

I was walking on Jana Kozielulskeigo in May 1987 when I heard beautiful singing a short way down the road. I followed the sounds to S. W. Stanislavska Kostki, the church of Father

[5] The characterization of "exaggerated individualism" is that of Gilles Lipovetsky, "May '68, or the Rise of Transpolitical Individualism," in Mark Lilla, ed., *New French Thought: Political Philosophy* (Princeton: Princeton University Press, 1994), p. 214. His portrait of 1968, though suggestive, is terribly one-sided.

[6] "In the course of its millennial history," Pope John Paul II has written, "Poland has been a state made up of many nationalities, many religions—mostly Christian, but not only Christian. This tradition has been and still is the source of a positive aspect of Polish culture, namely its *tolerance* and *openness* toward people who think differently, who speak other languages, or who believe, pray, or celebrate the same mysteries of faith in a different way." His Holiness John Paul II, *Crossing the Threshold of Hope* (New York: Alfred A. Knopf, 1994), p. 145.

Popieluszko.[7] In the churchyard were well over a thousand people. Most shaped the Solidarity "V" sign with their fingers, some held large Solidarity banners, all were singing national songs and church hymns as the priests led a slow procession around the perimeter of the church. By chance, I had stumbled on the "Mass for the Nation," worshipped the last Sunday evening of each month. At the time, such a contentious gathering could have taken place only on church ground. So the event underscored the very questions you and I had discussed earlier in the day about the relationship of secular goals and church means, hierarchy and democracy, communal skepticism about individualism, and the complicated, often exclusionary, meaning of "nation" in the Polish experience.

No such occasion could have taken place in Paris. For if Solidarity was attempting to change political structures in the name of Polish authenticity, May '68 had sought to authorize the individual against existing structures. But the two movements also were marked by more than a few likenesses. As vast fellowships of common sensibility, they valued freedom and they tethered large-scale goals to restricted means by miniaturizing the concept of revolution[8] and limiting its primary orientation to claims on behalf of civil society. They also linked socialism and liberty, each in its own way unwilling to give up the one for the other. Even in Poland, the continuing socialist and social democratic commitments of such opposition figures as Stanislaw Ossowski and Leszek Kolakowski in 1968 had helped refresh left-oriented options by rescuing them from their kidnappers, later embedding them inside KOR and Solidarity.

The legacies of these democratic movements are under threat from a new kind of mutual learning. Before Communism's fall, Western Europe's and North America's liberal political ethic gained strength from the contrasting existence of the rancid socialism of the East; in turn, dissident anti-Bolshevism

---

[7] Father Jerzy Popieluszko, a vigorous supporter of Solidarity, was kidnapped and then tortured and killed by state security police in October 1984.

[8] The phrase is Lipovestky's.

inside Communist Europe was nourished by the West's actually existing liberalism. During the past half-decade, a pathological hyper-individualism has moved east and neotribalist versions of communal identity have turned up with a vengeance in the West. Spasmodically violent nationalist neopopulist impulses now have fused with a market-worshiping commercialism to produce ugly assaults across the old divide on the values and type of politics you and I cherish.[9]

In circumstances marked by these aggressive strikes at social pluralism and liberal democracy and by the wholesale discrediting of socialism, the stunned intellectual incoherence of the left with which we both identify in the face of rightist forms of communitarianism and market sanctification is not just shocking but dangerous.[10] So as I sat in that delightful tea garden I also pondered the pressing task of discovering an ethical and political imagination sufficiently resourceful to grapple with current challenges and responsibilities.

We need, I believe, the kind of social knowledge public moralists produce.[11] Public moralists have ambitions broader than those of political theorists but are less marginal or estranged than critics who rail at society from the outside. Nor are they

---

[9] For a discussion of the consequences for political ethics of the obliteration of boundaries, see Keith Tester, *The Two Sovereigns: Social Contradictions of European Modernity* (London: Routledge, 1992).

[10] The post-Communist Polish intelligentsia, Michnik has observed, "seems to be as lost as in the worst of times—as though it had lost its own ethos, the image of itself and its own place in society." Adam Michnik, "The Three Fundamentalisms," July 1991; published as part of Adam Michnik, "Market, Religion, and Nationalism," *Politics, Culture, and Society* 8 (Summer 1995): 537–42.

[11] Stefan Collini, *Public Moralists: Political Thought and Intellectual Life in Britain, 1850–1930* (Oxford: Clarendon Press, 1991), pp. 2–3. The health of democracies depends not inconsiderably on the quality of the discourse public moralists produce. I agree with the political scientist V. O. Key, who concluded his major work on public opinion with the following caution: "Democracies decay, if they do, not because of the cupidity of the masses, but because of the stupidity and self-seeking of leadership echelons. . . . [T]he health of a democratic order consists in the beliefs, standards, and competence of those who constitute the influentials, the opinion-leaders, the political activists in the order. . . . If a democracy tends toward indecision, decay, and disaster, the responsibility rests here, not in the mass of the people." V. O. Key, Jr., *Public Opinion and American Democracy* (New York: Alfred A. Knopf, 1961), pp. 557–58.

mere rationalizers or publicists of given ideologies. Rather, they deploy their distinctive voice in public intellectual debate.[12] Solidarity and cognate movements in East Europe were led by people prepared to innovate in this space; that is, by intellectuals, scholars, and professionals who deployed their thought and sensibilities to characterize society, shape cultural and moral attitudes, deepen political argument, connect private troubles to public issues, and motivate responsible transformations while nourished by larger conceptions of decency and justice. For the public moralist, in short, "strong elective affinities connect conceptions of knowledge and responsibility with conceptions of politics,"[13] as theory, politics, procedures, and policy are seen to mutually constitute each other under conditions of uncertainty and flux.

Whereas most philosophers distinguish abstract, universal morality from situated, culturally sited ethics, the term "public moralist" signifies a refusal to abide by this distinction. Values appropriate to political action and the shaping of public philosophies germane to particular circumstances require a persistent oscillation between morality and ethics and a repudiation of attempts to separate judgment from experience of the kind characteristic, on the one side, of a strong Kantian philosophy abstracted from time and place or, on the other, of local, culturally circumscribed, and inevitably relativist ethical stances. Contingency, experience, experimentation, and a respect for distinctive historical configurations goes hand in hand with the knowledge that without significant universal standards we risk becoming hostages to the vagaries and violence of history as the sphere of values and norms is reduced to particularity. "Universal man" may not exist, but universal humankind does; in turn, Kant's formalistic conception of morality, though more appeal-

---

[12] For a discussion of literary criticism with public and normative aspects, see Morris Dickstein, *Double Agent: The Critic and Society* (New York: Oxford University Press, 1992).

[13] James T. Kloppenberg, *Uncertain Victory: Social Democracy and Progressivism in European and American Thought, 1870–1920* (New York: Oxford University Press, 1986), p. 145. The discussion immediately following is indebted to this excellent work.

ing than a utilitarian cost-benefit calculus, generates intentions that can have effect only if realized through practical action in specific times and places.

In the last quarter of the nineteenth century and the first quarter of the twentieth, a remarkable and diverse group of public moralists on the left under the umbrellas of progressivism, social democracy, and the "New Liberalism" worked the space where political imagination meets social and political theory. Innovative in epistemology, social science, and policy studies, figures as diverse as England's T. H. Green, Germany's Walter Rauschenbusch, France's Jean Jaures, and America's John Dewey sought to make liberalism more social and socialism compatible with liberal democracy while tempering both with a large dose of civic virtue. Their formative work—aimed at scholars, politicians, journalists, and the mass public—grounded politics and policy on the democratic left (including the New Deal and post–Second World War European social democracy) for much of the twentieth century. Though depleted, we still are living off the intellectual and political capital they produced. But we must do more than restock because this legacy's restriction of politics to the formal public sphere, indifference to vast inequalities of gender and race, and innocence about human potential for wrongdoing disqualify it as a sufficient guide for the left today. Yet what remains appealing, even inspiring, is the scope of that generation's radical project and the manner in which it gave voice to appealing aspirations.

Since the exhaustion and dissolution of the New Left, the right has dominated public morality and public discourse in the West and much of the East, urging a liberalism close to libertarianism and opposing equality to liberty. In the United States, assertive and capable intellectuals in think tanks, journalism, and higher education have deployed effective right-wing tools and ideas to alter the terms and content of political argument. By contrast, the left is demoralized, institutionally impoverished, and lacking in appealing ideas. Important public intellectuals on the left, primarily feminist and African American, exist, but they remain encamped in the universities where they speak to limited and artificially adulatory audiences; secure inside the world's most stable liberal regime, they have made the liberal tradition the central object of their often powerful social criticism while leaving the larger field of play to others.

In the 1960s, I unhesitatingly declared myself, as you did, a democratic socialist. I forswore the label "liberal" as tainted by racism, imperialism, militarism, and class domination, as did so many members of my generation. We implicated liberalism in the destructive myth of progress, in the deployment of universalism to mask a Western capitalist particularism, and in the silencing of dissent. We thought that the antitotalitarian anxieties of liberals had made the language of politics and the range of permitted debate increasingly Orwellian. We believed that liberalism as we experienced it lacked ethical content as it validated only pragmatic and short-term private interests and was too often tempted to treat social and political collectivities as heaps of individuals abstractly conceived. I think we were substantially correct in each of these respects even now, though I have come to value politics grounded in the liberal tradition. At the heart of the New Left's critique was an exasperation with the limited scope, formal institutions, hypocrisies, procedural emphases, and market economies of Western liberalism. As we marched the streets, disappointed in and then disdainful of authority, our cultural and political criticism targeted tired, smug academics, journalists, and political leaders; the limitations of formal democracy; the clumsy, bloated, and self-interested state bureaucracies of the West and East; an insistence on decorum and reasonableness in the face of vast inequalities and mass suffering; the militarization of our economy and politics in the age of a Cold War turned hot; the distortions and cruelties of racism and colonialism; and the arrogance of the American and Soviet empires. We were certain we composed a *new* left,

unbeholden to Stalinism and the old marxism, or to such ossified instruments of change as the Democratic party and its comfortable union allies.[14]

As the American New Left matured, say by the heyday of
1968 when its unruliness and growing anger still were contained by sharpening tools of analysis and connection to broad-
based movements for change, many of us had come to the
conclusion that the various targets of our concern were inter-
connected by the character and processes of capitalism. We discovered a usable marxism (reading groups on the *Grundrisse,*
Capital, and Gramsci's *Prison Notebooks* proliferated) as a tool for
unlocking capitalism's realities and secrets of oppression. Liberalism, most of us thought, simply was capitalism's benign
surface.[15]

When C. Wright Mills helped kick off the New Left with his
celebrated "Letter," he called for the development of fresh
"theories of society, history, and human nature" to promote opposition to the right wing, which was celebrating society "as it is,
a going concern." He went on to define what he meant by the
left:

> It means structural criticism and reportage and theories
> of society, which at some point or another are focused
> politically as demands and programs. These criticisms,
> demands, theories, programs are guided morally by the
> humanist and secular ideals . . . of reason, freedom, and
> justice. To be "left" means to connect up cultural with po-
> litical criticism, and both with demands and programs.
> And it means all this inside *every* country in the world.[16]

[14] For the text of SDS's Port Huron statement as well as commentary, see Richard
Flacks et. al., "Port Huron: Agenda for a Generation," *Socialist Review* 17 (May–August
1987).

[15] For a treatment of the early New Left as a revolt against nineteenth-century Marxism, see Paul Buhle, "The Eclipse of the New Left: Some Notes," *Radical America* 6
(July–August 1972).

[16] Mills, *New Left,* p. 67. The other challenge, for Mills the more important of the
two, was the identification of "ideas about the historical agencies of structural change."

By this measure, the democratic opposition in East Europe, speaking truth to power, was the very incarnation of "left." If you and your colleagues excited the Western right by your anti-Communism, you exhilarated a 1960s old-timer like me by your open and unafraid radicalism.

Like other visitors, I was transported to a charged community once characteristic of the New Left before its implosion and ugly demise when I first met Czech, Polish, and Hungarian members of the opposition in the mid-1980s. Of course, your circumstances were far more daunting than those the predominantly white American student movement had faced, except when its members had gone south to share hazards with black civil rights activists. Nonetheless, it was not just the remarkable hospitality I encountered that made me feel at home, but your familiar distrust of authority (even when it responded to your own demands),[17] as well as your sense of project, marriage of analysis and action, and rejection of established models. Your language and insurgency played on conversant instruments: personal commitment, collaboration between intellectuals and workers, the creation of free zones within civil society in spite of distortions of language and institutions outside, and the joining of culture to politics, of ethics to action. Even some of the music was the same; Joan Baez singing Bob Dylan, I recall, in the background of an intense discussion about the costs of paranoia in a Prague flat in 1987, just days after the secret police had picked apart the apartment.

In Warsaw, a week later, I set down my impressions of the dissident community after a long evening lubricated by plentiful drink at Aldona Jawlowska's home. The party was jammed with some thirty key members of the Polish opposition—including editors of *Krytyka* and *Res Publica*, organizers of under-

---

[17] I am thinking here of the sense of letdown Milan Simecka (whose wife had begun translating Orwell's *1984* into Czech in *1978*) felt in Bratislava when he discovered at the beginning of *glasnost* in 1984(!) that the Soviet Union's *Literaturnaya Gazeta* had begun to publish a Russian translation. Milan Simecka, "Newspeak and *glasnost*," *Times Literary Supplement*, January 6–12, 1989, p. 10.

ground art exhibitions, a film director, a secular Catholic devoted to the restoration of the city's Jewish monuments, and
leaders of Solidarity who had been either underground for a
period or involved in a recent hunger strike. I wrote,

> I found the evening's manifest passion for ideas and for
> the variety of means of human exchange and communica-
> tion, and the appreciation of the importance of precision
> and nuance in language revealed in the conversations that
> went on late that evening, nothing short of breathtaking.
> We in the West have the space to develop a critical culture,
> but we do so little with it. Our slackness and self-indul-
> gences are mocked by the creative sensibilities of Polish
> colleagues for whom each idea, each image, sometimes
> each word, and the timing of their use constitute a terrain
> of day to day struggle. Not since the movements of the
> 1960s have I experienced anything like the intensity and
> seriousness of these political exchanges.

But, of course, there was one vital difference: the status of
liberalism, not merely as an implicit premise but as a cluster of
political values and institutions. For Americans, liberalism was
a background condition, almost a fact of nature, a given many
of us had come to see as functioning not only as a mask for
power but as the routinized means to contain and limit full and
honest public discourse. By contrast, East Europe's antitotalitarian intellectuals and social movements placed high value on
just those features of the liberal tradition—including privacy,
property, and the protection of rights essential to a democratic
polity—that my generation in the West either had taken for
granted or had criticized as deceptive put-ons. For you, this critical position was not only impossible but nearly inconceivable
given the level of surveillance the state attempted (in the German Democratic Republic some 500,000 people served the
Stasi as employees or informers).[18] You embraced liberalism

[18] See Edward Martin, "In the Stasi Cesspit," *Times Literary Supplement*, February 21,
1992.

with affection and commitment[19] as an alternative not only to your region's party states but to the revisionist marxism of the 1960s to which you once had subscribed. While we had obsessed about the left and the right you were preoccupied with the liberal-totalitarian antinomy. Your liberalism had become an antimarxism, and you rejected talk of a "middle way" between the capitalism of the West and the socialism of the East, the in-between location thought at present to constitute an illusion.

Though the democratic opposition hardly thought with one mind, Karl Popper's *Open Society and Its Enemies* and Friedrich Hayek's *Road to Serfdom*[20] became the movement's modal political texts. You and your fellow activists exploited the limits of putatively totalitarian regimes to penetrate and control the private sphere in order to create free spaces characterized by great vitality, densely textured human relations, and, above all, a vigorous exchange of ideas about what the *public* sphere should be like. A fabulous incongruity was at work: the contingent and contested sphere of civil society produced powerful political theory—really, liberal political theory—in just those settings where most forms of political theorizing were seditious pursuits.

I think this legacy—that is to say, yours—is double-edged. It

[19] Just over a year before the Communist collapse, Michnik described the goals of the opposition to Erica Blair, an English interviewer, this way: "The point is that, as citizens, we in the democratic opposition don't want to be treated any longer as children or slaves. The basic principle of the anti-feudal movement was human rights, the idea that everyone has rights equal to that of the monarch. That's what we also want. We want everybody to enjoy the same rights as Jaruzelski, secured by the rule of law." "Toward a Civil Society: Hopes for Polish Democracy," *Times Literary Supplement*, February 19–25, 1988, p. 198. Also see Adam Michnik, "The Presence of Liberal Values," *Eastern European Reporter* 4 (Spring/Summer 1991).

[20] K. R. Popper, *The Open Society and Its Enemies. Volume I: The Spell of Plato; Volume II: The High Tide of Prophecy: Hegel, Marx, and the Aftermath* (London: Routledge & Kegan Paul, 1945); Friedrich A. von Hayek, *The Road to Serfdom*, fiftieth anniversary edition with an introduction by Milton Friedman (Chicago: University of Chicago Press, 1994). Antitotalitarianism, it is important to recall, has not been a monopoly possession of the right. In Germany alone, the rich array of socialist critics of totalitarianism included Max Horkheimer, Herbert Marcuse, Karl Korsch, Rudolf Hilferding, Ruth Fischer, Richard Lowenthal, Ernst Fraenkel, Franz Borkenau, and Franz Neumann.

teaches a deep skepticism of all illiberalisms (including soft illiberalisms that devalue liberal tolerance as potentially oppressive[21]) and demonstrates how communitarian, republican, socialist, Foucauldian, feminist, or other transliberal bases of
critique run profound, even dangerous, risks when they seek to
go it alone without being embedded within liberal principles
and practices. But in showing how an assertively liberal political
and moral public philosophy can matter, the dissident legacy,
by primarily focusing on negative liberty, also teaches less satisfactory lessons drawn mainly from Popper: that the liberal tradition is so vulnerable it must be guarded uncritically; that liberalism should be closed and autarchic, nervous about alliances
with traditions focusing on positive liberties; hence that positive
ideologies as normative conceptions should be feared because
they are susceptible to being mobilized on behalf of historicist
and potentially totalitarian grand narratives.[22] A worthy concern, but surrendering ideology and systematic programs for
positive liberty is perilous. Without positive ideology, it is hard
to see how we either can strive to shape a liberalism mindful of
inequality or can adequately protect liberalism against predatory adversaries.

I

You may wonder why I want to write about the possibility of a
public philosophy based in part on the amalgam of liberalism
and socialism. After all, virtually to a person our friends from

[21] As in Herbert Marcuse, "Repressive Tolerance," in Robert Paul Wolff, Barrington
Moore, Jr., and Herbert Marcuse, *A Critique of Pure Tolerance* (Boston: Beacon Books,
1965).

[22] This theme, of course, is also taken up by Isaiah Berlin in his celebrated "Two
Concepts of Liberty," in Berlin, *Four Essays on Liberty* (Oxford: Oxford University Press,
1969). The evidence for the connections he, like Popper, draws between the ideas of
philosophers and the later creation of authoritarian and totalitarian regimes, Perry
Anderson rightly notes, "is essentially circular: modern despotism proves the dangers of
the ideal of positive liberty, so that ideal must have contributed to the rise of despotism." Perry Anderson, "England's Isaiah," *London Review of Books*, December 20, 1990,
p. 4.

the pre-1989 opposition believe it naive and dangerous to hold on to socialism in any form. Must we follow them, putting aside the understanding to which you once gave voice that liberalism without socialism is a license for degradation? In mirror image, many on the Western left continue to think of liberalism simply as a veneer shielding the fundamental inequalities of class, race, and gender characteristic of capitalist societies.

One effect of 1989 has been that of forcing even the staunchly anti-Communist left to revisit its doctrinal heritage. If what we have been discovering cannot be categorized as the detection of a god that failed[23] since most of us on the democratic left never put our confidence in antiliberal Bolshevist ambitions, our introspection certainly has produced a loss of assurance inside our once stable pantheon.[24] This crisis of belief and opinion on the left, moreover, runs especially deep because it is embedded in a wider loss of faith in the assumptions of rationality, stable knowledge, and common standards. The confident spirit of the famous eleventh edition of the *Encyclopedia Britannica*, written "in the spirit of science" and "in the objective view,"[25] has been undermined by various postmodern trends in the academy, by the intensity of economic, spatial, and technological restructuring, and, of course, by the defeat of singular historical narratives.

Perhaps liberal socialism will prove an impossible subject, but I remain persuaded, as our hero George Orwell was, that it is an inescapable one, notwithstanding the staggering moral

[23] Richard Crossman, ed., *The God that Failed* (New York: Harper and Brothers, 1949). The essays in this celebrated volume were by Louis Fischer, André Gide, Arthur Koestler, Ignazio Silone, Stephen Spender, and Richard Wright.

[24] By contrast, the right seems exultantly secure in theirs. When the new Speaker of the House of Representatives addressed the assembled first-year Republican cohort in January 1985, he presented them with a reading list one book long: Hayek's *Road to Serfdom*.

[25] "Editorial Introduction," *Encyclopedia Britannica, Eleventh Edition* (New York: Encyclopedia Britannica, 1910), pp. xx–xxi. Today, by contrast, "consensus of all kinds in academia has broken down—left and right, political and aesthetic—broken down, worn out, or at best opened up." Sacvan Bercovitch, "The Problem of Ideology in a Time of Dissensus," in Bercovitch, *The Rites of Assent: Transformations in the Symbolic Construction of America* (New York: Routledge, 1993), p. 353.

and practical tensions characterizing their relationship. When he reviewed Hayek's *Road* in 1944, Orwell focused on his preferred version of liberalism based on a combination of planning and political liberty:

> Professor Hayek is probably right in saying that in this country the intellectuals are probably more totalitarian-minded than the common people. But he does not see, or will not admit, that a return to "free" competition means for the great mass of the people a tyranny probably worse, because more irresponsible, than the state. The trouble with competitions is that somebody wins them. Professor Hayek denies that free capitalism necessarily leads to monopoly, but in practice that is where it has led, and since the vast number of people would rather have state regimentation than slumps and unemployment, the drift towards collectivism is bound to continue. . . . Such is our present predicament. Capitalism leads to dole queues, the scramble for markets, and war. Collectivism leads to concentration camps, leader worship, and war. There is no way out of this unless a planned economy can somehow be combined with freedom of the intellect.[26]

Orwell's archaic endorsement of a liberal socialist space was simplistic, but his target clear. A decent politics and society cannot be constructed on the terrain of a strong, closed liberalism of the kind Hayek promoted, nor, in turn, certainly, on the ground of a strong, closed socialism.

In 1976, Noberto Bobbio addressed his *Quale Socialismo?* primarily to fellow members of the Italian left "to stimulate fresh debate on the old problem of the relationship between democracy and socialism." He devoted one chapter to the question "Why Democracy?" and the next he called "Which Socialism?"[27]

[26] Cited, without reference, in Bernard Crick, "Socialist Values and Time," Fabian Society pamphlet 495 (March 1984), p. 4.

[27] Noberto Bobbio, *Which Socialism? Marxism, Socialism, and Democracy* (Minneapolis: University of Minnesota Press, 1987), p. 103.

After 1989, it seems far more plausible to transpose the words to ask not why democracy, but which; not which socialism, but why. Perhaps, on examination, we will feel compelled to confirm Ralf Dahrendorf's forceful claim that "socialism is dead" and any vision of a "third way" a mirage, or Paul Starr's insistence that we draw an emphatic line between liberalism and socialism once and for all in order to avoid opening a Popular Front umbrella obscuring crucial differences.[28] From standpoints like these, the lessons of 1989 include jettisoning the priority of the left-right distinction and confirming that the liberal tradition uninvigorated and uncontaminated by socialism (or, for that matter, any other "ism") is autarchically capable of shaping a desirable political order when liberalism is properly understood and defended. Obviously, it makes no sense to find an appealing relationship between the liberal and socialist traditions if these seductive propositions prove persuasive. I think they are not. Indeed, I think they are worse than wrong, because they are inimical to the functioning of healthy democracies.

Certainly, the obsolescence of socialism and the affirmation of liberalism's capacities are important legacies of pre-1989 opposition thought, but not quite in the cartoon version Westerners with an axe to grind have used to portray these commitments. After all, 1989 imparts complex lessons: the dangers of some strands of the Enlightenment, but the Enlightenment's indispensability; the value of individualism, but the imperative of collective solidarity; the delegitimation of empire, but the costs of national self-determination; and, indeed, the welcome end of an ideology of grand narratives, but also the vacuity of democratic politics in the absence of the markers only political ideologies can provide. It is worth recalling, moreover, that when Steven Lukes introduced a collection of essays by Czech intellectuals written between the Charter's call for civil and

---

[28] Ralf Dahrendorf, *Reflections on the Revolution in Europe* (New York: Times Books, 1990), p. 42; Paul Starr, "Liberalism after Socialism," *The American Prospect* 7 (Fall 1991).

human rights in January 1977 and the rough persecution of its signatories, he observed that none of the authors, including Havel, Hejdanek, Benda, Hajek, and Kusy, "is explicitly unfriendly to the socialist idea or socialist principles." Rather, "most engage in the 'immanent critique' of so-called 'real socialism' for failing to live up to its principles, which none explicitly rejects," even though most did not incline to the Marxist socialist tradition. Lukes was in Warsaw in 1980, six months before Solidarity but four years after Jacek Kuron became the father of KOR. He asked Kuron "whether he thought contemporary Poland or Western capitalist countries were nearer to socialism." Kuron responded with a situational rather than a principled reply: "'What we have here,' he said, gesturing around him, '*is* socialism. We must use other vocabulary and talk, for example, of democratizing the state apparatus.'" Solidarity, which soon followed, was nourished by Catholic ethics, liberal democratic values, and Polish nationalism, and, as you know far better than I, forged a political theory grounded in the autonomy of civil society. Socialism of any kind was conspicuously absent.[29] Soon enough, the Czech opposition also put aside its once robust idea of socialism with a human face.

Dahrendorf's dismissal of socialism in 1990 resembled Kuron's and echoed Popper's. Dahrendorf stressed the tension characteristic of the antinomy of totalitarianism and the open society. Though he conceded that there is no single correct formula for an everyday politics within liberalism, he argued that once the binary choice between open and closed regimes is made, socialism (which at the constitutional level he identified with the "closed" option) has no special standing; "in normal politics a hundred options may be on offer, and three or four usually are. . . . But before we get to normal politics, the point has to be made unequivocally that socialism is dead and

[29] Steven Lukes, "Introduction," in Vaclav Havel, et. al., *The Power of the Powerless: Citizens against the State in Central-Eastern Europe*, ed. John Keane (Armonk, New York: M. E. Sharpe, 1985), pp. 14–15.

none of its variants can be revived for a world awakening from the double nightmare of Stalinism and Brezhnevism."[30]

Neither Kuron nor Dahrendof made clear whether this is a descriptive or a normative claim. Perhaps the distinction is now flawed; as Lukes points out, "one of the long-term achievements of 'real socialism' in the Soviet bloc may turn out to be the extinction there of the entire socialist tradition as a theoretical system worthy of serious consideration, let alone allegiance, wherever it is practised. (It has not exactly helped the prospects of socialism in the West either.)"[31] But would such a disappearance actually enhance "normal" politics situated within liberal political premises? Dahrendorf appears to think so because of socialism's "peculiar affinity to the state." Social democratic policies always mean more government, more planning, more bureaucracy; that is, the enhancement of "the democratic *nomenklatura.*"[32]

Dahrendorf also looks forward, more generally, to the end of ideology, convinced as many dissidents were before 1989 that differences between capitalism and socialism, and, less loftily, between left and right, are not meaningful ways to define political contention.[33] Rightly suspicious of simplistic utopian "isms," Dahrendorf moves seamlessly from a rejection of narra-

---

[30] Dahrendorf, *Reflections,* pp. 35, 42. For an argument that the current crisis of ideology is not just that of socialism but a general crisis produced by the immensity of demographic change and alterations to technology and systems of production, see Eric Hobsbawm, "The Crisis of Today's Ideologies," *New Left Review* 192 (March/April 1992).

[31] Lukes, "Introduction," p. 15.

[32] Dahrendorf, *Reflections,* pp. 56–57.

[33] For a particularly self-conscious consideration of the connections between Marxism and the emergent liberal opposition in East Europe, see Gyorgy Bence and Janos Kis, "On Being a Marxist: A Hungarian View," in Ralph Miliband and John Saville, eds., *The Socialist Register* (London: Merlin Books, 1980). They wrote, "We do not believe that a Marxist who wants to join the new opposition must at once deny Marxism. What we do maintain is that he no longer needs it and is quite unlikely to derive any relevant theoretical or political guidance from it" (p. 266). Soon, this relatively tolerant view hardened not only into an antimarxism, but into a more thoroughgoing antiideology, antipolitics stance. Bence reflected critically on this move at the first gathering of the New School democracy seminar network after Bolshevism collapsed, held in Budapest in the spring of 1990.

tives of "The Grand March"[34] to a problem-centered, pragmatic politics as the stance appropriate to the liberal democratic project.[35] By replicating a key aspect of dissident thought appropriate to the struggle against Bolshevism but displacing it to liberal political circumstances, I believe he leaves us rudderless in a genuinely posttotalitarian world.

"Ideology" soaks up a great deal of meaning. Perhaps for this reason alone we should do without it. But to reject ideology is to renounce an inherent component of a hearty democratic politics. Under Communism, ideology transcended politics by announcing utopian, transconflictual goals and worked to secure them under the tutelage of those in the know. In democracies, ideologies are sets of competing ideas that give order to politics in the here and now. By clustering choices in intelligible repertoires and by telling "stories" about state-society and state-economy interactions, as well as about the content of each of these key terms, ideological options compel judgment. For if under totalitarianism, as Havel has argued, it was impossible to "live in truth" within official ideology, so, paradoxically, it is not possible to "live in truth" in a democracy without ideology. Without ideological guideposts that combine professional knowledge with mass appeal, democratic politics would be so disordered as to be vulnerable to authoritarian and totalitarian possibilities. A formless pragmatism combined with democratic institutions does not constitute a recipe for a content-rich political life; a politics lacking in the coherent configurations provided by ideology has the potential to debase citizenship and the public sphere.[36] Even worse, the absence of a connection

[34] The term is Milan Kundera's, whose antipolitics in *The Unbearable Lightness of Being* sought to counter the totalitarian notion of "The Grand March," "the march from revolution to revolution." Milan Kundera, *The Unbearable Lightness of Being* (New York: Harper and Row, 1985), p. 99.

[35] For other versions of this argument, see Jeffrey Goldfarb, *Beyond Glasnost: The Post-Totalitarian Mind* (Chicago: University of Chicago Press, 1989); Jeffrey Goldfarb, *After the Fall: The Pursuit of Democracy in Central Europe* (New York: Basic Books, 1992).

[36] For a sensitive treatment of these transformations and their implication for the concept of civil society, see Bronislaw Geremek, "Civil Society Then and Now," *Journal of Democracy* 3 (April 1992).

between the visions of ideologies and everyday politics disorganizes normal day-to-day democratic life and threatens to leave the field of social movements and large-scale collective action to antiliberal mobilizations led by such crabby, anti-immigrant populists as Jean-Marie Le Pen and Patrick Buchanan. Rather than ask whether ideologies should be put to rest, I suggest that we ask what kind of ideologies, about what, for what?

Explicit in Dahrendorf's work is a claim advanced more fully by Stephen Holmes to the effect that liberalism possesses sufficient intellectual resources to pursue egalitarian goals without assistance from other traditions, including socialism.[37] There are two persuasive parts to this impulse toward liberal enclosure. The first is his case that liberalism, from the start, has possessed an affinity for an enabling, not just a negative, constitutionalism; that is, a constitutionalism that seeks not just to inhibit but to enable the sovereign. After all, "statelessness means rightslessness."[38] He also shows that liberalism is not inherently opposed to the use of state capacity to provide basic welfare resources to all citizens. "Misled by a deceptively clear dichotomy between latitudes and entitlements," he writes, "many detractors of liberalism assume that the classical liberal state was designed to protect freedoms without providing resources." Instead, he argues that "liberal hostility to 'entitlements' has been exaggerated by enemies on both the left and the right because "The plausibility of this charge ... disintegrates upon inspection. . . . Equal access to the law, while sometimes more an ideal than a reality, expresses a liberal commitment not merely to the provision but even to the *just distribution* of collective resources."[39] The welfare state, he thus avers, can be, indeed has been, built on liberal foundations.

Holmes convincingly stresses that liberals have considered

---

[37] Stephen Holmes, *Passions and Constraint: On the Theory of Liberal Democracy* (Chicago: University of Chicago Press, 1995). Also see his article, "The Liberal Idea," *The American Prospect* 7 (Fall 1991).

[38] Holmes, *Passions*, p. 270.   [39] Ibid., p. 12.

state power not only as a problem but also as a solution to dilemmas they have sought to confront. Yet by the end of his
book, his claim for the self-sufficiency of liberalism is denuded.
In showing that "it is perfectly plausible to interpret social provision as a faithful application of traditional liberal principles to
a new situation," he concedes that these

> considerations do not provide a moral or political justifica-
> tion of the redistributionist state. . . . They alone cannot
> compel us to support any specific public policy. . . . All that
> the historian of ideas can plausibly demonstrate, in fact, is
> that redistributive politics *should not be rejected* on the
> grounds that they are inherently illiberal or represent a
> betrayal of the great liberal legacy.[40]

One may ask, if liberalism permits welfarism as a counterweight
to inequality but is not itself the moral or political creator of
such institutions and policies, from where will these impulses
come? In the past, they have mainly come from outside the liberal tradition. With this question, the start of an answer to "why
socialism" can be discerned.

There is a more fundamental reason, moreover, to insist that
liberalism on its own cannot perform the autarchic role assigned by Dahrendorf and Holmes. Liberalism was born both as
a doctrine of religious toleration and as an attempt to free the
political from theological control. It did so by drawing lines
between the public and private, by reducing faith to belief, by
treating citizens as rights-bearing actors without regard to their
values or social attachments, and by refusing to choose between
competing visions of morality and virtue. Liberalism validated
a disjunction between power and opinion, and between what
philosophers today like to call the right and the good. By confronting and taming the demands of Christianity, liberalism
demarcated politics from important aspects of belief and conviction by promoting the process of secularization and the creation of new forms of state and governance.

[40] Ibid., p. 266.

These developments were ridden with tensions. Liberalism feared and imposed institutional limits on the states it elevated; and in the name of freedom, it came to be committed to a reduction in the space allotted not just to religious belief but to all normative opinion.[41] As a result, liberalism is capable of high promiscuity, willing and able to mate with a wide variety of ethical and political traditions provided they are amenable to playing by liberal rules; but liberalism also remains vulnerable to illiberal temptations by virtue of its principled thinness. Precisely those features many of us consider liberal virtues—its low-key approach to patriotism, its reticence in officially sanctioning communal origins, its commitments to individual autonomy—deprive liberalism of the resources with which to construct satisfying collective political and communal identities or normatively grounded guides to public policy. Liberalism thus finds itself exposed to the dangers of illiberalism. Not without irony, I believe liberalism needs socialism (though not only, and not just any, socialism) as a partner to provide moral and practical elements it cannot supply on its own to help guard its crooked circle against illiberal adversaries.

There exists, of course, a strong and familiar objection: the freedom valued by liberalism and the equality prized by socialism conflict. Socialists long have insisted that it is private property and market competition for gain that constitute central impediments to meaningful freedom and individuality for the great majority; but the reciprocal argument (made not only by many liberals but also by Marx) that liberty and equality are contradictory, that an increase in one of these values necessarily is purchased at the expense of the other, must be taken seriously. Should this view prove persuasive (as it currently seems to be) we would be propelled to choose between them, as

[41] "Does the 'indeterminacy' credited to our political regimes," Pierre Manent asks, "mean that we are seeing explicitly instituted the disjunction between power, knowledge, and right that is essential to freedom? Or does it rather bring to light the paradox of a state which, having wished to close itself off from Christianity's power, from the power of one particular opinion, is endlessly obliged to deprive any opinion of power?" Pierre Manent, *An Intellectual History of Liberalism*, trans. Rebecca Balinski (Princeton: Princeton University Press, 1994), p. xviii.

such celebrated anti-egalitarian libertarians as Hayek, Robert Nozick, and Milton Friedman have insisted we must.[42]

But they are wrong. As Steven Lukes has shown, such thinkers stack the deck by the way they specify equality as to make it appear an arbitrary imposition on outcomes produced via the functioning of liberty. Their definitions—which view equality simply as the coercively imposed redistribution of material things and liberty as the ability to choose freely and voluntarily—end any debate before it begins. If, however, these contested concepts are treated less tendentiously, the libertarian anti-egalitarian case collapses.[43]

So, too, does the softer position which argues that liberty and equality as discrete values must trade off; the argument that the pursuit of one requires a reduction in the scope of the other.[44] The problem with this quite common position, Lukes explains, is that liberty and equality are multifold, intertwined values. As a result, they can be treated neither as incommensurable, as the libertarians do, nor as simple outlooks that must trade off. Liberty is more than the freedom to act on beliefs and yearnings. It also is the freedom to reconsider and change one's preferences. Thus, "Assessments of the extent or degrees of the realization of freedom are unavoidably contaminated by judgments about what matters."[45] Equality also is a complex concept because of the heterogeneity of that which is to be equalized. Political theorists who have grappled with this issue have come up with different answers: for Rawls, primary goods; for Dworkin, resources; for Sen, capabilities. Further, liberty and equal-

---

[42] Friedrich Hayek, *The Constitution of Liberty* (London: Routledge & Kegan Paul, 1960); Robert Nozick, *Anarchy, State, and Utopia* (New York: Basic Books, 1974); Milton Friedman and Rose Friedman, *Free to Choose* (London: Secker and Warburg, 1980).

[43] Steven Lukes, "Equality and Liberty: Must They Conflict?" in Lukes, *Moral Conflict and Politics* (Oxford: Clarendon Press, 1991).

[44] The extent to which the independent values of liberty and equality are realized is thought to be susceptible to measurement "according to some scale that enables people to express a preference between such 'extents,' or indifference between them; or, alternatively, economic and social policies or institutions or systems can be seen as capable of producing different combinations of such 'extents.'" Ibid., p. 59.

[45] Ibid., p. 60.

ity cannot be characterized independently one of the other. On virtually all the accounts we possess of equality, liberty is one of the goods to be equalized, "a constitutive part of the *equalisandum.*" It patently is not true that the equalization of liberties must always lead to their reduction. Rather than treat liberty and equality as antithetical assets, we need ask "whose equality, whose liberty, what is equalized and which liberties are in question."[46]

II

I wish I had read "Conversation in the Citadel" before your questioning about socialism put me on the defensive when we were first introduced. After all, it was far more surprising that you would use the language of socialism in the middle 1980s than I.

When we met, I did not yet know your views were an exception. Seemingly oblivious to the cigarette burning to your fingertips as we sat at a corner table in the Victoria's massive dining room, you inquired about my politics with sardonic amusement. "I understand you are a person of the left, a socialist, with some interest in marxism." Unsure of my ground, I nervously muttered an imprecise reply stressing our shared commitments to liberalism and to democracy. Though this conversation was not anodyne, I regret we did not have a less lenitive dialogue about the relationship of liberalism and socialism.

I would have particularly liked to discuss two points. The first, about the nature of the socialism we might wish to have, is raised by the way you introduced "socialism" into the body of

[46] For Rawls, primary goods are "rights and liberties, opportunities and powers, income and wealth." For Dworkin, resources are "those features of body or mind or personality that provide means or impediments to a successful life." For Sen, capabilities are the "real opportunities faced by the person." John Rawls, *A Theory of Justice* (Oxford: Clarendon Press, 1972), p. 92; Ronald Dworkin, "Equality of Resources," *Philosophy and Public Affairs* 10 (Summer 1981): 303; Amartya Sen, *Commodities and Capabilities* (Amsterdam: North Holland, 1985), p. 5; Lukes, "Equality and Liberty," pp. 62–63.

your essay. The second, concerning the possibility of mutually satisfactory relations between liberalism and socialism, is entailed in your answer to Janusz Onyszkiewiewicz, who had responded to "Conversation in the Citadel" by stating, "Socialism is a thoroughly discredited term," and by asking, "Is it good that you use it in your conclusions?"[47]

When you enumerated guidelines for a political program in the concluding section of "Citadel," you followed each assertion, but one, with an elucidation of your reasons. When you addressed "socialism," you provided not a single word of your own. Instead, you invoked the authority of Leszek Kolakowski, quoting an (undated) citation from his socialist humanist phase. His text qualified your bald exhortation, "We need socialism." Leszek had written,

> We need a living tradition of socialist thought which in proclaiming the traditional values of social justice and freedom appeals solely to human forces. But here we do not need the ideas of any socialism. We do not need crazy dreams of a society from which all evil temptations have been removed or dreams of a total revolution which all at once will bring us a bliss of final redemption in a world devoid of conflict. What we need is a socialism that will help us find our way in the complex reality of the brutal forces that operate in human history, a socialism that will strengthen our readiness to fight poverty and social injustice. We need a socialist tradition conscious of its own limitations, because the dream of final redemption is despair dressed in the cloak of hope, the greed of power clothed in
> . the gown of justice.[48]

[47] Michnik, *Letter*, p. 333.

[48] Ibid., p. 328. Though Michnik gives no reference, I believe this is an excerpt from Kolakowski's "What Is Socialism?," an unpublished essay written in 1956 that was refused publication by the relevant authorities. It was written, Kolakowski has told me, in the form of a parody, answering its question in the form of listing the characteristics socialists should not want by naming the key features of the Communist regime. Michnik, however, remembers the citation coming from an article Kolakowski wrote in 1976 on ideology.

When you responded to Onyszkiewiewicz, you did not repeat Kolakowski's point that not just any socialism will do. Rather, you claimed that socialism complemented the other strands of political and ethical thought on which you relied:

I don't know how to give an unequivocal answer to this question, even to myself. Because, indeed, in Poland the word *socialism* is both discredited and ambiguous. From this point of view it should be abandoned. Nonetheless, the Polish workers' movement and its party, the PPS, which upheld the ideals of the rights of working people and of national independence, the principles of "Poland's freedom and the freedom of man in Poland," used the word for decades. It is true that the PPS's socialism was the child of another era, the product of different social and intellectual circumstances. But isn't the overall form of those ideological conflicts an archival phenomenon? Do we not often argue about the past, thinking that we are arguing about the truths of the present? Is it not the case that out of the melting pot of the past, new programs, new ideologies, new expressions of old conflicts are bound to emerge? Is it not the case that the plans which are being made today for a self-governing republic must be a synthesis of the motifs that clashed yesterday and could not be reconciled, but which today are complementary and natural allies, mutually enriching each other? I believe that this is exactly the case today. That is why I used the concept of "socialist tradition," in which I see an indispensable factor of our present-day hopes. And this is why I wrote "Conversation in the Citadel."[49]

In October 1994, I asked Michnik in New York why he had utilized Kolakowski's text rather than his own, and whether he would still write "we need socialism" today. He replied that "in 'Citadel' I was saying goodbye to socialism as a man does to his wife before a divorce." Respecting the values of the socialist tradition, he communicated regard; but given that the dictatorship had traduced those traditions, the language of socialism had lost its meaning for Poland.

[49] Michnik, *Letter*, p. 333.

Had I been aware of this essay when you challenged me to defend my politics, I would have agreed with Kolakowski about the *kind* of socialism we should wish to have, but I would have contested your sense of the ready complementarity of socialism with what you called its "natural allies." Kolakowski's, and your, position in favor of the right kind of socialism was and continues to be warranted by steep hierarchies of social and economic power about which liberalism has had nothing inherent to say.[50] These demand remedy; you rightly identified the endowment of a century and a half of socialist thought as an important source of repair. The coupling of socialism and liberalism, however, does not constitute an easy alliance, at least not without specification. After all, figures as incongruous as Sidney and Beatrice Webb, Michael Oakeshott, and Hayek have been included by historians of ideas within the liberal camp.[51] Socialism, too, is remarkably heterogeneous, encompassing impulses both for democratization and decentralization and for privileging a party vanguard charged to sanction strong statist centralization. As the great liberal historian Elie Halevy put it in his 1936 lecture on "The Era of Tyrannies,"

> Since its beginnings, in the early years of the nineteenth century, socialism has suffered from an internal contradiction. On the one hand, its partisans often present it as the outcome and fulfillment of the Revolution of 1789, a revolution of liberty, a liberation from the last subjection after all others have been destroyed: the subjection of labor by capital. But, on the other hand, it is also a reaction against individualism and liberalism; it proposes a new compulsory organization in place of the outworn institutions destroyed by the Revolution.[52]

---

[50] For a statement of his views, see Leszek Kolakowski, "Amidst Moving Ruins," *Daedalus* 121 (Spring 1992).

[51] Brian Lee Crowley, *The Self, the Individual, and the Community: Liberalism in the Political Thought of F. A. Hayek and Sidney and Beatrice Webb* (Oxford: Clarendon Press, 1987); Paul Franco, "Michael Oakeshott as Liberal Theorist," *Political Theory* 18 (August 1990).

[52] Elie Halevy, *The Era of Tyrannies* (New York: Anchor Books, 1965), p. 265.

In the face of this liberal and socialist diversity, is it possible to imagine how a productive relationship between liberalism and socialism could be designed? This is a pressing question not just for socialists who might be seen by skeptics as reaching for a citizenship and rights-based political liberalism as the last chance for a doomed world view ("Democracy," Ferdinand Mount claims, is "the Left's new alternative to socialism")[53] but for the left, understood broadly as Wright Mills did and with more precision as the political tendency oriented to the rectification of inequality and skeptical about the claims and portrait of an abstract and unembedded individualism.[54] By now, it should go without saying that a socialism not fixed firmly inside political liberalism is strongly inclined toward contemptible practices by unconfined elites. As you are discovering in Poland, however, liberalism cannot make coherent politics and policy on its own. The comeback of the ex-Communists and *nomenklatura* reminds us that vast inequalities must not be left unchecked, not only because they are intrinsically undesirable but because, as Orwell predicted, they help invoke antiliberal options on the right and the left. Though you might not think so today, you were right to believe that the renewal of the democratic left depends on delineating and mapping the site where liberalism and socialism meet.

It hardly is a fresh idea to aver that some combination of the best in liberal and socialist precepts ought to be assembled. Among others, John Stuart Mill, John Dewey, Karl Mannheim, Bertrand Russell, John Rawls, Michael Walzer, and Noberto

[53] Ferdinand Mount, "Vote, Vote and Vote Again," *Times Literary Supplement*, May 7, 1993, p. 15; for an earlier version of this theme, see his "The Left's Last Throw," *Times Literary Supplement*, March 8, 1991.

[54] Here I am following Steven Lukes, "What Is Left? Essential Socialism and the Urge to Rectify," *Times Literary Supplement*, March 27, 1992. In a stinging rejoinder, Roger Scruton upbraided Lukes for failing to come to terms with the relationship of all socialisms to the Communist tradition and experience. This, of course, is a complex and heterogeneous subject which Scruton's screed vastly simplifies. Does he wish by way of this association to eliminate all socialisms from normal democratic political life? Roger Scruton, "What Is Right? A Reply to Steven Lukes," *Times Literary Supplement*, April 3, 1992.

Bobbio have advocated one or another version of this project.[55] In the main, their attempts to develop and sustain liberal socialism have been more appealing as efforts to define attractive ends than successful as a doctrine, a movement, or a durable combination.

Socialists who have advocated ties with the liberal tradition have sought to persuade other socialists that this project is possible without sacrificing core socialist ideas and values; that is, that Perry Anderson is wrong to assert that the combination of liberalism and socialism is an "unstable compound," which, "after seeming to attract one another must end by separating out, and in the same chemical process the liberalism moves toward conservatism."[56] Thus, when Carlo Rosselli sought to persuade Italian socialists in his *Liberal Socialism* that "the day will come when this word, this attribute [liberalism], will be claimed with proud self-awareness by the socialist," he observed,

> The phrase "liberal socialism" has a strange sound to many of us who are accustomed to current political terminology. The word 'liberalism' unfortunately has been used to smuggle so many different kinds of merchandise and has been so much the preserve of the bourgeoisie in the past,

[55] For a consideration of the relationship between liberalism and socialism in the emergent American academy of the late nineteenth century, see Dorothy Ross, "Socialism and American Liberalism: Academic Social Thought in the 1880's," *Perspectives in American History* 11 (1977–1978). Ross traces the generation of thinkers who entered the universities and transformed American liberalism from classic laissez-faire to a statist, progressive orientation. Their road traveled through socialism. Ross asks why such thinkers as Richard Ely, John Bates Clark, and Henry Carter Adams engaged with socialism only to set it aside, and she argues that what forced these economists to return to the liberal camp was labor unrest and the repressive reaction to it that created public pressures against socialism.

[56] Perry Anderson, "The Affinities of Noberto Bobbio," *New Left Review* 170 (July/ August 1988): 36. For another set of assessments on recent attempts "to chart a relationship between liberalism and socialism," see Peter Osborne, ed., *Socialism and the Limits of Liberalism* (London: Verso Books, 1991). The remarkable heterogeneity of essays in this collection, based on a 1988 conference, is symptomatic both of the extent of the loss of confidence by socialists even before 1989 and of deep confusion over whether and how to join the socialist and liberal traditions.

that today a socialist has difficulty bringing himself to use it. But I do not wish to propose a new party terminology here. I wish only to bring the socialist movement back to its first principles, to its historical and psychological origins, and to demonstrate that socialism, in the last analysis, is a philosophy of liberty.[57]

Likewise, liberals who have promoted a more social liberalism usually have sought to persuade fellow liberals that their program represents a realization, not a negation, of the liberal enterprise. In a representative example, L. T. Hobhouse urged collaboration with socialism on the basis of shared "roots deep in the necessities of Democracy." A properly argued liberalism, he told other liberals, embodies "many of the ideas that go to make up the framework of Socialist teaching."[58]

In the main, these efforts have been vague about the alterations to liberalism and socialism required in order to make their joining transcend what Hobhouse called "a half-hearted and illogical series of compromises" or to overcome what Benedetto Croce thought to be a set of "easy conclusions, falling into the logical mistake of juxtaposing" liberalism and socialism to produce a union based on a "synthetic formula."[59] When liberalism and socialism are conjoined without sufficient specification, the result indeed can resemble Croce's dismissal

[57] Carlo Rosselli, *Liberal Socialism* (Princeton: Princeton University Press, 1994) (original edition, 1930), pp. 84–85. Rosselli wrote this text during his imprisonment on the island of Lipari in 1928–1929; it was first published in French in 1930 after he had fled to Paris.

[58] L. T. Hobhouse, *Liberalism* (Oxford: Oxford University Press, 1964) (original edition, 1911), pp. 109, 108. "Writing in 1911," Jack Lively has noted, "the radical liberal Hobhouse, rejecting the possibility of any reconciliation between liberalism and State socialism, nevertheless saw the possibility of a Liberal Socialism, provided it fulfilled two conditions—it must be democratic and it must 'make its account with the human individual'." Jack Lively, "Programmes for Progressives," *Times Literary Supplement*, November 3–9, 1989, p. 1200.

[59] Benedetto Croce, *L'idea liberale. Contre le confusioni e gli ibridismi.* (Bari: Laterza, 1944), pp. 16–20; and Croce, *Nuove pagine sparse* (Naples: Ricciardi, 1929), 2:195–96. These are cited in Nadia Urbinati, "Introduction to Another Socialism," in Roselli, *Liberal Socialism*, p. L.

of liberal socialism as "a hircovervus, a fabulous creature half-goat and half-stag, an absurd and aesthetically unpleasant combination that purported to attach the rough, rude, and shaggy body of socialism to the long and agile legs of liberalism."[60] To do better, we might inquire, as Hobhouse did, about the forms of socialism to which liberalism should relate and those "with which Liberalism has nothing to do"[61] (and, reciprocally, about the kind of liberalism with which socialism should wish to engage).

Hobhouse counseled his fellow liberals to reject what he called mechanical and official socialism. By mechanical, he meant a socialism of economistic reduction; by official, the doctrine that class struggle based on a simplified notion of class structure motors all history. He sought, in short, to set aside the core ideas, as he understood them, of marxism. He called instead for a socialism with the ability to formulate "not a system to be substituted as a whole for our present arrangements but a principle to guide statesmanship in the practical work of reforming what is amiss and developing what is good in the actual fabric of society."[62] I disagree with Hobhouse about the total inadmissibility of marxism and about the degree of his tilt away from critique toward simple, merely pragmatic reform, but I do think we must reason on the ground he staked out.

III

In introducing the translation of *Liberal Socialism* to American readers, Michael Walzer described Carol Rosselli as possessing "the state of mind of a socialist who has sailed away from Marxist seas and touched land on the shores of liberalism."[63] Walzer intended this representation to convey a sense of providential attainment. But his image, like your response to Onyszkiewie-

---

[60] Urbinati, "Introduction," p. L.

[61] Hobhouse, *Liberalism*, p. 88.

[62] Ibid., pp. 88–89.

[63] Michael Walzer, introduction to Carlo Rosselli, "Liberal Socialism," *Dissent* 41 (Winter 1994): 123.

wicz, lacks sufficient recognition, as it were, that locations where land and water meet are unstable, dangerous sites. Their interjacent geography demarcates zones where complexity is experienced, lived, and navigated.[64]

To take one's bearings in such environments there has to be an acknowledgment of the difficulties of such in-between places.[65] Unfortunately, it has been all too common for those on the left committed to build a relationship between liberalism and socialism to skip this step. Two years after he wrote his "Letter to the New Left," Wright Mills published a book to make marxism accessible to American readers. Though he made his distance from Stalinism crystal clear, he insisted he could find no contradictions between liberalism and marxism. Marx, he wrote, was a secular moralist, a rationalist, a humanist who believed in freedom. The doctrine he initiated, like liberalism, was an insurgent creed that, also like liberalism, had become conservative. Indeed, Mills argued,

> What is most valuable in classic liberalism is most cogently and most fruitfully incorporated in classic marxism. Much of the failure to confront marxism in all its variety is in fact a way of *not* taking seriously the ideals of liberalism itself, for despite the distortions and vulgarizations of Marx's ideas, and despite his own errors, ambiguities, and inadequacies, Karl Marx remains the thinker who has articulated most clearly—and most perilously—the basic ideals which liberalism shares.[66]

[64] "On the beach, where the sea wets the land, boundary disputes and ambiguities naturally pile up. . . . The seaman looks anxiously to his depth sounder as he closes with the shore, for land is always dangerous to ships, while the landsman fears the water— the tide fanning out at speed over the level sands, the undertow, the deep. The law of the land gets into trouble when it reaches the ocean, often being hard put to say where the land is, or if the land is." Jonathan Raban, "On the Waterfront," *New York Review of Books*, July 14, 1994, p. 37.

[65] For rich discussions of borderlands as temporal and topographical, situational and personal, see Martin Meisel, "Waverly, Freud, and Topographical Metaphor," *University of Toronto Quarterly* 58 (Spring 1979); and Ann Stoler, "Sexual Affronts and Racial Frontiers: European Identities and the Cultural Politics of Exclusion in Colonial Southeast Asia," *Comparative Studies in Society and History* (July 1992).

[66] C. Wright Mills, *The Marxists* (New York: Dell Publishing, 1962), p. 14.

Now, I continue to think that marxism "for all its profound
and infirming flaws as a total ensemble of understanding and
governance . . . remains a vital tool for understanding and
raising questions about key aspects of modernity"; and I still
maintain that "in the aftermath of the conclusive triumph of
liberal citizenship and markets over competing conceptions,
the analytical and critical dimensions of Marxism, albeit in a
manner far more modest than Marxists once hoped, may now
find a new significance as a source of intellectual and political
friction."[67] But Mills's correct assertion that both marxism
and liberalism are offspring of the Enlightenment and share in
the Enlightenment's commitments to rationality, logic, progress, and self-conscious human projects hardly exhausts what
can be said about their relationship. In particular, Mills demonstrated an insouciance about the illiberal, antidemocratic
elements Marx self-consciously embedded inside his own
writings.[68]

The example of Mills conveys just how tempted even manifestly democratic socialists have been to treat marxism as a relatively unproblematical set of resources while eliding its shadowy
features in doctrine and in practice. The failure by socialists to
make crisp distinctions between illiberal and liberal variants
has proved strongest when liberalism has seemed radically insufficient and when the left has felt itself isolated and besieged.
In the 1930s and early 1940s, claims like Max Horkheimer's
that the liberal era had been closed by fascism's pincers seemed
self-evident.[69] Even in the United States, liberalism's fate

[67] Ira Katznelson, *Marxism and the City* (Oxford: Clarendon Press, 1993), p. vii. An
argument developed along these lines is by Adam Przeworski, "Economic Constraints
on Political Choices: On the Continuing Relevance of Marxist Political Theory of Capitalism," ms., 1994.

[68] For discussions, see J. L. Talmon, *The Origins of Totalitarian Democracy* (London:
Secker and Warburg, 1952); Leszek Kolakowski, *Main Currents of Marxism: Its Rise,
Growth, and Dissolution* (Oxford: Clarendon Press, 1978, 1981); Pierre Birnbaum, "Uni-
versal Suffrage, the Vanguard Party and Mobilization in Marxism," *Government and Op-
position* 20 (Winter 1985); Jean L. Cohen, *Class and Civil Society: The Limits of Marxian
Political Theory* (Amherst: University of Massachusetts Press, 1982).

[69] On Horkheimer, see Brian Barry, "Liberalism and Private Property," *Liber* 1 (February 1990): 6.

looked uncertain. In 1939, Walter Lippmann attributed its deep crisis of legitimacy to "the accumulated disappointments of the post-War era," referring to Woodrow Wilson's promise of global peace, the Republican party's guarantee of permanent prosperity in the 1920s, and the New Deal's pledge, unredeemed in 1939, to end the Depression. "Three times in these twenty years the American people have had a great hope and three times they have been greatly disappointed."[70]

It was in the context of this exhaustion and liberalism's loss of élan that Harold Laski, the Labour party activist, public intellectual, and professor of political science at the University of London,[71] mounted the podium at the London School of Economics to deliver the tenth annual L. T. Hobhouse Memorial Lecture on "The Decline of Liberalism."

In his 1911 codification of the New Liberalism, Hobhouse had represented individualist liberalism from Locke to Mill as a wholly negative doctrine, obsessed with the propensity for depredation and tyranny by the modern state.[72] Its core instrument was freedom of contract; its central idea, individual

[70] Walter Lippmann, *The American Destiny* (New York: Life Magazine Press, 1939), p. 4. For another influential treatment of liberalism's crisis, see Edward Hallett Carr, *Conditions of Peace* (London: Macmillan, 1942). Carr thought the solution lay in taking the planning impulses of fascism and Communism and transmuting them to a reinvigorated liberal democracy. Lippmann, by contrast, advocated a reinvigorated anticollectivist laissez-faire. See his *The Good Society* (London: Allen and Unwin, 1937).

[71] There are two estimable recent biographies: Michael Newman, *Harold Laski: A Political Biography* (London: Macmillan, 1993); and Isaac Kramnick and Barry Sheerman, *Harold Laski: A Life on the Left* (London: Hamish Hamilton, 1993). As a treatment of Laski's scholarship, especially with respect to his early work on pluralism, neither surpasses Bernard Zylstra, *From Pluralism to Collectivism: The Development of Harold Laski's Political Thought* (Assen, the Netherlands: Van Gorcum and Company, 1968); or Herbert A. Deane, *The Political Ideas of Harold J. Laski* (New York: Columbia University Press, 1955). Also see E. J. Hobsbawm, "The Left's Megaphone," *London Review of Books*, July 8, 1993. In reviewing Newman and Kramnick and Sheerman, Hobsbawm underscored the significance of Laski's Jewishness and the manner in which he managed to combine admiration for Roosevelt's New Deal and Stalin's USSR.

[72] "It would be impossible to have the essential principles of any political creed more clearly stated than they are in this little book," *The Spectator* observed in its review; 107 (August 12, 1911): 248. At the time, Hobhouse was professor of sociology at the University of London. For a consideration of Hobhouse in context, see Stefan Collini, *Liberalism and Sociology: L. T. Hobhouse and Political Argument in England, 1880–1914* (Cambridge: Cambridge University Press, 1979).

choice. Though both were deployed in the service of liberty, the unsocial and coercive qualities of property, unequally held, and the inclination of market societies to monopoly, he argued, had put individualism in question. The answer lay in an enlargement of social control. Liberty is not just a matter of negative protections. It requires the enablement of members of society, understood as a fellowship. Mutual aid to provide such agency rights is the partner of individual freedom.[73]

In Hobhouse's rendering, the double aim of social liberalism is the enlargement of liberty and the promotion of harmony through the instrumentality of the state, seen as the organized expression of society as an organic community. He took pains to avow that the state, albeit "distinguished by its use of coercive power, by its supremacy, and by its claim to control all who dwell within its geographical limits," should be regarded "as one among many forms of human association for the maintenance and improvement of life." Its utilization to these ends "not only involves no conflict with the true principle of personal liberty, but is necessary to its effective realization." In sum, he concluded, "Liberty and compulsion have complementary functions, and the self-governing State is at once the product and the condition of the self-governing individual."[74]

Three decades later, Laski sought to address liberalism's crisis. "We must, if we are to be honest, admit that the liberalism for which Hobhouse battled so bravely has suffered an eclipse as startling and as complete as that which attended the doctrine of the divine right of kings after the Revolution of 1688." Everywhere, he noted, the validity of liberalism's ideals was being "passionately renounced" as its incapacity to deal with the world crisis became increasingly manifest.[75]

---

[73] Hobhouse, *Liberalism*, p. 67.

[74] Ibid., pp. 71, 78, 81. In his work, as in his key predecessor T. H. Green's (the Idealist Oxford philosopher for whom will, not force, is the basis of the state), the intellectual foil for the New Liberalism's "positive freedom" was Mill's harm principle, the foundation of "negative liberalism." T. H. Green, *Lectures on the Principles of Political Obligation* (London: Oxford University Press, 1941) (original edition, 1882).

[75] Harold Laski, *The Decline of Liberalism*, L. T. Hobhouse Memorial Trust Lectures, no. 10 (London: Oxford University Press, 1940), pp. 3, 4.

Why so? His answer was straightforward. Liberalism had grown comfortable with the privileges capitalism accorded to the middle classes, who had provided its early social base. Faced with mass pressures by the labor movement and democratic politics, these classes grudgingly had conceded reforms, "forced to be generous where . . . not prepared spontaneously to be just." But what they had not permitted was a deeper questioning of the social and economic foundations of inequality. The result was the deep disaffection of the masses. Liberalism's leaders "did not understand . . . that men think differently who live differently, and that a simple faith in the power of reason to win common ground will not do because between those who live so differently there is not, in fact, a common language." Liberalism made the mistake of believing "that its procedures were eternal. It failed to understand that no procedures have that quality unless men who live by them accept the results to which they give birth."[76]

Starting from this acute diagnosis, Laski proposed a project we still badly require: "a refreshment and a reinvigoration of the doctrinal content of liberalism comparable in magnitude to the work of the Benthamites a century ago." Working from a (simplified) marxist analysis of the contradictions wrought by capitalism between the material and social relations of production, he insisted liberalism could be saved only by replacing individual with social property, and by substituting planning aimed at abundance for markets based on scarcity.[77] The manner in which he sought to construct this undertaking, however, constitutes a leading example of a search for remedies to the insufficiencies of liberalism without due consideration for the terms of the union of liberalism and socialism.

[76] Ibid., pp. 16, 15, 21.

[77] Ibid., pp. 22–23. For a contemporaneous approach, of which Laski almost certainly was aware, see John Dewey, *Liberalism and Social Action* (New York: G. P. Putnam's Sons, 1935). "I have wanted to find out," Dewey wrote, "whether it is possible for a person to continue, honestly and intelligently, to be a liberal, and if the answer is in the affirmative, what kind of faith should be asserted today" (pp. 5–6). He sought to rescue liberalism's individualism, stress on liberty, and values of free inquiry and expression from the clutches of capitalism and property and from the dictatorship of class.

Laski believed he had moved beyond Hobhouse and the New Liberals by deploying marxist tools to stare hard at class and state power. In fact, he had managed only a one-eyed squint. For the very dissolution of the separation of property and sovereignty Laski advocated in keeping with marxism's core ideas signified more than a deep disagreement with core liberal designs. It invited the utilization of the state not to dissolve but to conjoin economic and political privilege. The union of political liberalism and marxism he advocated, moreover, made nonsense of both. There is quite a distance between marxism as a critical tool with which to interrogate capitalism and prod liberalism to a reflexive recognition of its limits and silences and marxism as a formula for social organization and revolutionary transformation.

Marxism necessarily must derogate what it sees as the mystifications of civil and political rights and procedures in class-ridden societies based on property; liberalism necessarily must reject marxism's consequentialist ethics, anti-individualism, demotic self-sufficiency, and hierarchy of objects of struggle. Liberalism values toleration and ethical pluralism; marxism seeks to pierce the sham of forbearance and empower a single universal class. For political marxism, property rights provide the basis for domination, degradation, and social power; for liberals, they "define the space of opportunity within which he or she can seek to shape their lives."[78] For marxists, property rights are arbitrary impositions; for liberals, entitlements. Peering at each

---

[78] John Dunn, "Claims and Contexts," *Times Literary Supplement*, May 5–11, 1989, p. 489. This view is contested by Brian Barry, who argues, more, I believe, as a wish than as a grounded account, that property cannot be central to liberal rights because it is enjoyed only by a minority. He does see markets as essential to liberalism, but he seeks to sever their ties to property by arguing that the essence of markets is a system that disseminates information. He thus asks that we focus, in rather a utopian fashion, on the potential compatibility of liberalism, democracy, and noncapitalistic markets. Brian Barry, "Liberalism and Private Property," *Liber* 1 (February 1990). Mancur Olson grounds the contrary claim historically, arguing that "The conditions necessary for a lasting democracy are the same necessary for the security of property and contract rights that generate economic growth." Mancur Olson, "Dictatorship, Democracy, and Development," *American Political Science Review* 87 (September 1993): 567.

other across a divide, liberals and marxists see confirming images of tyrannical impositions, complacency about power, and failures to take "authentic" democracy seriously.[79] All this Laski's Hobhouse lecture left out of consideration.[80]

This evasion produced remarkable contortions in Laski's consideration of Bolshevism (reminiscent of the way some liberals have sought to find a place for a wide variety of despotic anti-Communist regimes), most notably in his 1943 volume, *Reflections on the Revolution of Our Time*.[81] Laski believed that Burke's aristocratic prejudices had rendered him incapable of seeing the future; by contrast, he believed he had successfully discerned an irresistible socialist future, one whose history had begun in 1917.

Laski's assessment of the Soviet Union was tellingly disjointed.[82] Based on liberal political presumptions, the first part of the relevant discussion in *Reflections* contains scathing denunciations of Bolshevism's traducement of basic human liberties. Laski showed how the dictatorship of the proletariat had become the dictatorship of the party and how the party had assimilated itself to the state. Permitting no threat to their unity, both were prepared to use all means, including bloody purges and the penetration of society by secret police, to protect their power. The Bolsheviks monopolized information and its dissemination. "Elections are a farce"; "there is arbitrary arrest"; "there is long imprisonment, and even execution, without

[79] For a still valuable discussion, see Franz Neumann, "On the Marxist Theory of the State," in Otto Kircheimer and Franz Neumann, *Social Democracy and the Rule of Law* (London: Allen and Unwin, 1987).

[80] Similarly, John Dewey's Page-Barbour Lectures of 1934 argued that "the cause of liberalism will be lost for a considerable period if it is not prepared to go further and socialize the forces of production, so that the liberty of individuals will be supported by the very structure of economic organization," without inquiring about whether his formulation "that socialized economy is the means of free individual development as the end" was characterized by antagonistic contradictions. John Dewey, *Liberalism and Social Action*, pp. 88, 90.

[81] Harold J. Laski, *Reflections on the Revolution of Our Time* (New York: Viking Press, 1943).

[82] An earlier treatment can be found in Harold Laski, *Communism* (London: Frank Cass, 1968) (orig. ed., 1927).

trial." Travel is restricted. Prisoners lack rights of *habeas corpus.*
Trials are held in secret with no real defense allowed. Children
are eulogized for denouncing their parents. Laski's eloquent
indictment ran on over the course of many pages to conclude,
"I know no justification of these things which seems to me ra-
tionally based. It can only be justified for those in whose eyes
the rules of the Soviet Union can do no wrong."[83]

Immediately, however, his apologies began. "Despite many
and grave errors," he observed, the Soviet Union's rulers did
not "maintain personal power for its own sake merely. The
great end of the Revolution remains in being. . . . And it is
proper to note that the habits of the dictatorship appear to
seem far less evil to millions of Soviet citizens than they do to
the outside observer." Further, for the Soviet citizen, faith in
the regime holds "high its standard on behalf of the unemanci-
pated masses elsewhere." For Laski, the USSR remained part,
perhaps the most important part, of the socialist grand narrative; its violations of liberal process he thought secondary to
this purpose. With this view in hand, Laski was keen to distinguish fascism, as well as right-wing big business in the capitalist
West, as part of the inherently antidemocratic counterrevolu-
tion, from the Soviet experience. He argued, remarkably, that
"the difference is the vital one that there is nothing in the nature of the Bolshevik state which is alien from the democratic
ideal." He insisted, not without some merit, that the realization
of what he saw as the Soviet Union's progressive course "has
been halted, in the main, because its experiment . . . has never
been conducted in an atmosphere of security"; but in this way
he dismissed Bolshevism's responsibilities for its own action.
Once the tensions surrounding the safety of the revolution dis-
sipated, he predicted, "its true character as a genuine search
for democracy and freedom . . . can verify itself in experience"
and serve as a model for the elimination of private property by
popular mandate in the West. Socialism and liberalism then

[83] Laski, *Reflections,* pp. 57, 69–70.

would be fused. The only alternative, he believed, was super-fascism.[84]

This panegyric, reminiscent of the previous decade's *Soviet Communism* by the Webbs,[85] alas was no fluke or aberration. Because property, capital, and exploitation by the bourgeoisie are the principal sources of social power, and the capitalist state, irrespective of the rights it upholds, acts as the force of coercion for those holding such power, the exercise of planned authority by the state against capital and the elimination of private property are the only feasible instruments with which to achieve egalitarian goals. Embedded in this world view, Laski seemingly forgot his prior warnings about state despotism. In spite of a profession to the contrary, he ended up by claiming that socialist ends really do justify distasteful means.[86]

[84] Ibid., pp. 71–71, 301. I think it significant to note that the late Ralph Miliband—Laski's student and arguably his most important heir on the recent British left to the effort to draw substantially on marxist tools of analysis while holding to the values of political liberalism—took a very different position on Communist regimes. Published on the eve of Communism's fall, Miliband's "Reflections on the Crisis of Communist Regimes," a title, given his lineage, not chosen lightly, assessed Bolshevism in practice and found it terribly wanting. He lambasted its "savage repression" and observed that "the system entailed an extreme inflation of state power, and, correspondingly, a stifling of all social forces not controlled by, and subservient to, the leadership of the party/state." The lesson he drew for Western socialists was that, at minimum, this was a road not to take. "The simple fact of the matter is that capitalist democracy, for all its crippling limitations, has been immeasurably less oppressive and a lot more democratic than any Communist regime, whatever the latter's achievements in the economic, social, and other fields." Ralph Miliband, "Reflections on the Crisis of Communist Regimes," *New Left Review* 177 (September/October 1989): 29, 31. Also see the 1958 essay by Miliband, "Harold Laski's Socialism," and the memoir by his wife, Marion Kozak, "How It All Began: A Footnote to History," in Leo Panitch, ed., *Why Not Capitalism: Socialist Register 1995* (London: Merlin Press, 1995).

[85] Kramnick and Sheerman report that Laski was lifted out of his depression by planning for a trip to the Soviet Union in early 1944. He served as a director of the Anglo-Soviet Public Relations Committee and uncritically praised the Soviet regime in popular articles in the *New Statesman* and *Daily Herald* for creating a new civilization marked by industrialization, mass literacy, and an end to unemployment. "Beatrice Webb, still vigorous in her eighties, wrote to Laski to say how thrilled she was about his articles on the 'heroic Soviet resistance' and Russian 'scientific humanism.' She asked him to look over the proofs of a new edition of *Soviet Communism*, and just before her death in April 1943 she asked Laski to be one of the executors of her will." Kramnick and Sheerman, *Laski*, pp. 465–66.

[86] Strikingly, Laski never advocated transliberal means or processes for his England,

To be sure, it would be unreasonable to make Laski a stand-in for other socialists, as if we all have shared assessments of the Soviet experience. Most of the non-Communist left railed against Bolshevism and Stalinism from the moments of their appearance and sought to draw a sharp line between good and bad socialism. Nonetheless, it would be too self-congratulatory for us not to see that social democracy and Communism have not inhabited separate universes. Grounded in a common doctrinal lineage, even critics on the democratic left often have seen Communism as the wayward member of a single progressive family. Such, alas, proved the case in Czechoslovakia in 1947, on the threshold of the Communist coup. That year, President Benes told the journalist Leo Lania of his confidence that the partnership of social democrats and Communists could work against indecent alternatives. "Czechoslovakia," he declared, "is perhaps the best example that there can be co-operation between Communists and non-Communists. . . . We have a coalition government with the Communists as the strongest party, and you have seen for yourself that Czechoslovakia has not betrayed a single principle, a single idea, of true democracy. We have no censorship and no police state."[87] These are not easy sentences to read.

IV

"Self-limiting revolution" was the name you and Kuron assigned to the program you conceived as an alternative both to direct confrontations with Communist state power (of the kind

---

where he certainly was prepared to live with parliamentarism and the vagaries of elections. For a discussion of the relationship among planning, the New Deal, and the American left's fascination with the USSR, see Lewis S. Feuer, "American Travelers to the Soviet Union 1917–1932: The Formation of a Component of New Deal Ideology," *American Quarterly* 14 (Summer 1962).

[87] William Shirer, *Midcentury Journey: The Western World Through Its Years of Conflict* (New York: Farrar, Strauss and Young, 1952) p. 26, citing Leo Lania, *The Nine Lives of Europe* (New York: Funk and Wagnalls, 1950).

crushed in Hungary in 1956) and to reform from above (like that employed by the reform Communists of the Prague Spring). This project aimed at mobilizing independent communal and social life as sources of pressure and freedom by conceding the state sphere to the leading role of the Communist party. Czechoslovakia, in particular, you wrote in "A New Evolutionism" in 1976, had taught "that change is possible and that it has its limits. Czechoslovakia is an example of the fragility of totalitarian stability, and also of the desperation and ruthlessness of an empire under threat. The lesson of Czechoslovakia is that evolution has its limits and that it is possible." You observed that though the limits of evolutionary change in Poland were imposed by the Soviet political and military presence, a skillful policy of maneuver could find and exploit room for change.[88] With a social base in the working class, the Church, and youth, you perspicaciously saw openings for a democratic opposition where others might only have grasped all-or-nothing alternatives. "In searching for truth," you concluded, "or to quote Leszek Kolakowski, 'by living in dignity,' opposition intellectuals are striving not so much for a better tomorrow as for a better today. Every act of defiance helps us build the framework of democratic socialism, which should not be merely or primarily a legal institutional structure but a real, day-to-day community of free people."[89]

The considerable power and insight of this self-limiting but ambitious point of view, Jean Cohen and Andrew Arato point out, was that it simultaneously was strategic and normative. It broke "with the revolutionary tradition whose logic was understood to be undemocratic and inconsistent with the self-organization of society" both in order to achieve what you then called

[88] For an assessment of very similar moves made by nineteenth-century nationalists in India who discovered room for a war of maneuver against the colonizer, see Partha Chatterjee, *Nationalist Thought and the Colonial World* (Tokyo: United Nations University Press, 1986).

[89] Adam Michnik, "A New Evolutionism," in Michnik, *Letters from Prison*, pp. 139, 147, 148.

democratic socialism and because you thought it a superior political-ethical stance. Though revolutionary in the sense of aiming to be transformative, the posture you adopted disconnected itself from key aspects of the revolutionary tradition. As Cohen and Arato observe,

> All major revolutions from the French to the Russian and the Chinese not only demobilized the social forces on which they originally depended but also established dictatorial conditions that were meant to block the reemergence of such forces at their very root for as long as possible. The project of "self-limiting revolution" has, of course, the opposite goal: the construction from below of a highly articulated, organized, autonomous, and mobilizable civil society.[90]

My views concerning socialism have been nourished by your qualified and restricted approach. Both as a normative and strategic matter the left requires a socialism that is self-limiting. This claim implies more than expressing a preference for one *conception* of socialism over another (as, say, Karl Kautsky did in his disagreements with Eduard Bernstein over the qualities of late-nineteenth-century German social democracy), but a recension of beliefs and ambitions within the *concept* of socialism itself. Socialism must undergo an astringent tapering. Reciprocally, but not symmetrically, if this revised socialism is to connect with liberalism more than grudgingly—that is, if it is to be suffused by the central values and practices of the liberal tradition without losing its own demanding powers of critique and invention—it must wage important battles not, as in the past, about the fundamental concepts of political liberalism, but about specific conceptions of such concepts as property, public, private, and autonomy.[91] How socialism becomes self-limiting

[90] Jean L. Cohen and Andrew Arato, *Civil Society and Political Theory* (Cambridge: MIT Press, 1992).

[91] The distinction between a concept and conceptions of the concept is discussed by

thus is not indifferent to the type of liberalism within which it might come to be inserted.

Specifically, I think three related dimensions of revision to the concept of socialism and to conceptions of liberalism are especially vital if the difficult project of liberal socialism is to have a fighting chance:

First, socialism must come to terms unequivocally with the permanent separation of the zones of property and sovereignty, resting content to negotiate the terms of their institutional relationship and degree of overlap. In turn, it should press for particular conceptions of property as a general, inclusive right and as a relational construct that must reckon with the conditions and entitlements of the propertyless and nearly propertyless.

Second, socialism must give up the impossible dream of a future entirely without exploitation and scarcity and settle for meliorative, but not necessarily inconsiderable, goals, while recalling to liberalism the inherently social qualities of its own cherished norm of human autonomy.

Third, socialism must recognize the indispensability of the distinction central to liberal citizenship between public and private spheres. In so doing, however, it should remind liberalism of its own doctrinal commitment to understand and regulate the public aspects of putatively private activities and insist on a robust extension of liberalism's understanding of the scope and content of what counts as political.

So you see, Adam, I still think you were correct in your formulations in "Citadel," but their specification remains to be accomplished.

John Rawls, *A Theory of Justice* (Oxford: Clarendon Press, 1971), pp. 5–11; Ronald Dworkin, *Taking Rights Seriously* (Cambridge: Harvard University Press, 1978), pp. 134–36, 226; and Jeremy Waldron, *The Right to Private Property* (Oxford: Clarendon Press, 1988), p. 52. The idea of competing conceptions of a concept is connected to the discussion of conceptual disagreement in W. B. Gallie, "Essentially Contested Concepts," *Proceedings of the Aristotelian Society* 56 (1955–56): 167. Also see J. N. Gray, "Political Power, Social Theory and Essential Contestability," in David Miller and Larry Siedentop, eds., *The Nature of Political Theory* (Oxford: Clarendon Press, 1983).

V

Property is an institution with rules, procedures, and norms; it comprises a bundle of rights, enforceable in law, which permit private owners to do generally as they wish with what they own (while diminishing the freedom of those who do not own).[92] The state and the law take actions that define and secure property rights; that is, the terms of ownership and control. This terrain has been the site of energetic contest between socialists and their adversaries. Ever since Proudhon's famous polemic, socialists have asserted, as did he, that "Every argument which has been invented on behalf of property, *whatever it may be*, always and of necessity leads to equality; that is, to the negation of property."[93] Though socialists have disagreed about matters of pace and scope, socialism traditionally has sought to transform property from a private to a collective holding. They have understood that property separates private appropriation from public responsibility; hence that capitalism privatizes political power, impels the devaluation of citizenship, and compromises democracy by inhibiting political participation by privatizing decision making that affects public life fundamentally. Further, they have insisted that property cannot be central to civil and political rights because it is possessed by relatively few.[94] By contrast, most liberals anchor the fences they build to protect

[92] See Armen A. Alchian and Harold Demsetz, "The Property Rights Paradigm," *Journal of Economic History* 33 (March 1973); Avner Offer, *Property and Politics, 1870–1914: Landownership, Law, Ideology and Urban Development in England* (Cambridge: Cambridge University Press, 1981), p. 5; and G. A. Cohen, "Capitalism, Freedom and the Proletariat," in Alan Ryan, ed., *The Idea of Freedom: Essays in Honour of Isaiah Berlin* (Oxford: Oxford University Press, 1979).

[93] Pierre-Joseph Proudhon, *What Is Property?* (New York: Dover Publications, 1970), p. 66. See the nuanced discussion of Proudhon in Waldron, *The Right to Private Property*, chap. 9.

[94] For particularly elegant formulations of this position, see Ellen Meiksins Wood, "The Separation of the Economic and the Political in Capitalism," *New Left Review* 127 (May–June 1981); and her "Capitalism and Human Emancipation," *New Left Review* 167 (January–February 1988). Also see Jennifer Nedeslsky, *Private Property and the Limits of American Constitutionalism* (Chicago: University of Chicago Press, 1990); and Brian Barry, "Liberalism and Private Property," p. 6.

against incursions of state power on the foundation of property. Liberals have been preoccupied with private property both as a basis for selfishness and on behalf of the virtue of limiting the hubris of the state.[95] For most liberals, assaults on private property long have been considered attacks on liberty because liberty rights and property rights are thought to amount to one and the same thing. Property limits the hubris of the state by providing and securing a zone within which owners act freely, insulated from public intervention and decision.

In light of this contrariety, if socialism were to relinquish its long-standing ambition to transcend the property system, would it not have to end its useful life by dissolving into corrosive liberal surroundings? Much depends on what we mean by useful. The separation of property and sovereignty has been so basic to Western modernity and the demonstrated costs of trying to undo it have been so considerable that any socialism worth having no longer can pursue this project. But this learned abnegation does not leave socialism purposeless. A self-limiting socialism would refuse the imperialist move that "employs a conception of property that gobbles up all rights, no matter how little they have to do with liberal ownership."[96] It also would revisit the justifications liberal theorists have deployed to account for the initial establishment of private property; it would require a close and recurring examination of the effects of the distribution of property; it would insist that liberalism recognize that its own history of ideas provides fertile ground for debate about the regulation of property; and it would strongly prefer solutions with an egalitarian tilt to the balance between private and common property. The antinomies of private versus public ownership and of markets versus

[95] For discussions, see Nathan Tarcov, "A 'Non-Lockean' Locke and the Character of Liberalism," in Douglas MacLean and Claudia Mills, eds., *Liberalism Reconsidered* (London: Rowman and Allanheld, 1983); Nedelsky, *Private Property and the Limits of American Constitutionalism*; and Mancur Olson, "Dictatorship, Democracy, and Development."

[96] Gerald F. Gaus, "Property, Rights, and Freedom," *Social Philosophy and Policy* 11 (Summer 1994): 239–40.

planning would be replaced by the understanding that there is a range of institutional variations and combinations.

Just as liberal political theorists have had to justify political authority, so liberal theorists of private property have had to explain and validate initial, unequal distributions of property rights.[97] Rousseau did so by recourse to shared values; the distribution of property is subject to society's general will.[98] Locke defended private property as the outcome of acts of individual enterprise and appropriation that are legitimated by the manner in which a person through the use of labor invests in transforming nature.[99] A self-limiting socialist approach, by contrast, would reject such efforts to provide a moral justification for the assignment of property rights, agreeing instead with Hume that historical distributions of private property are mainly arbitrary.[100] Property is based on vastly unequal power relations by which some people gain and maintain belongings while others cannot, and on the legal enforcement, as Hume put it, of "abstinence from the possessions of others."[101] The rules of property, for Hume, did not develop by way of an intentional design based on principles, but slowly based on the pursuit of interest. On this understanding, he rejected notions of distribution based on moral merit or equality. If socialists cannot agree with liberals in ethically legitimating initially unequal distributions of property (whether in terms proposed by Rousseau or by Locke), they can do so despite Hume's inegalitarianism, within a Humean framework that recognizes that property rights and distributions are neither natural nor moral.

[97] This discussion about foundations draws on Jeremy Waldron, "The Advantages and Difficulties of the Humean Theory of Property," *Social Philosophy and Policy* 11 (Summer 1994).

[98] Of course, I am simplifying a complex point of view, which included important elements that were antiproperty. Jean Jacques Rousseau, *The Social Contract* (London: Penguin Books, 1968), book 1, chaps. 6–9. The flaw in this position is historical; no such consensus about the acquisition and allocation of property has ever existed.

[99] John Locke, *Two Treatises of Government* (Cambridge: Cambridge University Press, 1968), *Second Treatise*, chap. 5, secs. 27ff.

[100] David Hume, *A Treatise of Human Nature* (Oxford: Clarendon Press, 1988), book 3, part 2, sec. 4, p. 514.

[101] Ibid., sec. 2, p. 490.

A liberal socialism requires, in turn, that socialism forgo its traditional claim that there is only one proper property regime: common property. It must tilt strongly, however, in the direction of regulations and policies capable of providing a counterweight to the conception privileging private property as an exclusive right. Such alternatives can draw on neglected aspects of the liberal tradition. Liberalism, in fact, has been far more accommodating to intermediate and inclusive property norms than most liberals today or their critics acknowledge. The meaning of property rights for liberalism has a complex, contested history. Currently, we tend to treat property exclusively; that is, as the legitimate ability "to exclude others from the control and use of resources" rather than as the right "to be included in the use of resources necessary for life or livelihood." But we are wrong to limit our understanding of liberal usage in this way. As Thomas Horne's excellent study of arguments for property rights in Britain decisively shows, liberalism's natural law discourse contained *both* the exclusive and inclusive senses of property.[102] Liberalism has been identified too narrowly with the qualification of owners to restrict access to property and to do with it what they want. From Locke forward, the liberal tradition has not, in fact, been characterized by a one-dimensional view that the possessors of property must have untrammeled and unregulated use of it as the basic underpinning of liberty and human autonomy. "Virtually every defense of the right to exclude written during this period carried with it a self-limiting feature under which exclusion could no longer legitimately occur. . . . The problem of liberal property rights was and is to find ways to recognize both aspects of the right to property."[103]

Locke's individualist justification of property imposed two constraints—against waste and demanding that the taker leave "enough and as good" for others. Taken together, these guidelines open up quite a wide scope for disagreement and contest.

---

[102] Thomas A. Horne, *Property Rights and Poverty: Political Argument in Britain, 1605–1834* (Chapel Hill: University of North Carolina Press, 1990), p. 5.

[103] Ibid., p. 7.

Locke's injunction about waste is permissive; it only weakly in-
hibits egotistical conversions of common property to private
ownership. But the second of his restrictions restrains private
property far more than strong defenders of exclusive property
rights would want.[104] It was this aspect of Locke's approach to
property that authorized some (albeit a minority of) liberal
thinkers to develop expansive views concerning the public in-
gredients of private property and the diversity of permissible
property regimes.[105]

For natural law theorists like Locke, the right to property preceded the formation of governments; God gave humankind
property, which it has owned in common. For Locke, human
labor justified the transfer of parts of this commons to private,
unequal, possession. Nonetheless, Locke felt constrained to
consider situations of inheritance, conquest, and poverty where
property arrangements might deny to human beings their natural independence.[106] Property rights thus are not absolute.
When a childless father dies, Locke thought, private property
should revert to the commons. Additionally, the propertyless
possess a right to subsistence and are eligible to take from the
surplus of the wealthy that which they need to escape extreme
deprivation. "Men, being once born, have a right to their preservation, and consequently to Meat and Drink, and other such
things, as nature affords for their subsistence."[107]

A natural law understanding of property entails legal and
moral restraints and provides grounds for an egalitarian thrust
within the liberal tradition.[108] Because there was an original
common, natural law liberals could understand property as not
only an exclusive but an inclusive right. Human beings have an

---

[104] For a discussion, see Richard A. Epstein, "On the Optimal Mix of Private and
Common Property," *Social Philosophy and Policy* 11 (Summer 1994).

[105] See, for a consideration of this aspect of American jurisprudence, Paul Kens,
"Liberty and the Public Ingredient of Private Property," *The Review of Politics* 55 (Winter
1993).

[106] Horne, *Property Rights*, p. 55.

[107] Locke, *Second Treatise*, p. 25.

[108] Natural law understandings thus shaped a far more egalitarian set of possibilities
for liberals than Hume's rightless world of power and prudence.

obligation to preserve the common property God has given them. On this basis, for example, Hume was sharply criticized by Thomas Reid and other Scottish Enlightenment figures who stressed the inclusive side of property rights.[109] Lockean notions of the right to subsistence were extended by many nineteenth-century liberals who argued that the poor possessed a welfare right based on a claim to the wealth of the nation.

Separately, utilitarian liberals who did not ground their doctrine in natural rights also developed quite a spread of opinion about property. While most utilitarians, like Bentham, emphasized the exclusivity of property, some cultivated a strong inclusive bent in the name of minimizing suffering and securing social peace. Thus, anticipating John Rawls (himself an antiutilitarian) by nearly a century and a half, William Forster Lloyd's *Two Lectures on the Justice of the Poor Laws* in 1837 argued that inequalities based on property can be justified only if they insure that everyone shares in the benefits generated by inequality.

Late-eighteenth- and nineteenth-century radical liberals, including Tom Paine, returned to the natural rights tradition as a basis for their moral outrage about how propertied inequality undercuts human independence. Though they strongly defended property rights, they deployed their readings of Locke to argue for a more inclusive right to property as a basis for justice, autonomy, and human identity. Current maldistributions, they argued, were not products of an open process of appropriation but results of distortions introduced by class and state power. The liberal welfare state that Hobhouse and the other New Liberals of the late nineteenth and early twentieth centuries advocated was promoted on the basis of these intellectual underpinnings.

The liberal tradition, in short, possesses a great deal of in-

---

[109] To be sure, Reid was on the "left" side of the Scottish Enlightenment. Even when "they did not defend individual inclusive property rights, they continued to work from the central assumption of the natural law tradition that the earth was given for the preservation of human life and that all systems of property rights were to be judged by their ability to meet this standard." Horne, *Property Rights,* p. 122.

determinacy about private property. Its range can be located in the space defined by two versions of a key formulation of Locke's that was quoted by Thomas Hodgskin, a radical political economist, in his 1832 text, *Natural and Artificial Right of Property Contrasted.* Locke had written: "As much land as a man tills, plants, and improves, cultivates and can use the product of, so much is his property"; but Hodgskin changed the punctuation by moving a comma to make the sentence read, "As much land as a man tills, plants, and improves, cultivates and can use, the product of so much is his property."[110] Inside this zone, there is much room to propose a more just and inclusive system of access to and control over private property's rights, powers, and duties.[111]

VI

Overcoming scarcity has been integral to the socialist conception seeking to eliminate the divisions separating property from sovereignty and the private sphere from the public. Traditional socialism claimed to possess a holistic alternative to capitalism unmarked by these partitions. Unfortunately, this postcapitalist utopia has been more than a pleasant fable. Throughout much of this century, but especially under Stalinist and post-Stalinist Bolshevism, this ambitious program for human emancipation promising liberation from the fetters of material necessity

---

[110] Cited and discussed in ibid., p. 239.

[111] It is tempting to try to discover in constitutional rights to privacy an alternative to property as the main bulwark against a potentially predatory state or tyrannical democratic majorities. Jean Cohen, for example, sees the "new privacy" as "protecting what property can shield no longer, namely, fundamental personal liberties." She argues that whatever the potency of property rights in the past, in post–New Deal America property and freedom of contract no longer can perform this protective role because these bases of protection have been devalued. In this setting the normative shift in constitutional jurisprudence to enhanced privacy rights is especially important and welcome. Though I share her appreciation of the significance of privacy, I think it is unpersuasive to have this contested concept bear the weight of the function traditionally performed for liberalism by the deeply inscribed institutions of property and contract. Jean Cohen, "Redescribing Privacy: Identity, Difference, and the Abortion Controversy," *Columbia Journal of Gender and Law* 3, 1 (1993): 109.

(which has been achieved nowhere) authorized a perfectionist morality judging acts by their effects on this ultimate, if elusive, goal. Since the objective of transcending material want seemed so manifestly desirable as a radiant contrast to daily struggles, anything and anyone who stood in its way became fair game. This morality of ultimate ends made liberal notions of rights and procedures appear irrelevant hoaxes at best or dangerous impediments to a shining future.[112]

By contrast to such a socialism of exceptional ambitions and long time-horizons, liberal socialism as an ethos and political program must strive in the here and now sharply to limit and modify the mendacious advantages conferred by property and class position. Guided by an egalitarian ethical compass and sensibilities, it focuses on shaping institutions and policies to secure the abilities of all citizens. While agreeing with the hierarchical ordering of John Rawls's two principles of justice ("the first of which requires equality in the assignment of basic rights and duties, while the second holds that social and economic inequalities, for example inequalities of wealth and authority, are just only if they result in compensating advantages for everyone, and in particular for the least advantaged members of society"),[113] a liberal socialism would insist on a strong egalitarian reading of the second principle to resolve its ambiguities by emphasizing its tilt toward the least advantaged rather than its justification of inequality, and by going further to press actively for the elimination of unwarrantable inequalities. In pursuit of these goals, unlike its more ambitious brethren, a liberal socialism must come to possess presently relevant programmatic ideas joined to administrative and fiscal means; without these, its public philosophy is reduced to empty gesturing and risks licensing unpleasantness on a large scale.[114]

---

[112] An extended discussion can be found in Steven Lukes, *Marxism and Morality* (Oxford: Clarendon Press, 1985).

[113] John Rawls, *A Theory of Justice* (Cambridge: Harvard University Press, 1971), pp. 14–15.

[114] These formulations owe a lot to Crick, "Socialist Values and Time."

Political liberalism is substantively indeterminate in the sense that it confers no special standing on a self-limiting socialism, or any other contending ideology. But there do exist conceptions of liberalism that are particularly conducive to a mutual relationship between the two traditions; and there is a long history of partnership under the rubric of the welfare state. These are worth attending to, both to identify opportunities for collaboration and for the design of public policy. At the level of doctrine, I have in mind such efforts to develop liberal theory as Ronald Dworkin's attempt to connect the rectification of market distributions to key principles of liberal theory and Joseph Raz's effort to elaborate on liberalism's long-cherished notion of human autonomy. At the level of social policy, I am thinking of the diverse models of welfare state development characteristic of Western countries since the late nineteenth century.

Dworkin observes that liberals have valued economic markets as one set of means to secure liberalism's core value of the equality of regard and standing for all citizens. But markets, he notes realistically, produce not only such inequalities as are required for their own functioning, as those that reflect the differential costs of goods, but also those that cannot be defended by liberal principles of equality. As a result, he claims, liberalism is required, based on its own commitments, to invite schemes of redistribution that curtail the production of impermissible inequality.[115]

Likewise, Joseph Raz's important work on liberalism and autonomy develops a potentially egalitarian conception of liberalism. Individual well-being, in this formulation, is measured not exclusively by success in achieving goals but in terms of the availability of a multiplicity of desired objectives from which people can freely choose. "The ruling idea behind the ideal of personal autonomy," Raz writes, "is that people should make

---

[115] Ronald Dworkin, "Liberalism," in Stuart Hampshire, ed., *Public and Private Morality* (Cambridge: Cambridge University Press, 1978).

their own lives. The autonomous person is a (part) author of his own life. The ideal of personal autonomy is the vision of people controlling, to some degree, their own destiny, fashioning it through successive decisions throughout their lives."[116] The goals people choose may cohere in a unified project or be heterogeneous and diverse; they may be consistent or change over time. What matters, from this perspective, is the uncoerced and genuinely open qualities of the process of choice. This requires certain conditions to make human agency meaningful. Because human beings possess the reasoning capacities to assess their lives, the key authorizing conditions are structural: the existence of an adequate selection of morally acceptable options from which to choose (where genuine variety matters more than the number of alternatives), and access to a threshold level of information and resources that substantively actuate the capacity to make independent choices.

This type of argument, Raz stresses, is quite different from the kind of individualism that produces a theory of limited government that regards states mainly as dangers to liberty. Raz's autonomy-centered individualism "regards [states] also as a possible source of liberty. They can create conditions which enable their subjects to enjoy greater liberty [which Raz understands as enhanced autonomy] than they otherwise would."[117] From the premise of autonomy, governments become subject to "duties to provide the conditions of autonomy for people who lack them." The state thus has a double role: to use coercion to prevent agents—individuals, groups, corporations—from diminishing the autonomy of others, and to act to broaden the range of meaningful options available to its citizens.[118]

---

[116] Joseph Raz, *The Morality of Freedom* (Oxford, Clarendon Books, 1986), p. 369.

[117] Ibid., p. 18.

[118] Recent work on equality by the economist Amartya Sen parallels and reinforces Raz's autonomy-based liberalism. It is not enough to advocate equality, Sen argues; it is necessary to answer the question, "equality of what?" Every political and ethical theory argues for the equalization of something—political rights, liberties, income, wealth, property, life-chances, and so on—but in practice the choice of any of these must trade

Though there is ample room for debate about what, precisely, a strong reading of Rawls's difference principle, Dworkin's equal regard, and Raz's robust autonomy require by way of specific policies and programs,[119] clearly they authorize within the ambit of liberalism vigorous measures "either to influence, or to interfere with, or to supercede the free play of market forces in the interest of welfare."[120] Their work is consistent with Hobhouse's insight that the welfare state's attempt to provide its citizens with minimum standards marks the crossroads of liberalism and socialism because it identifies impediments within capitalism and markets to the realization of liberalism's cherished goals of equal citizenship and the production of citizens who possess the ability to author their lives and make reasonable choices about their interests.

At a time when socialism no longer persuasively can claim to be a complete alternative system of economic organization, and when the right trumpets the market as an institutional panacea, it is especially pressing that the left focus assertively on the control of capital, the organization of markets, and the rectification of market distributions and reiterate that since "the market is not there to keep an eye on justice," that task must be pursued elsewhere.[121]

The separation of property and sovereignty entails more

---

off against some others. Rather than choose between them, he pushes to the deeper level of the equalization of capabilities to pursue and achieve objectives. For all but the tiny minority of human beings incapable of reasoning and moral reflection, well-being, in the first instance, depends not on what an individual has accomplished, but on the person's capabilities to succeed as an autonomous agent. Like Raz, Sen advocates a participatory view of liberalism, one that can be secured only if human freedom to achieve desired ways of life is undergirded by a provision of the elements sufficient to its exercise. Amartya Sen, *Inequality Reexamined* (New York: Russell Sage Foundation, 1992).

[119] For a discussion, see David Johnston, *The Idea of a Liberal Theory: A Critique and Reconstruction* (Princeton: Princeton University Press, 1994).

[120] This is the famous definition of the welfare state in T. H. Marshall, "The Welfare State: A Sociological Interpretation," *Archives Europeennes de Sociologie* 11, 2 (1960): 288.

[121] For a discussion along these lines, see Robert Heilbroner, "The Triumph of Capitalism," *The New Yorker*, January 23, 1989. The citation is from Michnik, "The Three Fundamentalisms."

than the persistence of the division between them and the continued existence of private property. It also implies a refusal to cede sovereign capacities to private capital and to insist on the accountability of capital to more than its shareholders. Thus, a central arena for political contest and conflict concerns the capacities of liberal states to create institutions and policies that regulate and deploy property rights and coordinate economic production and exchange. Most liberal economic analysts have tended to neglect how the state's institutional structure and repertoire of policies shape capitalism's characteristics conferred by property rights because they have been so insistent on property's freedoms just as many socialists, by stressing how private property constrains public policy, have insufficiently attended to the range of possible ways in which state action can influence the way capitalism is organized and runs.[122] For a very long time, social democratic debate, as, say, in the British Labour party, oscillated between a commitment to public ownership, at least of the commanding heights of the economy (stopping short of centralized economic planning of the Soviet type), and the management of economic demand as the main active element of government policy. Yet between these poles there is a host of potential mechanisms available with which to coordinate and temper capitalism. A liberal socialism—in full knowledge "that private ownership of capital limits the range of outcomes that can ensue from the democratic process" and that "private property pretty well is a distribution of freedom and unfreedom"[123]—seeks to act without making socialism inseparable from common ownership because it understands that the elimination of private property is neither possible nor desirable. But its policy repertoire need not be reduced to a program that begins to act only after capital has. Instead, it

[122] This discussion draws on John L. Campbell and Leon N. Lindberg, "Property Rights and the Organization of Economic Activity by the State," *American Sociological Review* 55 (October 1990).

[123] Adam Przeworski, "Economic Constraints on Political Choices: On the Continuing Relevance of Marxist Political Theory of Capitalism," ms., 1994, p. 2; G. A. Cohen, "Capitalism, Freedom and the Proletariat," p. 15.

must insist on the manipulation and enforcement of property rights to create pressures on capital to temper its inherent destructiveness. The current counterprogram of the right, which, in the United States, includes a deregulatory assault even on the safety of food and water, is an indication of just how much can be achieved to inflect capitalism's cruel and violent tendencies. The "trick" of course is to do so by cultivating rather than eliminating incentives to invest by discovering and deploying an appropriate mix of policy instruments, for enhanced capitalist success is a requisite for a meaningful liberal socialism in the absence of alternatives capable of generating an economic bounty. Although the selection of such policies is limited by the state's structural dependence on capital, this reliance is not fixed in scope or content, as the range of existing and imagined options in Western capitalist countries attests.

A liberal socialist economic project thus needs to experiment with property rights actions through contract law, antitrust activity, sectoral regulation, tax policy, and other rules determining conditions of ownership and the location of economic activity to affect the organization and performance of the economy, the patterning of economic governance, the spatial distribution of economic growth, and the degree of inequality present in the economic system. It is committed to the proposition that capitalism's lock on the state and the political process is not absolute and that transactions between the state and capital can be renegotiated and transformed in an egalitarian direction.[124] This working hypothesis is confirmed, I believe, by the ferocity of the current assault by capital on so many of the rules and regulations concerning state-economy transactions. This power-grab aimed at the contraction of government and collec-

---

[124] Adam Przeworski and Michael Wallerstein, "Structural Dependence of the State on Capital," *American Political Science Review* 82 (March 1988). Przeworski now believes they were too optimistic about political room for maneuver, but his reasoning in "Economic Constraints" leans too hard in the other direction. Certainly, in the United States, a still largely enclosed continental economy, the capacity to impose regulations at the federal level without killing the goose that lays our eggs is very considerable.

tive democratic authority and the expansion of private prerogatives does more than threaten growing economic inequality; for
it narrows the scope of democracy and mocks the meaning of
liberal rights.

A renewed focus on capital and production is no substitute
for continuing attention to issues of distribution at a moment
when the welfare state too is under fierce attack. Socialists have
had a long history of wariness about the welfare state. After
all, it was antiliberal conservatives—in Bismarck's Germany, in
influential papal encyclicals, and under Italian fascism—and
not socialists who were the most significant early innovators in
social policy at a time when the large majority of liberals conceded to social policy only a very modest, residual role.[125]
Before the 1930s, most European socialists tended to resist a
welfare role for the state. Especially under predemocratic or
antidemocratic conditions, they rightly considered the state to
be deeply class-biased, preferring instead to build independent
working-class capacity for future struggles. Only during the interwar period did an increasing number of socialists begin to
try to utilize the combination of democracy and social policy to
craft a peaceful strategy for the transition to socialism. The regulation of capitalism and the rectification of its inequality
within normal politics, they thought, could move socialism toward its long-range goal of overcoming capitalism.[126]

This kind of social democracy now is well beyond our grasp;
it was premised on the now discredited notion that socialist
planning and coordination mechanisms can substitute effectively for the price system and market signals. Nonetheless, important legacies from this tradition of socialist social policy
remain.

---

[125] Gosta Esping-Andersen, "Citizenship and Socialism: Decommodification and Solidarity in the Welfare State," in Martin Rein, Gosta Esping-Andersen, and Lee Rainwater, eds., *Stagnation and Renewal in Social Policy: The Rise and Fall of Policy Regimes* (Armonk, New York: M. E. Sharpe, 1987). Also see Gosta Esping-Andersen, *The Three
Worlds of Welfare Capitalism* (Princeton: Princeton University Press, 1990).

[126] For a discussion, see Adam Przeworski, *Capitalism and Social Democracy* (Cambridge: Cambridge University Press, 1985).

Over the past six decades, the historical indeterminacy and potential range of welfare states have become increasingly clear. Welfare states vary not only in social spending but in other significant dimensions: the nature of the political coalitions supporting them; the degree of universality of their programs; their fiscal mechanisms; their relationship to property rights; their trade-offs of income and welfare; their effectiveness in altering market allocations; the extent to which they extend the limits markets impose on policy choices; their impact on class structures, gender, and other bases of stratification; the extent to which they are integrated with the economy and with economic decision making; and their visions of social citizenship as a right. In short, together with a renewed focus on property rights and the rules of transaction governing relationships between the state and the eonomy, there is ample room for a vigorous and meaningful politics of concerned with social policy and the welfare state pivoting around these issues.[127]

The right, of course, has attempted with a good deal of success to make even this self-limiting program of the left appear utopian. The welfare state, it is said, exacts inefficiency costs that are too high, acts as a drag on economic growth, exceeds our fiscal abilities in an age of deficits, and hurts international competitiveness; hence we will have to put up with rising inequality as the price of more general prosperity.[128] These arguments, however, are not persuasive. The wide array of empirical studies of social policy we possess demonstrate that the vast majority of welfare state programs do not reduce the quantity or quality of the supply of labor. There is no systematic relationship between the size of a country's welfare state and its trade competitiveness or growth rate (the United States has one of

---

[127] For a largely positive evaluation of the welfare state achievements of the democratic left, see Nicos Mouzelis, "The Balance Sheet of the Left," *New Left Review* 200 (July–August 1993).

[128] I draw in this discussion on Richard Freeman, "W(h)ither the Welfare State in an Epoch of Rising Inequality?" in Keith G. Banting and Charles M. Beach, eds., *Labour Market Polarization and Social Policy Reform* (Kingston: Queen's University, 1995).

the worst growth records and trade imbalances in the West yet one of the smallest welfare states and comparatively low rates of taxation). The constraint of scarcity does invalidate traditional socialism's most expansive dreams, but so long as economic growth is taking place, the distribution of government revenues and welfare-state benefits constitutes a political question rather than a fixed barrier. After all, in the United States the steep increases in budget deficits experienced in the 1980s and 1990s have been the result of a combination of high defense spending and reductions to the tax rates of the rich, not of falling revenues or economic decline. The brute politics of the right is based on the humbug of deploying ideological versions of economic theory to place the central issues of economic accumulation, growth, and distribution outside the ambit of democratic politics.

VII

Commercial billboards now have replaced party slogans on Poland's main roadways, but in June 1987, when I drove to the industrial area west of Krakow, long red banners with white lettering festooned the highways' overpasses. They proclaimed Communist party ambitions. I was particularly struck by the one announcing, in effect, that the reach of the party was complete and unencumbered: "A socialist government," it stated, "unites the nation on the basis of Marxism-Leninism in all of its activities." By then, of course, this bone-chilling totalism had become an empty slogan, certainly with few adherents in these Solidarity strongholds of coal mines and steel plants. The sign's hubris, nonetheless, did more than proclaim an aspiration. It summarized a long-standing socialist suspicion of liberalism's insistence on a borderline dividing private from public matters as an essential buffer against predatory rule. Liberty, liberals long have understood, requires the existence of this partition in order to secure private pursuits from public intrusion and coercion.

You know rather well that this liberal dualism not only has been a focal point for old left socialist critics who treat it as a cloak for class oppression, but also has been a favorite target of an array of liberalism's critics. The New Left proclaimed the personal to be political. Feminists have argued that liberalism's public sphere is gendered and that its private zone protects patriarchy in matters of sexuality and family life. Communitarians and republicans have bemoaned the reduction of politics and the thinning of its content. Post-modernists have been suspicious of all binary categories and have discovered, following Marx and Foucault, that power is not confined to the public domain, and it is merely privatized, released, and refined in bourgeois liberal orders.

These influential lines of criticism, Carole Pateman has observed, have been "primarily directed at the separation and opposition between the public and private spheres in liberal theory and practice."[129] They effectively target the oppressive effects, mystifications of power relations, displacement of politics, and devaluation of citizenship that result from treating the sphere of the private as if it were situated wholly outside politics. They insist that the public and the private are mutually constitutive. They have shown how restraining the scope of power to the public realm protects the worst aspects of capitalism by artificially delinking the political economy from the public domain and how the distinction between public and private facilitates the privatization of political power by leaving the allocation of power in significant areas of human life unexamined and beyond the scope of effective remedy. Social coercion thus is cloaked in the appearance of consent.[130]

---

[129] Carole Pateman, "Feminist Critiques of the Public/ Private Dichotomy," in S. I. Benn and G. F. Gaus, eds., *Public and Private in Social Life* (London: Croom Helm, 1983), p. 281.
[130] The most vigorous location for recent critiques of this kind has been feminist theory. For representative examples, see Bonnie Honig, *Political Theory and the Displacement of Politics* (Ithaca: Cornell University Press, 1993); Susan Okin, *Justice, Gender, and the Family* (New York: Basic Books, 1989); Deborah L. Rhode, "Feminist Critical Theories," *Stanford Law Review* 42 (February 1990); Cass Sunstein, ed., *Feminism and Political*

If the division between public and private is the centerpiece of a host of unjust social, political, and economic relations, the remedy has seemed clear-cut: eliminate, not just rebalance, the distinction in order to deepen liberty and equality. Yet as that chastening banner over the Polish highway signified, such a program of transcendence is naive and potentially insidious. The strong version of the criticism of the divide between public and private focuses on the notion of an opposition and insists on mandatory remedies. But in so doing, it risks authorizing tyrannies imposed either by democratic majorities or by authoritarian rulers; and it refuses the urgent task of discovering a balance recognizing the profound inequalities that inhabit the zones liberalism traditionally has consigned to the private sphere with an appreciation of the protections against domination and control provided by the semifiction of a public-private split.

There is a good deal of ambiguity in the antidualist position. Both the extent of the assault and the character of the remedy are not entirely clear. When Anne Norton, for example, critiques the distinction between the public and the private for giving men in the private sphere the aristocratic authority they have lost in the public domain, thus securing a subaltern position for women, she calls not for the end of liberalism, but for a liberalism "mindful of difference." Yet there can be no liberalism at all without some version, however provisional, permeable, and contested, of the separation she denounces.[131] When Pateman remarks that feminists, like other critics of the public-

---

Theory (Chicago: University of Chicago Press, 1990); Carole Pateman and Elizabeth Gross, eds., *Feminist Challenges: Social and Political Theory* (Boston: Northeastern University Press, 1987); and Sylvia Walby, "Is Citizenship Gendered?" *Sociology* 28 (May 1994).

[131] Anne Norton, "Engendering Another American Identity," in Frederick M. Dolan and Thomas L. Dumm, eds., *Rhetorical Republic: Governing Representations in American Politics* (Amherst: University of Massachusetts Press, 1992), p. 136. Likewise, when the constructivist feminist Judith Butler entered public debate in the letter page of the *New York Times* (June 8, 1995) to contest conservative assaults on "gangsta rappers," she deployed a distinction between reality and represenation in order to make an appeal for the alleviation of "social distress" and stake out a clear divide between "private" culture and "public" authority. I am indebted to David Plotke for pointing this out.

private distinction, object to liberalism's "separation" and "opposition," she fails to note that these are not the same thing. Separation need not imply opposition. Public and private manifestly are diverse, internally complex, contested concepts. Whether in fact they are, or need be, opposed one to the other; or, indeed, how they are, or might be, connected and interrelated, are contingent matters. The total antiliberal critique about their separation and opposition thus is rather too blunt an affair, for it has the effect of closing off possibilities and of covering over some of the most difficult and challenging questions. The prescriptive side of the critique is indefinite. Is the effect of eliminating the separation of public and private intended to require public action in such putatively private arenas as the bedroom and the family, for example, in order to secure equality between men and women or merely authorize some interventions under determinate and well-circumscribed conditions?

In fact, the liberal tradition possesses heterogeneous conceptions about the relationship and terms of linkage between the public and the private. As the political theorist Donald Moon has pointed out, critics of liberalism's treatment of public and private artificially narrow our understanding of the range of options liberalism actually possesses. Most liberal theorists, he shows, have not reproduced Aristotle's "distinction between the household and the political association." Rather, they have considered the public-private split as "a distinction of institutional context and of the forms of rule appropriate within each sphere." For a good many liberals, Moon argues, the difference is not defined by institutional locations but by activities; that is, "between those activities that are properly subject to authoritative direction and control (i.e., rulership) and those not so subject. It is a distinction between areas where rulership is legitimate and where it is not."[132]

---

[132] J. Donald Moon, *Constructing Community: Moral Pluralism and Tragic Conflicts* (Princeton: Princeton University Press, 1993), p. 151.

Thus what Moon identifies as the dominant liberal view does not require that oppression in the "private" sphere be left undisturbed by public precept. The location of activities in the "private" zones of the household or the factory does not exempt them a priori from public scrutiny and regulation. On this understanding, a Lockean approach authorizes the treatment of such matters as child abuse and marital rape, though located in the household, as public matters because "to the extent that a nonpolitical exercise of power impinges on someone's civil interests, on one's life, liberty, health indolency of body, or possessions, it falls within the public sphere. . . . Inasmuch as human rights can be violated in the personal sphere, the liberal agrees that the personal is political."[133] Likewise, liberalism as a doctrine has provided far more room for the public organization and regulation of conditions of work and the wage relation than most liberals have been prepared to credit. Reciprocally, liberalism consigns other activities that have a public countenance to the unregulated zone of the private. Religious worship is the leading example. Organized religions convene congregants to pray in public, yet how they do so is a matter of private faith. It is just this reduction of religion to the private sphere that permits its unimpeded and tolerated public expression. The public sphere, in short, is the zone where the activities of people are entwined necessarily with those of others; hence such activities must be constrained and shaped by public principles and authority. The private realm, in turn, inheres

---

[133] Ibid., p. 152. Moon takes this language from Locke's *Letter Concerning Toleration*, in which he writes that "Civil interests I call life, liberty, health, indolency of body; and the possession of outward things such as money, land, houses, furniture, and the like." John Locke, *Letter Concerning Toleration* (Indianapolis: Hackett Publishing Company, 1983) (original edition, 1689). For a suggestive consideration of urban-spatial change and its impact on the categories of public and private, see M. J. Daunton, "Public Place and Private Space: The Victorian City and the Working Class Household," in Derek Fraser and Anthony Sutcliffe, eds., *The Pursuit of Urban History* (London: Edward Arnold, 1983). Daunton treats both the impact of the move away from the cellular pattern of closed quarters with shared public space to the private house and outward-looking streets more open to public regulation and the impact of these changes on the functional specificity of the working-class house and on the changing role of women.

not in institutional locations or in specific spheres of society but in the privacy rights of individuals with multiple identities, roles, and institutional locations who possess the capacity to author their lives free from regulation by principles of conduct decided by state managers or by democratic majorities.

To be sure, liberals often have been confused about the difference between locations and activities (a great deal of American jurisprudence, for example, hinges on sorting this out), and, in practice, liberalism has tilted in the direction of yielding far too much unregulated power to "private" actors. But the liberal conception, at least as grounded in Locke, permits far more public intervention than most feminists and socialists have been prepared to recognize. There is no simple dichotomous polarity opposing the public to the private; rather there are intersections and relationships. Both liberals and their critics must learn to recognize that the public-private split is a compound of constitutional rights and never-ending contests over boundaries and content. Within a liberal political frame, there is no single correct way to distinguish these zones. Rather, these are appropriate subjects for moral reasoning and political conflict provided the concepts of the private and of rights to privacy remain intact.[134]

A liberal and self-limiting socialism thus would insist on a particular liberal conception that does not entail a thin version of civic powers provided that citizens possess civil and political rights that cannot be taken away. It would assert an approach to the sphere of the public that could encompass economic and social relationships too rigidly consigned by many liberals to unregulated private activity. Reciprocally, it would continue to emphasize the significance of the public-private divide as a protector not only of liberty understood in rather general and abstract terms, but of liberty as the preserve of alternative, even competing, understandings of how to live a good life. A fabu-

---

[134] I have relied a good deal in this discussion on Stanley I. Benn and Gerald F. Gaus, "The Public and Private: Concepts and Action," and their "The Liberal Conception of the Public and Private," in Benn and Gaus, ed., *Public and Private in Social Life.*

lous paradox is at work. For liberalism, the very idea of a zone of the public shared by all citizens on the basis of consent constitutes a nonneutral concept of the good that insists on the neutral application of rules and governance. The zone of the private, by contrast, depends on public neutrality about competing ways of life, but in so doing it authorizes nonneutral configurations of values and practices.

Inside this complex field, liberalism's political originality has been its institutional treatment of the links between state and society as a region of representation, characterized literally by the re-presentation of civil society within the state.[135] Representative political institutions have been liberalism's deft strategy for stabilizing substantive transactions between the state and civil society and for securing equal respect among citizens given the heterogeneity of interests and identities.[136] A liberal, self-limiting socialism can concur with these assumptions and arrangements but finds them insufficient and potentially ingenuous. Liberals stress the manner and process of rule; socialists stress who rules on behalf of whom. The left has learned and experienced far too much to fall again into the trap of opposing these issues as if they are trade-offs. But the left can play a role in insisting that the institutions and practices of liberal representation be open to participation by all; that each citizen possess threshold levels of resources, including access to politically active secondary associations, to become effective political players; that the democratic qualities of public space be undamaged and undistorted by money, gender, race, and other bases of privilege; and that systematically inegalitarian constraints on citizenship be affirmatively addressed.

In short, the left must insist that popular sovereignty itself be repoliticized to focus debate on what is required to make the concept more than a frequently breached background myth.

---

[135] See Hannah Pitkin, "The Concept of Representation," in Hannah Pitkin, ed., *Representation* (New York: Atherton Press, 1969).

[136] Dworkin, "Liberalism," p. 125; Francois Furet, "From 1789 to 1917 and 1989," *Encounter* 75 (September 1990).

Liberals rightly have understood that the state as a site of congealed power can never be a liberal institution, and that democracy contains imperfections and dangers; hence they often have focused on the potential threat to liberty posed by mass participation. A liberal socialism would stipulate that the best way to constrain the state is by enhancing and enlarging liberal representation, and that the most effective check on mass irrationality is the creation of a thick, institutionalized democratic politics underpinned by an inclusive sense of property and welfare rights aimed at securing a capable citizenry. The liberal socialist contribution asserts the possibility of respecting liberty while seeking equality in full knowledge that it will never be possible to eradicate entirely the differential character of citizenship in a capitalist context. Without a robust socialist countercurrent, however, class and other bases of exclusion from full political incorporation tend to become only more rigid and effective barriers to democracy.

The traditional socialist critique of democracy has been uncertain about "whether the limits on representative democracy are necessary or unnecessary deficiencies. Either representative democracy is fatally destined to a contraction of its substance; or it is potentially amenable to an amplification of that substance. Both cannot be true at the same time."[137] A self-limiting socialism has no choice but to wager on the latter and do battle on behalf of an elaboration of the character and scope of political representation. Such a socialism understands there is no substitute for representative democracy and rights but insists they be supplemented by forms of representation that explicitly take class relations into account and extend democratic practices to those areas of the state, economy, and civil society now commonly thought to be outside the range of ordinary politics. Whereas the political right in Western Europe and North America has utilized an ambitious market vocabulary as an instrument to depoliticize the institutions and relationships in civil society and the economy, the left must find a persuasive

[137] Anderson, "The Affinities of Noberto Bobbio," p. 26.

way to recognize that social antagonisms cannot be packaged neatly or contained within formal political institutions because every site of human relations is characterized by relations of power.[138]

Such a politics requires more than most social democratic and reform parties of the left have been willing to countenance with respect to both substance and means. Certainly the American right recently has demonstrated how the assertion of a broad world-view, the elaboration of detailed policy knowledge, the willingness to do the hard work required for effective party politics, and the mobilization of social movements can combine and mutually reinforce. By contrast, the mainstream left has been increasingly reticent to announce broad goals, cautious in its policy ideas, and wary of movement politics outside the control of party elites. It has shied away from audacious, non-utopian statements of principles and visions and has come to be afraid of seeming to propose too much. And it has worried about the disruptive, expressive, unpredictable qualities of social movements.[139]

None of these elements of public philosophy, policy prescription, party mobilization, and movement politics alone is the key to reverse the left's current decline, but each is required for any possible new liberal socialist constellation. Such a proj-

---

[138] For a discussion of these issues to which I am indebted (even as I differ from its radical constructivism and from its insistence that "we have to break with rationalism, individualism and universalism"), see Chantal Mouffe, *The Return of the Political* (London: Verso Books, 1993); the citation is from p. 7. For an anthology developing these themes, see Chantal Mouffe, ed., *Dimensions of Radical Democracy* (London: Verso Books, 1992).

[139] Commenting on the dramatic, open movement politics of "moments of madness," Zolberg observed that "the prevailing negative view which focuses on obstacles and reactions distorts the truth. It neglects the lasting political accomplishments that are perhaps made possible only by the suspension of disbelief in the impossible which is characteristic of moments of madness. As a general proposition, it can be asserted that the Utopian project is a feasible strategy of social and political change, even a necessary one. . . . The moments do not collapse the distance between the present and the future, as those who experience them yearn to do. In that sense, moments of Parisian madness and others like them are always failures. But they drastically shorten the distance, and in that sense they are successful miracles." Zolberg, "Moments of Madness," p. 206.

ect is both more modest and more assertive than traditional social democracy. Its socialism is calibrated and compressed. Yet it also is more enterprising in coming to terms with the barriers capitalism throws up to democracy and equality and more ambitious in redefining conventional understandings of property, political economy, and the public-private divide. There is no lack of policy blueprints for the left. On my desk as I write is a detailed 1985 programmatic manifesto for the future of the welfare state, a prescient 1988 Jackson campaign document outlining a substantial plan to revamp the federal budget, a stunning 1987 article pointing to an egalitarian restructuring of social policy to promote economic investment and growth, and a remarkably impressive 1979 manifesto of the European Trade Union Institute specifying what a high-wage participatory economics might look like as an alternative to unchecked economic power.[140] Social democrats in the past erred on the side of pretentiousness in declaring ultimate aims but were too temperate in identifying means. Today, faced with the right wing's successful capture of the meaning of 1989, they have lost ambition and initiative. Can we do no more than hold our breath while witnessing the onslaught on the welfare state, the campaign to install an unbridled capitalism as humanity's highest good, and the crusade to eliminate public and democratic counterweights to naked class power? As we find our place in the post-Communist world, is it too late to relearn and apply the lessons signified by the icons on my kitchen wall?

La lutte continue!

Yours,

I K

---

[140] Barbara Ehrenreich and Frances Fox Piven, "Toward a Just and Adequate Welfare State: Philosophical and Programmatic Perspectives," paper presented at the Ford Foundation Wingspread Conference on Future Social Policy Options, 1985; "Paying for Our Dreams: A Budget Plan for Jobs, Peace, and Justice," Jesse Jackson 1988 Campaign (drafted primarily by David Gordon); Fred Block, "Social Policy and Accumulation: A Critique of the New Consensus," in Martin Rein, Gosta Esping-Andersen, and Lee Rainwater, eds., *Stagnation and Renewal in Social Policy*; European Trade Union Institute, "Keynes Plus a Participatory Economy," Brussels, May 1979.

Two: The Storehouse of Power and Unreason

Dear Adam,

"In the Balkans," you began, "reason is asleep while monsters are waking up." I have been haunted for months by your New School lecture of last fall on former Yugoslavia; not just by its depiction of aggressive nationalism, the absence of just borders, the widening syndrome of organized hatred, or the destruction of dialogue and the spirit of democracy, but by your deep and uncharacteristic pessimism.[1] You saluted Nbojsa Popov, the Belgrade sociologist, for his heroic effort to thwart his government's murderous designs, yet you are too much of a realist to believe individual valor can effectively obstruct such ugliness.[2] As your writings have stressed for a long time, without a plausible compound of ideas and institutions your cherished goal of combining liberalism with pluralism cannot be realized.

Like the frontier where liberalism and socialism meet, the borderland of liberalism and difference constitutes a site of danger and possibility. Prodded by their adversaries in the late nineteenth and early twentieth centuries, liberals defended and enlarged their doctrine against the socialist challenge. Liberalism's fate today is bound up more with recognizing, appreciating, and managing human difference.[3] Not only dreadful

---

[1] I want to acknowledge a debt at the outset. I owe much of the framing of issues in this letter and my sense of irresolvable tensions to a discussion by Partha Chatterjee of the relationship between communal struggles and the role of the state in religious affairs in India and the qualities and limits of liberal theory, which I read when I was finishing my first draft. Chatterjee, "Secularism and Toleration," *Economic and Social Weekly*, July 9, 1994, pp. 1768–77. "My problem," he wrote, "is to find a defensible ground for a strategic politics both within and outside the field defined by the institutions of the state in which a minority group, or one who is prepared to think from the position of a minority group, can engage in India today" (p. 1775).

[2] Adam Michnik, "Dignity and Fear: Dialogue with a Friend from Belgrade," New School for Social Research, October 31, 1994.

[3] Jacek Kuron recently has stressed how this test has become far more difficult in the absence of the bonding ideologies and circumstances of the Cold War. See the interview with him entitled "Being Here, Being There: The Global Village," *2B* 3, 5–6 (1995): 9.

fanaticisms of nationality and religion but far more appealing perspectives rightly descry the liberal tradition's insufficient recognition of moral conflict, community, gender, and race, and they refuse the absorption of such categories of identity into the general species of liberal citizen.[4] These are challenges to more than the consistency or power of liberal doctrine or to its normative proclivities. To the extent liberalism fails to wrestle with these subjects and objections, it becomes more vulnerable to integral nationalism, religious fundamentalism, and other forms of chauvinist parochialism.

As I listened to you gamely read your New York talk on the Balkan bloodletting, I was particularly sorry you had been unable to join the democracy seminars' annual meeting in Stupava a few months earlier.[5] We heard chilling firsthand reports about pogroms directed at Romania's and Slovakia's Hungarians, challenges to the identity and cultural institutions of Bulgaria's Turks, anti-Semitic outrages in Armenia, evictions of the Czech Republic's Romany population, and the systematic rape of Muslim women by Serb forces in Bosnia. We quickly discovered that virtually nothing in our group's arsenal of experience and doctrine had prepared us for such dispiriting developments so soon after the putative triumph of liberalism, democracy, and "European" values. Overwhelmed by these admonitory catalogs of cruelty, we shifted the subject of our meeting to consider whether liberalism does or can be made to possess the requisite capacity to tame the great storehouse of unreason.

[4] A useful, if rather blunt-edged, critique of liberalism along these lines is Ronald Beiner, *What's the Matter with Liberalism?* (Berkeley: University of California Press, 1992). More nuanced assaults on liberalism for promoting an individual without attention to difference can be found in Sheldon Wolin, *The Presence of the Past: Essays on the State and the Constitution* (Baltimore: Johns Hopkins University Press, 1993); and Anne Norton, *Reflections on Political Identity* (Baltimore: Johns Hopkins University Press, 1988). Also see Judith Butler and Joan Scott, eds., *Feminists Theorize the Political* (New York: Routledge, 1992), for an anthology of key issues and questions for liberalism raised by feminist political theory.

[5] Stupava lies just outside Bratislava. This gathering was the annual meeting of representatives of the New School's network of democracy seminars, whose origin, goals, and character are described in the preface.

We did not get very far beyond a mixture of lamentation and concern. Our discussions of current events were marked by a gnawing uncertainty. Historical reality and liberal doctrine seemed so out of mesh that we wondered whether liberal reason and moral purpose constitute no more than a set of pious principles in the face of the sensations of identity and community.

The day I returned to New York, I discovered draft chapters on my desk of a brilliant dissertation on constitutionalism, slavery, and gender in the United States. It argued, in effect, that the goal of a plural liberalism is a pipe dream. Liberalism cannot be seriously pluralist because it represents a choice instead of an arena of multiple, plural choices. Liberalism's abstract, disembodied treatment of individuals and their rights, it argued, is disengaged from context and tradition. By privileging post-Cartesian reason and placing "nature" outside modernity as prior to it, liberalism finds it difficult to credit the full, wide range of human rationality and practice. On this reading, liberalism not only undermines human heterogeneity but invites the deployment of oppositional portraits of identity that turn biology into destiny.[6] We can see these tendencies at work even in this century's liberal masterwork, John Rawls's *A Theory of Justice*, which deduced its famous principles of justice by placing individuals in a hypothetical, nonparticularistic "original position" where they were shielded from knowledge of who they are and how they are situated in society; and which characterized a desirable society as one based on normative agreement. Everyone, Rawls wrote, "has a similar sense of justice and in this respect a well-ordered society is homogeneous. Political argument appeals to this normative consensus."[7]

Manifestly, the assertion of liberal values, especially those based on such an imputation of agreement, is not enough to stem the hysteria, fear, and killing generated by ethnic and

[6] Catherine Holland, "The Body Politic: Nature, Politics, and the Body in American Political Culture, 1776–1875," Ph.D. dissertation, Department of Political Science, The Graduate Faculty, New School for Social Research, 1995.

[7] John Rawls, *A Theory of Justice* (Cambridge: Harvard University Press, 1971), p. 263.

national identifications, but is it credible to think liberalism should not anchor any imaginable decent set of political and social arrangements? Is there a better nonliberal option on offer? If, in light of its very checkered history and theoretical limitations, we were to cast liberalism aside, what resources could we deploy to favor difference but stop the killing? We face the choice you left implicit in your lecture. Either we defer to history's convulsions or we respond to liberalism's more thoughtful critics by trying to fashion a liberalism more capable of bringing the parameters of difference inside its frame.

There is no good alternative to an expansive liberalism as pluralism's best available resource. For all its infirmities and hypocrisies, liberalism first fashioned as a response to the cruelties of religious warfare and the dissonance of moral belief remains the only great political tradition to affirm and contain moral and group pluralism.[8] Since its origins, liberalism has been a response to modernity's irreducible moral and cultural discord. Though the application of liberalism's values, rights, and protections has been extraordinarily irregular, it is universally available as a self-limiting political doctrine that disqualifies itself from making ethical choices about ways of life that cannot be measured on a single scale (unless political liberalism itself is seriously threatened). More than any other political outlook, and in spite of its own history of accommodating to vicious exclusions, liberalism has learned to embrace ethical and cultural pluralism while continuing to insist that "*being*

[8] Certainly, the socialist tradition has been weak in these respects, in spite of the fact that socialists have valued fraternity and community. Kymlicka has ably summarized why most socialists have been hostile to cultural pluralism and minority rights. First, as an evolutionist theory, socialism has traced the expansion of social units from the local (the family and tribe) to the regional, the national, and the global. "Smaller cultural communities, therefore, must give way to larger ones." Second, socialists have tended to judge cultural diversity through the lens of politics, "asking only whether cultural identities promote or retard the political struggle for socialism. And most socialists have assumed that ethnic and national identities are a political hindrance." Third, many socialists also have considered such identities to be barriers to the kind of socialist solidarity required for shared sacrifices in the transitional period between capitalism and socialism. Will Kymlicka, *Multicultural Citizenship* (Oxford: Clarendon Press, 1995), pp. 69, 72.

human [is] a universal category, applicable to each individual human being, confirmed by the inviolability, irreplaceability, and unexchangeability of the person."[9]

I am burdening you with yet another long letter because my thinking about these questions is marked by the ambition and character, even by the shortcomings, of your text, now two decades old, on *The Church and the Left*.[10] You wrote as a critic to conjure combinations of memory, identity, and tradition within the specific historical, sociological, and strategic setting of mid-1970s Poland to advance a tolerant liberal order. Writing in the spirit of the rich rabbinical cosmography about the passage— believed to exist beneath the Temple of Jerusalem—to the Tehom, the abyss of the world, and the abode of mystery and disorder, you understood that modernity has not sealed off the pathway to this bottomless depth of sorrow and chaos.

Your sober polemic gathered intensity from your vantage point inside yet aside the central tendencies of your culture. Your insider-outsider status facilitated your capacity to hear and attend to nonliberal claims that liberalism truncates moral pluralism without yielding essential liberal principles. As a secular radical, a Pole in a thoroughly Catholic culture, and a Jew inhabiting a world of ghosts, you read the center from its experiential and philosophical margins without severing connections to it, having earned the right to outrageousness.[11]

The work in the liberal tradition best suited to grapple with the conflicting philosophical and moral claims of groups and

---

[9] Leszek Kolakowski, "Why Do We Need Kant?" in *Modernity on Endless Trial* (Chicago: University of Chicago Press, 1990), p. 53.

[10] Adam Michnik, *The Church and the Left* (Chicago: University of Chicago Press, 1991).

[11] I owe this formulation to Seyla Benhabib, "Facing the 21st Century: The Struggle over Values and the American University," Aims of Education Lecture, New School for Social Research, September 1992. Similarly, Michael Camille shows how the margins of illuminated manuscripts critically commented on the cultural core of their civilization. By placing the perimeters of difference inside the visible frame of the manuscripts, medieval marginalia constituted an arrangement of critical commentary secured to the period's dominant texts. Michael Camille, *Image on the Edge: The Margins of Medieval Art* (London: Reaktion Books, 1992).

nations likewise has been characterized by the sociological realism, marginality, and pervasive scent of fear that are prominent features of your text. These traits, I believe, recommend John Locke's writings on toleration from exile or Isaiah Berlin's nonrelativist pluralism informed by the pain and humiliation of the modern Jewish experience and distinguish these efforts from the flatter and narrower considerations of diversity such as those by John Stuart Mill and John Rawls.

In his *Leben des Galilei*, Brecht quotes Galileo as saying, "If there are obstacles the shortest line between two points may well be a crooked line."[12] There is no straight route connecting liberalism and pluralism; it is a meandering, serpentine path characterized by surprises and pitfalls that we must learn to tread. In addition to *The Church and the Left*, I suggest some other companion guides: from history, the extension of Europe and encounters between European explorers and non-European people and between Europe's Christians and Jews; from philosophy, *Epistola de tolerantia*, the first of John Locke's four letters on toleration, John Stuart Mill's *On Liberty*, and contemporary scholarship by Anglo-American political theorists on the ties between liberalism and pluralism; and from recent events, the decolonization of the globe and the decline of Europe's hegemony.

My argument, you will see, comes in four interlocking parts. First, I briefly trace the large-scale processes that shaped the creation and character of liberalism in early modern Europe. These include the making of Europe itself as a distinctive cultural zone; the differentiation of European society after feudalism into the increasingly separate institutional spheres of sovereign states, economies, and civil societies; the polarization of Christendom and marginalization of the Jews; the formation of a Europe-centered world as a consequence of global conquest; and the creation of a new specialized class of secular intellec-

---

[12] Cited in Partha Chatterjee, *Nationalist Thought and the Colonial World* (Minneapolis: University of Minnesota Press, 1986), p. vii.

tuals. Liberalism's origins were entwined with these developments. Liberalism's doctrine commented on them.

Liberalism's problems and capacities continue to be marked by these beginnings. From the start, liberal thinkers assumed that Europe as the site of reason was different from other global locations; hence that the rights and responsibilities they sketched applied only to a limited fraction of humankind. The diversity they recognized pivoted on the management of Christian religious differences within a statist framework that, otherwise, stressed the common traits of citizens. Inside these states, liberalism focused on ways to empower states against other theaters of coercion while regulating the state's capacity to transact with civil society and the economy. This complex legacy has been challenged by decolonization and democratization, forcing liberalism in our times to come to terms with human differences of race, gender, nationality, and culture far more diverse than those for which it originally was deployed.

Second, I claim that this pressing project can be advanced by making choices about the value of different strands within liberalism's intellectual heritage and between alternative kinds of liberal theory. To clarify these options, I distinguish the views of Locke on toleration from those of Mill. It has become commonplace for liberalism's critics to show how both thinkers exemplify liberalism's infirmities in dealing with questions of difference. In turn, many liberal theorists concede the case on Locke but find in Mill's writing, as you do, a strong affirmation of the value of diversity. I claim to the contrary that it is Locke, not Mill, who endows a genuinely plural liberalism.

Third, in examining the best present work on moral and group pluralism by liberal theorists, I assert that they want to extract too much from liberal doctrine and too little from history, sociology, and politics. I prefer the doctrinally less ambitious but historically less antiseptic approach of Berlin to that of Rawls and other liberals who want to keep difference in its place by distinguishing too starkly between the public and private spheres and by insisting to the point of impossibility on a strong notion of state neutrality. Currently, we seem torn between this purified, hygienic liberalism and quite a heterogeneous collection of antiliberal critiques. Instead, we need to forge a liberalism that is more than an umpire but less than a full substantive morality and that tilts more in the direction of innovation in institutions and policies than of ever more fine-grained refinements to liberal philosophy.

Fourth, in pursuit of these ends, I build on the type of liberal political theory exemplified by Locke and Berlin to identify elements for a plural liberalism with broadly common standards but capable of diverse application across disparate instances. I do so by trying to thicken and deepen liberalism's understanding of toleration in genuinely multicultural settings. I ask: How are the units of toleration to be conceptualized: as the friends of communtarian thought, as the individuals of classical liberal thought, or, as Susan Mendus prefers, as neighbors whose mix of contact and seclusion is a variable?[13] Preferring the latter, I argue that a hallmark of neighborliness is the freedom not to provide reasons for one's values and practices provided they respect and do not transgress certain limits. By recognizing a zone of relations outside any single ontology or system of reason, the approach of neighborliness can make room for diversity in a thoroughgoing, nonbanal sense of the term while insisting on common rules. I try to suggest how we might think about what such rules, embedded in institutions, should aim at.

This letter hardly constitutes a set of prescriptions for bringing enduring peace to Bosnia, preventing deathly outrages, or assuring respect for diverse cultures, values, and ways of life. Rather, it is an effort to clear ground, assert the value of a particular manner of political thought, and suggest some solutions to problems that have bedeviled liberal efforts to deal with the heterogeneity of values and cultures. How we ask questions,

---

[13] Susan Mendus, "Strangers and Brothers: Liberalism, Socialism, and the Concept of Autonomy," in W. Watts Miller and D. Milligan, eds., *Liberalism, Citizenship, and Autonomy* (Aldershot: Avebury, 1992).

how we see and represent the world, how we secure standards of judgment matter a great deal.

I begin with *The Church and the Left* because its strengths and weaknesses can help guide the renewal of a pluralist liberalism. You introduced the English-language edition with cautionary words about the untranslatability of the Polish experience for American readers. "The United States," you observed, "is a country of many religions. It is multi-ethnic and pluralist; multicultural almost by definition."[14] By contrast, Poland, has been artificially homogeneous since the genocide and border changes imposed by Hitler and Stalin. You were unduly fearful of irrelevance. Your quest for an effective plural liberalism in mid-1970s Poland struggled with liberalism's capacity to be mindful of difference: the conditions of its engagement with ethical systems different from its own, the rules it insists on for entry into the realm of liberal citizenship, and the range of toleration it can offer within the ambit of what you called the "pluralistic unity" of a culture—that is, with issues that continue to press heavily on those of us in the United States and elsewhere who want to revalue the liberal tradition. But just this phrase betrays my reservations about the mix of noise and silence in your text. You assumed a framework characterized sufficiently by shared tacit knowledge that dialogue and goodwill could overcome the sharp differences of value that divided the secular left from the Church. Correlatively, the grounding of your work in a deep and nearly unitary sense of Polishness helped you focus the text more on the clash between the values of individuality, toleration, and rights and the domain of the Church than on the problem, once so pervasive in Poland, of how to forge a political nation that could include the one in ten citizens (and one in three residents of Warsaw) who were not Catholics but Jews, while leaving open the choices located at, and between, the pillars of Jewish cultural assimilation and separation.

---

[14] Michnik, *The Church and the Left*, p. xi.

I

On a walk from the Hotel Victoria to the University of Warsaw in 1987, I caught sight of you, reverent, in front of the statue of Stefan Cardinal Wyszynski. I watched, stunned, I confess, not by your deference[15] but by your act of genuflection (by a self-described "Pole who has never hidden his Jewish origin").[16] In what meaning a Pole, I thought? In what significance a Jew? Sincerity often is thought to imply no imitation, yet here, by making the sign of the cross, your conduct paid homage within the idiom of the other, crossing divides separating the Catholic and Pole from the Jew, the secular person from the religious, the public from the intimate. The syncretism of your behavior distinguished your stance from the usual liberal cosmopolitanism or socialist internationalism or from a communitarianism so thick that only insiders qualify. In effect, you announced the mutual constitution of cultures and the ambition of belonging not just to a single enclosed tradition but to combinations of experience.

---

[15] After all, Wyszynski is a national hero who, after his release from three years in prison in 1956, secured a remarkable degree of autonomy for the Church.

[16] When Michnik spoke in April 1991 at the pulpit of New York's Central Synagogue to accept the Shofar Award "for leadership on behalf of justice, equality and commitment to the rights of the individual, in the finest tradition of Judaism and the Jewish people," he indicated a certain embarrassment: "I would like to thank you very much for this unusual honor. And I would like also to tell you about my problem. What is to be said here in this noble place by a Pole who has never hidden his Jewish origin?" He continued, "All my life for all foreigners I was and I wanted to be a Pole. In this way I introduced myself; here in America, in Europe and in Israel. In all my documents on the question of nationality I have always written Polish. But at the same time whenever Polish public life was overshadowed by anti-Semitism, I always clearly and explicitly stated that my origin is Jewish, that my grandparents were Jews. Because being a Pole, I always wanted to be a Jew to anti-Semites. . . . I am a Pole and now I must explain why I have accepted this award given to Jews. I have accepted it in the name of solidarity." He explained, "It is not solidarity with Jewish history or religion. It is not solidarity with Jewish tradition and customs. Neither is it solidarity with the Jewish nation or the country of Israel. Then to describe this complex and intimate feeling, it is solidarity with Jewish adversity." It is not right to judge such heartfelt statements, but when I read them I thought, so many recusals, so little affirmation; are Jews merely a metaphor for suffering? The text is cited in Jonathan Rosen, "Adam Michnik's Jewish Problem," *Forward*, April 26, 1991, p. 11.

Just after *The Church and the Left* appeared in English, it oc-
curred to me that this public/private act shed a good deal of
light on the text's ambitions as well as what I see as its shortcomings. Though you drew no attention to yourself and intended no particular witness, by making these connections you
declared a disdain for fixed identities and cultural compart-
mentalization while displaying regard for the form and content
of Polish tradition. You rightly implied that unless universal
principles of justice and rights connect to the local and the
emotional, they will evanesce as timeless dreams. At the same
time, your act of devotion proclaimed—it seemed to me—the
intent to transcend without incorporating Jewish particularity
into the Polish nation.

The Church and the Left superseded its immediate strategic aim
of forging a broad-based anti-Communist coalition. It signified
your disinclination to embrace the liberal legacy of the Enlightenment by juxtaposing knowledge to superstition. Instead, you
demonstrated regard for nonliberal values and institutions.
Your search for a properly defended liberalism treated issues of
culture and commitment neglected by Western liberalism's
rather abstract portrayal of civil society as essentially consensual
and composed of rights-bearing individuals living outside of
context and community, meaning and belief. You appreciated
that unless the liberal tradition is succored and enriched it will
lack the ability to figure out how people in variegated situations
with different values, histories, and commitments can learn to
live with one another.

Religious difference provides the archetype for the playing
out of these questions in *The Church and the Left*. Church-and-
state, of course, is liberalism's oldest concern. Soaked in the
blood of religious warfare, the regulation of religious difference after the Reformation became Europe's most pressing
issue. Liberalism's solution of toleration had three main aspects: the reduction of religious culture to religious faith; the
relegation of religion to the private sphere; and the replace-
ment of scriptural by political judgment within the realm of the

state.[17] No wonder Catholicism resisted so fiercely liberalism's retraction of the Church's scope and claim.

Your text began with two sharply etched views: yours and Cardinal Wyszynski's. Yours was rights-based. Arguing that Catholics deserve religious, cultural, and political rights not because they constitute a majority, but because "Catholics are due the same rights as other citizens, whether Protestants, Muslims, or atheists," you asserted that "From the standpoint of state law, religious conviction should be a purely private matter. Secularization to me means the following: complete separation of church from state, and complete civil rights for all."[18]

Cardinal Wyszynski, of course, saw things quite differently. Secularization's aim, as a post-Enlightenment tendency, he wrote,

> was to create, with the help of the state, both secular schools and a secular morality, and to bring about the secularization of all state, social, and political establishments. . . . If we still read and hear so much about the secular state today, this is just so much reheating of the old food, which a modern man simply cannot swallow. These are obsolete concepts. The state has no right to forcibly propagate, with the help of social and public institutions, secular rights or a secular morality, particularly in a society that is Catholic through and through.[19]

---

[17] For discussions, see J. C. Davis, "Religion and the Struggle for Freedom in the English Revolution," *The Historical Journal* 35 (September 1992); C. John Sommerville, *The Secularization of Early Modern England: From Religious Culture to Religious Faith* (New York: Oxford University Press, 1992); Susan Mendus, *Toleration and the Limits of Liberalism* (London: Macmillan, 1989); Susan Mendus, ed., *Justifying Toleration: Conceptual and Historical Perspectives* (Cambridge: Cambridge University Press, 1988); Owen Chadwick, *The Secularization of the European Mind in the 19th Century* (Cambridge: Cambridge University Press, 1975), chaps. 1 and 2; and Kirstie M. McClure, "Difference, Diversity, and the Limits of Toleration," *Political Theory* 18 (August 1990).

[18] Michnik, *The Church and the Left*, p. 139. The critical distinction, Michnik has written more recently, distinguishes between the place of the Church in a democratic as opposed to a confessional state. In the former, the Church professes and appeals to individual conscience; in the latter it imposes, thus restricting the rights of others. Adam Michnik, "Confessional State or Personal State?" February 1992.

[19] Stefan Cardinal Wyszynski, *Kazania Swietokrzskie* (Sermans of the Holy Cross)

In effect, you asked whether it is possible to find a framework that respects and learns to live with the irreconcilability of liberal and Catholic claims by protecting civil society from the forcible propagations of the Church while simultaneously protecting the Church from the forcible propagations of nonbelievers and non-Catholics. How, you wanted to know, could liberalism and the Church coexist in a manner protective of a liberal order of rights and choice without stipulating that the Church submit without complaint to a creed it abhors? If liberalism, you insisted, must take moral conflict seriously, the Church, like Aristotle, sees "conflicting moral beliefs as a mark of ignorance, never as a recognition of conflicting moral requirements."[20] Whereas liberalism aims at obedience to secular law while encouraging criticism of it, religion commands submission; whereas liberalism marks all citizens as equal irrespective of their religion, religion wants the state to do what is morally correct; and whereas liberalism is premised on norms of rationality, religion focuses on the transrational.

You understood that the Church was right: liberalism in practice has not been very good at pluralism, and the pluralism it has sanctioned has been confined mainly to nonconflictual diversity or to incompatible views that can be traded off one against the other. But liberalism, the Church has known, is less than comfortable with situations where "trade-offs become unavailable because there is no common currency . . . or scale on

---

(Rome: Rycerza Niepokolanje, 1975), pp. 51–52; cited in Michnik, *The Church and the Left*, pp. 139–40. Similarly, Pope John Paul II has written that as a consequence of the Enlightenment, "*man was supposed to live by reason alone, as if God did not exist.* Not only was it necessary to leave God out of the objective knowledge of the world, since the existence of a Creator or of Providence was in no way helpful to science, it was also necessary to act as if God did not exist, as if God were not interested in the world. *The rationalism of the Enlightenment was able to accept a God outside of the world primarily because it was an unverifiable hypothesis. It was crucial, however, that such a God be expelled from the world.*" His Holiness John Paul II, *Crossing the Threshold of Hope* (New York: Alfred A. Knopf, 1994), p. 53.

[20] Steven Lukes, *Moral Conflict and Politics* (Oxford: Clarendon Press, 1991), p. 3. See especially his chapters on "Making Sense of Moral Conflict" and "Taking Morality Seriously."

which conflicting values can be measured." In such settings, conflicts cannot be resolved by an appeal to a single set of values, experiences, or traditions. Rather, "however one decides, it will be *from* and not just *for*, one of the viewpoints in contention, or from a further viewpoint that is no less contentious."[21] This is a truth much recent liberal theorizing has sought to avoid.

But what to do in such circumstances? Your recurring call for dialogue might well have been enough within the setting of a culturally homogeneous civil society struggling against an ugly Communist order, but even in Poland this has not proved a sufficient formula under democratic conditions. When the Catholic leadership makes claims against the secular state for its own reasons, indeed when it tries to erase the boundary between the secular and the profane, how far does liberal toleration stretch? What principles can be invoked to regulate this engagement? Can the demands made by the Church properly be resolved by democratic, majoritarian politics? More and more, I note, your writings have been warning about the dangers of a religious fundamentalism in Poland, whereas not so long ago you directed your cautionary words at the anticlericalism of the left.

What you are discovering, I suspect, is that the main principles of liberty (guaranteeing the freedom to practice religion), equality (which requires the state not to give preference to any particular religion), and neutrality (demanding the state not tilt toward the religious or the nonreligious), which the liberal tradition has deployed, often prove insufficient as guides in specific historical settings where there are many gray areas.[22] When these values are applied in specific cultural, communal, political, and institutional contexts, it quickly becomes clear

---

[21] Ibid., pp. 11–12. For stimulating discussions, see Emmet John Hughes, *The Church and Liberal Society* (Princeton: Princeton University Press, 1944); and R. Bruce Douglass and David Hollenbach, eds., *Catholicism and Liberalism: Contributions to American Public Philosophy* (Cambridge: Cambridge University Press, 1994).

[22] I draw in this discussion on Chatterjee, "Secularism and Toleration," p. 1771.

that they raise virtually as many practical and ethical questions as they resolve. The freedom to practice religion obviously must be constrained by other basic rights the liberal state is pledged to protect, but where are the lines to be drawn or the judgments made, and by whom? The stipulation of equality works in vastly different ways in settings where there are many faiths and religious establishments, as in the United States, and in settings, such as India, Israel, and Poland, where there clearly exists a majority religion. Further, the separation of church and state implied by neutrality can never be applied absolutely; even in the United States, which arguably is more committed to this principle than any other country, the state finds itself entangled with religion in numerous ways, including the tax system, the symbolic deloyment of public space, and collaborative social welfare efforts. In any specific set of circumstances, universalist liberal guides to religious liberty, equality, and neutrality run the risk becoming pious homilies that hover above the fray or that, in settings of power, get attached to discourses and policies that do not seem legitimate or fair to many citizens.

Now that a good part of the Polish Church is seeking to put a stamp on the state and is rejecting the spirit of dialogue you once asked the left to extend to the Church, we need to do more than counterpose a vision of a state "in which all citizens enjoy equal rights independently of the religions they profess" and the Church "professes its faith in dialogue with the surrounding world."[23] It is easy to agree heartily with these words of yours, but in the absence of more sharply etched guides to doctrine, institutions, and practice they do not take us very far.

Nonetheless, you will see that I think such an effort can build on your book's treatment of the clash of secular and religious ontologies and rationalities in Poland, which was distinguished by your receptivity to the perspectives of others without losing your own standards of judgment and by the combination of a normative doctrine with a historically grounded, sociologically

---

[23] Adam Michnik, "Confessional State or Personal Faith?" February 1992.

informed realism. What remains impressive about *The Church and the Left* is your rejection of an individualism or a culturalism that is too strong, and your recognition that a decent liberalism must resist both the repudiation of difference and the deification of it. You have been suspicious of liberalism suspended in a cultural void and lacking in regard for values of tradition and trust, just as you have been wary of cultures so encompassing that they negate human autonomy, stifle reason, promote dogmatism, and impose the suspicion of difference. For these reasons, you have been careful to counsel the avoidance of the most common moves the left has made in reaction to strong romantic reactions on the right to the Enlightenment's precepts: the kind of strong republicanism repressing difference that has been characteristic of the French left since the revolution, or the kind of multiculturalist pluralism developed as a countercurrent to individualist liberalism in the United States that risks a paralysis of judgment.

I share many of your reservations about the tribalization of politics; but I was dissatisfied, I confess, by the reductive treatment of the single example of group pluralism *The Church and the Left* actually takes up: the case of Poland's Jews. I found your writing to be more compelling when it deals with ethical pluralism within the "unity" of Catholic Poland than with Polish anti-Semitism and the role of the Church in mediating Polish-Jewish relations. Because your emphasis on the diversity of opinion and ethics rather than on cultural heterogeneity is characteristic of liberal orientations more broadly, *The Church and the Left* contributes cautionary as well as exemplary lessons.

By describing the Church's record as blemished but largely meritorious, you aimed to demonstrate that Polishness and the toleration of difference are not mutually exclusive. Of course I know you believe the Church fell far short of its moral responsibilities in March 1968 (fearing to get too far ahead of its parishioners) and that you have condemned anti-Semitism and other forms of chauvinism and racism assertively countless times (you broke with Walesa, in part, in 1990 because he was prepared to profit from anti-Jewish themes).[24] I am aware that you reject any simple understanding that Pole equals Catholic, stressing instead how prewar Poland gathered energy from its polyglot qualities when there were Jews everywhere. I understand why you would want to emphasize the progressive stance of some figures in the Church during such ugly moments as the Kielce pogrom at the conclusion of the Second World War or the March 1968 purge of Jewish intellectuals when the party blamed "Zionists" for student unrest and some 20,000 Jews left the country. I am sympathetic to your effort to locate Polish anti-Jewish violence in the more general context of violence in Polish society and to distinguish Poland's largely peasant, folk anti-Semitism (which today has become an anti-Semitism without Jews) from Nazi Germany's scientific, racist, and genocidal version.[25] Nonetheless, even while allowing for the tactical requirements of the mid-1970s and the desire to entice the Church and the broader Polish public into a common project with the democratic opposition, I am still put off by the treatment in *The Church and the Left* of anti-Semitism primarily as an aberrational blot on Polish culture rather than as part of a more inherent, if complex, story of cultural collision and difference and by the way you downplayed Church complicity in anti-Jewish outrages, mainly by the route of silence.[26] On these subjects the text is surprisingly aseptic; very different, say, from the vocabulary of outrage and responsibility deployed by Jan

[24] Adam Michnik, "My Vote Against Walesa," *New York Review of Books*, December 20, 1990. Raised in an assimilated, secular household, Michnik had neither experienced anti-Semitism nor had a consciousness of being different or treated differently before the regime-inspired anti-Semitic purges and outrages of March 1968.

[25] Michnik, *The Church and the Left*, pp. 61, 97–112. For a treatment of anti-Jewish pogroms in the context of Russian peasant violence, see I. Michael Aronson, *Troubled Waters: The Origins of the 1881 Pogroms in Russia* (Pittsburgh: University of Pittsburgh Press, 1991).

[26] For a critique along these lines, see Jeffrey C. Isaac, "Adam Michnik: Politics and the Church," *Salmagundi* 103 (Summer 1994). In "Confessional State or Personal Faith?" Michnik does take note of sermons by priests after 1935 who approved the boycotting of Jewish businesses and the demand by conservative students, frequently attended to in practice, that Jews be placed on "ghetto benches" (separate seating areas) in university classrooms.

Blonski to recall pre-Holocaust Poland or characterize current circumstances where only shards of Jewishness remain in once thriving centers like Katowice, Lublin, Lodz, Bialystock, and Warsaw. Jewish blood, he has written, "remains on our walls and is soaked into the ground, whether we like it or not. It has soaked into our memory, into ourselves. We must boldly and honestly face the question of our responsibility."[27] In Warsaw as in Berlin, the postwar city literally was reconstructed on a foundation of Jewish bones. But it is less a matter of evocative expression or even of responsibility that I have in mind. Rather, I think your treatment of the Jewish question inadvertently gives expression to the liberal tradition's ambivalence about a resonant cultural pluralism. Like many liberal thinkers, your keen appreciation for the force and nuances of moral conflict is not matched, at least not in this text, by an equal affinity for the value of deep cultural diversity.

Because your writings on anti-Semitism have been geared mainly to a strategy of defense and the expression of outrage, you have parried romantic and racialist assaults on Poland's Jews by asserting rationalist and universalist principles,[28] but in so doing, you have downplayed Jewish culture and particularity. Though certainly unintentional, this emphasis implies a reduc-

[27] Cited in Barry Newman, "In a Freer-Speech Era, Poles at Last Confront Ghosts of the Ghetto," *Wall Street Journal,* January 4, 1989, p. 4. Blonski's essay on Polish corespon-sibility, which first appeared in 1987 in the liberal Catholic newspaper *Tygodnik Pow-szechny* as part of a broader effort to grapple with the heritage of anti-Semitism, caused an uproar, was rejected even by a leading opposition lawyer-activist as a piece of anti-Polish propaganda, but was effective both in facilitating a Catholic-Jewish dialogue and in making the point that it is possible for victims not to be free of their own guilt. Blonski was recently echoed by the heroic mayor of the once half-Jewish village of Tykocin who erected, against spirited opposition, a new stone memorial to the village's Jews, declaring, "We must never, never forget them." Cited in "Never Forgetting," *The Economist,* November 9, 1991, p. 44. At the time, *The Economist* noted, nearby Bialystock, once a city with 40,000 Jews, was scarred by graffiti reading "Jews to the gas chamber" when it was home to only six. Of course, that hardly makes more than the mad person who daubed it culpable, but why, one might ask, do such words linger unerased?

[28] I have been helped in thinking about these issues by two suggestive papers: Barbara Kirschenblatt-Gimlett, "Erasing the Subject: Franz Boas and the Anthropological Study of Jews in the United States, 1903–1942," ms., 1986; and Igor Barsegian-Kokkei, "The Epistemology of Identity," ms., 1994.

tion in the scope of desirable cultural difference uncomfortably similar to John Stuart Mill's claim that liberal institutions are only possible within the framework of common language, customs, literature, traditions:

> Among a people without fellow-feelings, especially if they read and speak different languages, the united public opinion necessary to the workings of representative institutions cannot exist. . . . [It] is in general a necessary condition of free institutions that the boundaries of governments should coincide in the main with those of nationalities.[29]

Similarly, T. H. Green, who pioneered England's socially oriented New Liberalism, argued that political obligation could be expected only by people who feel bound to the state by "ties derived from a common dwelling place with its associations, from common memories, traditions and customs, and from the common ways of feeling and thinking which a common language and still more a common literature embodies."[30] Indeed, not only Mill and Green, but most liberals (and, indeed, most communitarians) have found it difficult to find a place for a heterogeneity of cultures within a common political community. In T. H. Marshall's rendering in his famous essay on the history of civil, political, and social rights in England, "citizenship requires a bond of a different kind, a direct sense of community membership based on loyalty to a civilization which is a common possession."[31] Of course, if rights are contingent on membership in a community (rather than in natural law), they can readily be revoked.

This strand of liberal thought, Will Kymlicka notes, insists

---

[29] John Stuart Mill, *Considerations on Representative Government*, in H. Acton, ed., *Utilitarianism, Liberty, Representative Government* (London: J. M. Dent, 1972), pp. 230–33; cited in Kymlicka, *Multicultural Citizenship*, p. 52.

[30] T. H. Green, *Lectures on the Principles of Political Obligation* (London: Longman's, 1941), pp. 130–31; cited in Kymlicka, *Multicultural Citizenship*, p. 52.

[31] T. H. Marshall, "Citizenship and Social Class," in Marshall, *Class, Citizenship, and Social Development* (Westport, Connecticut: Greenwood Press, 1963), p. 101.

that "since a free state must be a nation-state, national minorities must be dealt with by coercive assimilation or by the redraw-
ing of boundaries."[32] Certainly David Bromwich's very recent
insistence that liberalism must focus on individual independence and mount a challenge "to *all* bargains with cultural
identity" (arguing that what he calls culturalism places liberals
in the impossible position of showing regard for illiberal cultures in situations where cultural attachments rarely are benign) is far more consistent with the dominant trajectory of
the liberal tradition than Kymlicka's more attractive position,
which understands that individualism on its own can provide
no basis for confronting the variety of cultural and political situations of humankind; hence that liberalism is doomed to irrelevance unless it can come to terms with transindividual loyalties,
practices, and ways of life about which Mill was so distrustful
because of their propensity to conformity.[33] At stake is whether
we can discover a way to treat humankind as a single unity without eliding or destroying its marks of difference and whether
the pluralism liberalism is willing to put on offer is far-reaching
or narrowly gauged.

Though you obviously recoil from the implications of the
Mill-Green-Marshall line of reasoning, you implicitly adopt kin-
dred thinking. To be sure, there was passion to spare in your
1991 essay on "Poland and the Jews" when you denounced a
post-1989 wave of anti-Semitism as a menace to Poland's fledg-
ling post-Communist democracy. Your solidarity, you wrote, was
"with the Jewish fate . . . the fate of a threatened people who
have suffered many blows, who know the taste of humiliation,
of defeat, and who have always faced hard choices. It is finally
the fate of a people who have been rejected and persecuted."
Commenting on this text, the political theorist Jeffrey Isaac has
written,

---

[32] Kymlicka, *Multicultural Citizenship*, p. 52.

[33] David Bromwich, "Culturalism: The Euthanasia of Liberalism," *Dissent* (Winter
1995): 96.

But what does it mean to say that anti-semitism is dangerous because it threatens Polish democracy, and that the
Jewish fate is persecution, humiliation, defeat? It is to
declare Jewish existence and thriving to be somehow in-
essential. Michnik's speech act is astonishing. Sincerely
denouncing anti-semitism, he is unable to affirm that Judaism is a civilization that persists not as an example of righ-
teous suffering for people of good (Christian) will, but as
a living civilization, with its own values, culture, and integrity. Michnik's language, the language of his Poland,
seems unable to think this, just as it seems unable to think
the possibility of a Polish Jew in the same way there are
German-Jews or Jewish-Americans. In the end its holy
trinity—Poland, Church, Christ—seems to leave little
room for Jews as a living people.[34]

Perhaps Isaac ignores that you were seeking a stratagem to
check anti-Jewish sentiment at a particular juncture (hence that
you were constrained to operate within given cultural assumptions), but I fear he is right to see traces in your prose of Poland's long-standing difficulty as a traditionally Christian environment in discovering a full commensurate place for Jews and
their distinctiveness irrespective of individual choices about assimilation or conversion. In Christian Europe, Jews have been
liminal, ambiguous figures who neither wished to be, nor could
be, wholly absorbed.[35] As the consummate other, Jews have fit
awkwardly into Catholic worldviews. As antecedents of the true
faith, Jews occupied a determinate place in the Christian grand
narrative, defined in sacral rather than secular terms. Within
the embrace of an enveloping Christendom, Jews (in Poland as

[34] Isaac, "Adam Michnik: Politics and the Church," pp. 210–11. The references to
"Poland and the Jews" are drawn from citations in this article.

[35] As alien and suspect, Jews, Anne Norton has written, have been "preeminently
liminal, being a people without land, residents of every nation yet having none of their
own, . . . the antithesis of volkish nationality." Anne Norton, *Republic of Signs: Liberal
Theory and American Popular Culture* (Chicago: University of Chicago Press, 1993), p. 82.

elsewhere) suffered blood libels and massacres, were forced to endure recurring humiliations, and lived on sufferance, if never wholly outside society. Their spatially segregated position at the edge of Christian fellowship reinforced an isolation they by and large desired for themselves, and it legitimated their performance of activities vital to the larger economy, state, and social system.[36]

In this context, anti-Semitism served as a boundary-guarding mechanism. When the German juggernaut came and with it a more systematic, scientific, genocidal anti-Semitism, no segment of Polish society (with the exception of a small number of heroic individuals), notably including the Church, betrayed sympathy for the Jews. As Jan Gross has shown, while the vast majority of Poles certainly did not condone murder, they approved the confinement of the Jews in ghettos and did not understand anti-Semitism to be sinful. Arguing effectively against cost-benefit approaches to explain Polish reticence in helping or finding solidarity with threatened Jewish brethren, he demonstrates that the causal arrow actually pointed the other way: "Because the Poles were not ready to assist the Jews, and, by and large, refrained from doing so, the death punishment for harboring Jews was meted out by the Germans systematically and without reprieve."[37]

---

[36] See Pierre Birnbaum and Ira Katznelson, "Emancipation and the Liberal Offer," in Pierre Birnbaum and Ira Katznelson, eds., *Paths of Emancipation: Jews, States, and Citizenship* (Princeton: Princeton University Press, 1995); Alan Ryan, "Letting Them Live," *London Review of Books*, August 4, 1988; Robert Bonfil, "Aliens Within: The Jews and Anti-Judaism," in Thomas A. Brady, Jr., Heiko A. Oberman, and James D. Tracy, eds., *Handbook of European History, 1400–1600: Late Middle Ages, Rennaissance and Reformation. Volume I: Structures and Assertions* (Leiden: E. J. Brill, 1994); Joshua Trachtenberg, *The Devil and the Jews: The Medieval Conception of the Jew and Its Relation to Modern Antisemitism* (New Haven: Yale University Press, 1943); Robert Chazan, ed., *Church, State, and Jew in the Middle Ages* (New York: Behrman House, 1980); and Salo W. Baron, "The Jewish Factor in Medieval Civilization," in Robert Chazen, ed., *Medieval Jewish Life: Studies from the Proceedings of the American Academy for Jewish Research* (New York: Ktav Publishing, 1976).

[37] Jan T. Gross, "Polish-Jewish Relations during the War—an Interpretation," *Dissent* (Winter 1987); Jan T. Gross, "Polish-Jewish Relations during the War," *Archives Europeenes de Sociologie* 28, 2 (1986): 207.

A nuanced discussion of these issues recently appeared in a discussion in *Gazeta*

With the Jews now physically gone, anti-Semitism, you recognize, still lingers as a way of defining limits and exclusions, but now it is directed against modernity and liberalism itself. But by adopting Polishness as your own idiom and by making the Church central to it without fully confronting its traditional role in keeping Jews in their place, you make yourself vulnerable to Isaac's not fully fair charge of valuing ethical pluralism without a concurrent component of cultural and group difference. If forced to select between discriminatory particularity and a universality of standards and rights (with the implication for Jews that these alternatives entail, respectively, a precarious isolation or wholesale assimilation), it is clear why you would choose the latter. But this I believe to be an impoverished choice.

II

As Mill's, Green's, and Marshall's texts on nationality, culture, and political boundaries suggest, the option of rightslessness for people outside culturally homogeneous national frameworks is embedded in liberal thought even for thinkers committed to respect far-reaching ethical differences inside a given national culture. This tension has recurred in liberal theory since its origins because it owes its existence to a constellation of circumstances and large-scale historical processes that marked lib-

---

Wyborcza concerning Andrzej Wajda's decision to film the short story "Holy Week" (*Wielki Tydzień*) by Jerzy Andrzejewski, written in the aftermath of the destruction of the Warsaw Ghetto. Wajda, Adam Michnik, and Tadeusz Sobolewski conducted an illuminating roundtable to assess the legacies of indifference and responsibility for the circumstances in which Warsaw's Gentiles prepared for Easter while watching the ghetto burn. In their conversation, which also touched on Jan Blonski's discussion of Polish-Jewish relations, Michnik observed that when he is in the West he reacts sharply to "idiotic" generalized statements about Polish anti-Semitism, but that this kind of defense does not take us very far. Indeed, he noted, the widespread negative reaction to Blonski's "J'Accuse" shows that no causistry can erase the fact that during the German occupation Polish anti-Semitic attitudes helped underpin the detachment of most Poles to the fate of the Jews, even as the situation itself was structurally impossible. This discovery, Michnik noted, "was shocking for me." "From Our Side of the Wall," *Gazeta Wyborcza*, June 10/11, 1995.

eralism's inception and the problems of stateness, differentiation, diversity, and toleration it initially sought to confront. Liberalism's past continues to inform its present.

The creation of Europe as a meaningful cultural and political construct was the first of these processes. For the four centuries after A.D. 950, conquest, colonization, and cultural diffusion from the core areas of France, Germany west of the Elbe, and northern Italy transformed the differentiated Latin Europe of the early Middle Ages into a reasonably well integrated region marked by an increasingly manifest cultural identity. Europe Europeanized. This pattern, Robert Bartlett has observed, shared many qualities with postmedieval overseas expansion, but with the subordination left out:

> When Anglo-Normans settled in Ireland or Germans in Pomerania or Castilians in Andalusia, they were not engaged in the creation of a pattern of regional subordination. What they were doing was reproducing units similar to those in their homelands. The towns, churches, and estates they established simply replicated the social framework they knew from back home. The net result of this colonialism was not the creation of "colonies," in the sense of dependencies, but the spread, by a kind of cellular multiplication, of the cultural and social forms found in the Latin Christian core.[38]

This process entailed a reduction in diversity. Though the growing uniformity of Europe was resisted, often violently, by the time the high Middle Ages passed, the vast differences between places on the map were tempered by their insertion into a meaningful European unit integrated by ideas, faith, armies, institutions, and networks of economic, political, and social elites.

The second great historical process was the accumulation and concentration of sovereignty into national territorial states.

---

[38] Robert Bartlett, *The Making of Europe: Conquest, Colonization and Cultural Change, 950–1350* (Princeton: Princeton University Press, 1993), p. 306.

These states, which emerged as the dominant institutional form of coercion and coordination, were distinguished from their medieval predecessors by claiming a unique authority within their borders, by arraying power in a systematic hierarchy, and by recognizing boundaries demarcating comparable units. By the middle of the seventeenth century, these forms of political organization had trumped their key competitors, which included feudal arrangements dominated by the nobility, the church as a translocal community of believers, the Holy Roman Empire claiming superiority over local and national rulers, the Hanseatic League which confederated key cities engaged in long-distance trade, and the Italian city-states.[39] The national state became more lawful, more abstract, more distinct from the person of the king or prince, and more respectful of the distinction between public and private morality. International relations became distinguishable from domestic politics, and an international state-system provided a framework for war, peace, and economic relations.

This consolidation of sovereignty into particular kinds of increasingly centralized political units that standardized laws, coinage, taxation, language, and responsibility for security inside clearly demarcated boundaries provided the basis for cultural and national differentiation within Europe at the same time as it had the effect of reducing heterogeneity inside the terrain of any given state. Typically, a state's claims to territoriality and sovereignty preceded the creation of a singular cultural nation of subjects or citizens; it was the existence of states themselves that shaped nations as a result of self-conscious efforts by states that sought in a variety of ways—including military

[39] See, for discussions, Charles Tilly, ed., *The Formation of National States in Western Europe* (Princeton: Princeton University Press, 1975); Charles Tilly, *Coercion, Capital, and European States, A.D. 990–1990*. (Oxford: Basil Blackwell, 1990); J. H. Shennan, *The Origins of the Modern European State, 1450–1725* (London: Hutchinson, 1974); Orest Ranum, ed., *National Consciousness, History, and Political Culture in Early-Modern Europe* (Baltimore: Johns Hopkins Univesity Press, 1975); Richard Bonney, *The European Dynastic States, 1494–1660* (New York: Oxford University Press, 1991); and Hendrik Spruyt, *The Sovereign State and Its Competitors: An Analysis of Systems Change* (Princeton: Princeton University Press, 1994).

service, efforts directed at creating linguistic uniformity (at least among elites), and explusions (as in the case of Jews, who also were taxed disproportionately and frequently had their assets expropriated)—to homogenize their populations.

A corollary third process was that of a growing structural set of separations inside national boundaries distinguishing the realm of property from that of sovereignty and the state as an entity separate from, if intimately tied to, civil society. National states created between the fourteenth and seventeenth centuries came to possess sovereignty, based on law, and with it legitimate force within a distinctive territory; an ensemble of institutions; and a vision and articulation of the common good. With these attributes, the state under the conditions of the postfeudal division of property and power emerged as a calculating actor vis-à-vis an increasingly differentiated economic sphere and a newly distinguishable civil society.

The key break point in the development of capitalism as the dominant framework for economic development in the West came only with the concentration of sovereignty, the liberation of the political order from direct control of production relations, and the establishment of an authoritative framework for property rights and economic transactions on a large scale. Separated from property, and concentrated in authority, the states of postfeudal Europe also had to forge new, and uncertain, ties to civil society. With the breakup of the tightly knit juridical, economic, and social units characteristic of feudalism, states could not simply impose their will by despotic imposition. Instead, it was a condition of their effectiveness that they transacted with society and coordinated aims with other "private" powerholders. State-society relations become reciprocal.

The development of a distinctive set of knowledge producers concerned with the new sets of transactions—the creation of intellectuals in a modern sense—constituted the fourth process essential to the birth of liberalism. This knowledge elite thought itself to be separate from the mass of society. "It was at the threshold of modern times," Zygmunt Bauman observes, "that the dominant and the dominated had become *culturally* estranged, with the dominant defining their own way of life as 'cultured' and thereby superior." This distinction identified the mass of the population "as the object of either a protracted civilizing crusade or of close surveillance, control, and—as an ultimate measure—of confinement."[40] Intellectuals were cast in the role of trainers in a double sense: to point rulers toward more effective transactions among the state, the economy, and civil society, and to improve the institutions and endowments of the mass of the population. As in the exemplary case of Machiavelli, these secular intellectuals advised the prince, created a modern science of government, and sought to police the population in order to improve its character.[41]

The fifth big process was the polarization of Christendom culminating in the Thirty Years War (the first general European war, settled at Westphalia in 1648), and with it the recognition of a new set of linkages between organized religion and the state. The Church's monopoly of doctrinal and institutional authority was ended by the rapid appeal and extension of Reformation revisionism, especially under Lutheran and Calvinist auspices. In effect, three schisms and sets of connections were established: between the vision of one Church and many; between Christian and heathen others (with a special status combining wariness, distancing mechanisms, and regard for the Jews who were essential to the Christian narrative); and between the religious and state-focused secular realms. Each of these relationships became politicized. At issue was the balance of forces, the degree and content of toleration, and the character of institutional ties characterizing these interdependencies.[42]

[40] Zygmunt Bauman, "Love in Adversity: On the State and the Intellectuals, and the State of the Intellectuals," *Thesis Eleven* 31 (March 1992): 82.

[41] For one of his best discussions of these matters, see Michel Foucault, "Governmentality," *m/f* 3 (July 1979).

[42] For discussions, see Robert Wuthnow, *Communities of Discourse: Ideology and Social Structure in the Reformation, the Enlightenment, and European Socialism* (Cambridge: Harvard University Press, 1989); J.H.M. Salmon, *The French Religious Wars in English Political*

Colonial conquest constituted the last, arguably the most important, of the large-scale processes shaping the development and content of early modern liberalism. Six decades after Columbus's voyages, Francisco Lopez de Gomara described the discovery of the Americas as "The greatest event since the creation of the world (excluding the incarnation and death of Him who created it)."[43] Characterized by huge disparities in power, the history of cultural collision and exploitation that followed the extension of Europe produced catastrophe for indigenous peoples and imported slaves and established "the beginning of Eurocentric world history, of the conviction that a few Western and Central European countries were destined to conquer and rule the globe, of Euromegalomania."[44]

Thoughtfully assessing the 500th anniversary of Columbus, Eric Hobsbawm reminded his readers that the asymmetries of power between the colonizers and colonized help mask the reciprocal impact of the Americas in the Old World. The expansion of Europe transformed trade, the availability of foodstuffs and commodities, and cultures.[45] But these new cultural contacts also altered Europe's own visions of politics and society. Whereas medieval Europeanization had made the continent more uniform, external colonization introduced an unprecedented cultural pluralism into the heart of Europe. Alien influences were absorbed, if not always intentionally; relationships across cultural divisions were forged; racial, sexual, and cultural hybrids were created; and Europe's knowledge about the

---

Thought (Oxford: Clarendon Press, 1989); and Richard S. Dunn, *The Age of Religious Wars, 1559–1715* (New York: Norton, 1979). For an acutely drawn case study of these elements, see the discussion of Galileo's martyrdom and his destruction of the Church's claim to authoritative access to all human knowledge by Pietro Redondi, *Galileo: Heretic* (London: Allen Lane, 1988).

[43] Francisco Lopez de Gomara, *General History of the Indies* [1552], cited in Peter Burke, "Religion and Secularisation," in Burke, ed., *The New Cambridge Modern History, XIII: Companion Volume* (Cambridge: Cambridge University Press, 1979), p. 293.

[44] Eric Hobsbawm, "Goodbye Columbus: 1492 and Its Cultural Consequences in Europe," *London Review of Books*, July 9, 1992, p. 15. A useful view of the colonization process is provided by Wolfgang Reinhard, "The Seaborne Empires," in Brady, Oberman, and Tracy, eds., *Handbook of European History.*

[45] Hobsbawm, "Goodbye Columbus."

world's surprisingly different ways of life was extended and elaborated.[46]

Together, these developments shaped liberalism's agenda and possibilities by creating new bases of differentiation: between an increasingly well-integrated Europe and other regions of the world; between different kinds of Christians; between Christians and Jews; and between the state and the other massive macrostructures of the economy and civil society. These transformations allowed liberals to support ductile states while erecting barriers to protect members of civil society from the willful imposition of state power; and to support ethical heterogeneity in the name of religious toleration while favoring reductions in their own countries' cultural diversity.

More than any other factor, liberalism's understanding of difference and its orientation to the pluralism of groups and cultures was shaped by Europe's massive colonial project. With the widening and deepening of European knowlege about human experience, sharp debates quickly emerged about the character and desirability of cultural pluralism. These had two aspects. The first concerned whether the terms of contact should be characterized as constituting a hierarchy of civilizations, with Europe at the summit, or in terms of a multiplicity of cultures. The second concerned whether the degree to which large-scale differences in ways of life would be tolerated. These two axes did not always go hand in hand. At the famous debate in Valladolid, Spain, in 1550, Juan Gines de Sepulveda upheld the superiority of Christian Europe against the claims of Bartolome de Las Casas, who vindicated the worth of Indian culture.[47] Though Sepulveda supported Spanish conquests because of the precedence of Europe's Christian way of life, he took the plurality of Indian ways of life seriously in order to up-

---

[46] See Urs Bitterli, *Cultures in Conflict: Encounters between European and Non-European Cultures, 1492–1800* (Oxford: Polity Press, 1989).

[47] There is a discussion in Tzvetan Todorov, *The Morals of History* (Minneapolis: University of Minnesota Press, 1995), p. 34. For the distinction between civilization and culture, see Marshall Sahlins, "How 'Natives' Think," *Times Literary Supplement,* June 2, 1995, p. 13.

hold his thesis of European superiority. By contrast, the more tolerant Las Casas justified his toleration by trying to show that the Indians actually shared and lived Christian values. Tzvetan Todorov acutely has noticed how this debate highlights the elusiveness of standards for a culturally pluralist world characterized by vast differences of power: "the egalitarian attitude threatens to be transformed into an affirmation of sameness, whereas the perception of difference runs the risk of being swallowed up in the brutal affirmation of the superiority of one culture over another."[48]

The post-sixteenth-century Europeanized world vastly extended possibilities for cultural understanding, awareness, syncretism, and toleration while producing new forms of racism, massacre, and barbarism, including a globalized system of chattel slavery.[49] Liberalism coped with the extraordinary post-sixteenth-century extension of contacts between cultures by naturalizing human difference and by making only a minority of Europeans eligible liberal citizens. Well into this century, liberalism's standards branded most of the world's population as not qualified. Indeed, it was just such a construction of the un-

[48] Todorov, *The Morals of History*, p. 35.

[49] The human cost was astonishing. In Peru, for example, the Spanish conquest had the effect of reducing the native population as a result of war and disease according to the high end of estimates from 8 million in 1530 to 1.3 million sixty years later. In Mexico, the Indian population was diminished even more dramatically from an estimated 25 million in 1519 to 2.6 million by 1568. Even if these figures are high, no one contests the astounding scale of devastation. Recent scholarship hypothesizes that just under 10 million slaves were transported to the New World, with the resultant loss of population in West Africa of between 12 million and 15 million depending on the demographic assumptions applied. See Nathan Wachtel, *The Vision of the Vanquished* (London: Hassocks, 1977); Nathan Wachtel, "The Indian and the Spanish Conquest," in L. Bethell, ed., *The Cambridge History of Latin America; vol. 1: Colonial Latin America* (Cambridge: Cambridge University Press, 1984); Herbert S. Klein, "Eighteenth Century Atlantic Slave Trade," in James T. Tracy, ed., *The Rise of Merchant Empires: Long Distance Trade in the Early Modern World* (Cambridge: Cambridge University Press, 1990); Johannes Menne Postma, *The Dutch in the Atlantic Slave Trade: 1600–1815* (Cambridge: Cambridge University Press, 1990); Philip Curtin, *The Rise and Fall of the Plantation Complex: Essays in Atlantic History* (Cambridge: Cambridge University Press, 1990); Joseph E. Inikori and Stanley L. Engerman, eds., *The Atlantic Slave Trade: Effects on Economies, Societies, and Peoples in Africa and the Americas, and Europe* (Durham: Duke University Press, 1992); and Bitterli, *Cultures in Conflict*, p. 37.

qualified savage that provided "the ideological justification for colonial appropriation of non-European territories, particularly in the Americas," and that legitimated colonial rule more generally.[50] Liberalism's concern for human autonomy and self-development at home soon came to be matched by an indifferent tolerance for the suffering of others, especially those demarcated from Europe by markings of physiognomy.[51] "The difference of cults and of nations," Diderot observed in his denunciation of colonialism, "has familiarized even the grossest minds with a spirit of indifference for the objects which would once have startled their imagination."[52] In Christian Europe the strengthening of liberal political norms and institutions proved entirely compatible with the disappearance of taboos against unethical behavior directed at the excluded. The conquest, expulsion, and enslavement engendered by colonialism made of all the world a community of Jews.

III

Nearly thirty years ago I heard Isaiah Berlin lecture about ethical and group pluralism at Cambridge's Mill Lane Lecture Rooms. Ever since, when I read his prose I think of Durer's magnificent copper-engraving "Melancholia," completed in 1514. Portraying a brooding winged genius overcome by anxi-

[50] Peter Hulme, "The Spontaneous Hand of Nature: Savagery, Colonialism, and the Enlightenment," in Peter Hulme and Ludmilla Jordanova, eds., *The Enlightenment and Its Shadows* (London: Routledge, 1990), p. 17.

[51] David Eltis recently has asked why Africans and not Europeans were enslaved for a labor supply. Skeptical of answers based on relative profitability, he argues that European capitalists could have used existing penal institutions as a labor source; instead, they purchased slaves in Africa. He argues that the key reasons were ideological, as more and more whites became insiders in European politics. In northwest Europe, where local people were most protected from forced labor, the most harsh, closed systems of black slavery were tolerated. David Eltis, "Europeans and the Rise and Fall of African Slavery in the Americas: An Interpretation," *The American Historical Review* 98 (December 1993).

[52] Cited in Anthony Padgen, "The Effacement of Difference: Colonialism and the Origins of Nationalism in Diderot and Herder," in Gyan Prakash, ed., *After Colonialism: Imperial Histories and Postcolonial Displacements* (Princeton: Princeton University Press, 1995), p. 140.

ety and dejected amidst his scientific instruments, this figure has been represented by Panofsky as grappling with the limits of human capacity and the defeat of reason in the face of "intellectual finiteness."[53] Whereas a melancholic temperament had been repulsive to the medieval imagination, Durer's humanist rendering transformed pensive despondency into a chastening recognition of the limits placed on human rationality by aggression, avarice, and conceit.[54]

Berlin not only looks like Durer's dour scholar; he has taken on equivalent burdens. Though a partisan of the Enlightenment, his skeptical liberalism combats the Enlightenment's tendency to flatten cultural differences in the name of reason and utterly rejects the idea that reason permits the discovery of one true way of thought and life. Berlin has struggled to defend a deep and wide pluralism of "many objective ends, ultimate values, some incompatible with others, pursued by different societies at different times, or by different groups in the same society, by entire classes, churches or races, or by particular individuals within them"[55] while abjuring a relativism so complete that we become captives of history who lack the capacity to consider, evaluate, and judge. Berlin has sought to find footing in moral universalism for the toleration of difference without subscribing either to the project of a singular pattern of enlightenment or to the view that anything authentic is acceptable.

Cultures, he understands, are never unitary, never indivisible, never organic, always assemblages of distinctive ideas, elements, patterns, and behaviors. While only the immersion in specific cultures can give individuals access to the universal (none of us lives life in general), only universal standards can

---

[53] Erwin Panofsky, *The Life and Art of Albrecht Durer* (Princeton: Princeton University Press, 1955), p. 168. Also see Keith Moxey, *The Practice of History: Poststructuralism, Cultural Politics, and Art History* (Ithaca: Cornell University Press, 1994), chap. 4.

[54] After Noah's flood, "the Lord said to Himself, 'Never again will I doom the earth because of man, since the devisings of man's mind are evil from his youth.'" *Genesis* 8:21.

[55] Isaiah Berlin, "Alleged Relativism in Eighteenth-Century European Thought," in Berlin, *The Crooked Timber of Humanity* (New York: Alfred A. Knopf, 1991), pp. 79–80.

provide means for evaluating specific aspects of cultures from outside the framework of their own exclusivity. Berlin insists that pluralism and relativism not be conflated because he rejects cultural hierarchies enforced by power and is concerned about the prospect of a cultural egalitarianism that can lapse into licensed barbarity. Though we must break with Europe's old habit of ranking whole cultures, we must not give up on the appraisal of specific cultural practices.

If Panofsky's interpretation is compelling, Durer's melancholic figure anticipated the shift from the practical philosophy of the sixteenth century to the theoretical conception of philosophy after Descartes. This change was marked by a turn from particular cases to general principles, from concrete diversity to abstract axioms, and from time-bound historical configurations to the timeless and the permanent.[56] What later became a hallmark of Enlightenment thought—the capacity of reason, science, and institutional design to provide for human improvement—was not so much rejected by such sixteenth century figures as Montaigne (and, in our time, by Berlin) as confined by irony, skepticism, and a penchant for ambiguity; that is, by a deep appreciation for the possibilities and pitfalls of pluralism and differentiation, the instabilities of truth, and an acknowledgment that even successful attempts to remedy flaws in human institutions cannot permanently prevent evil from trumping reason.

Liberalism mainly has placed its bets on the abstract, timeless ambitions of the post-Cartesian program. As such, late in humanity's most bloody, ugly century, it is vulnerable to the charge of being light and simple. In the face of a demonstrated human capacity to act out its most monstrous nightmares, liberalism appears as a credulous attempt to institutionalize decency. Perhaps we must transcend rather than deepen the decontextualized, disembodied, universalist features of the

---

[56] Stephen Toulmin, *Cosmopolis: The Hidden Agenda of Modernity* (New York: The Free Press, 1990), pp. 30–35.

Enlightenment and its liberal (and socialist) progeny.[57] This is
the advice of many anti-Enlightenment thinkers who find liberalism to be innocent of history, irrelevant to a politics of identity and difference, and incapable of taming the ferocity of
human attachments and the vitality of situated, particularistic
passions.

As Berlin understands, these criticisms of the Enlightenment's legacies as shallow, utopian, and disrespectful of difference have great force, but an anti-Enlightenment punch line is
insupportable normatively and practically. A radical attack on
the Enlightenment is an indulgence we can ill afford. Attacks
on reason and objectivity cannot be limited to normative purposes of which we approve.[58] The view that the liberal tradition
is irrevocably hostile to human diversity or irrelevant to the
prevention of cruelties based on indifference or domination
amounts to a counsel of despair. To the extent the left has
bought into this line of thinking, as in some versions of multicultural and postcolonial discourse that highlight the Enlightenment's impositions of power while deliberately eschewing a
critical standpoint, it is unprepared to confront the vast abyss
of untamed, unmanaged difference; yet to the extent we do
not face up to the insufficiencies of the liberal tradition in dealing with difference, we risk the reciprocal ugliness of trying to
face down intolerant zealotry with soft versions of cultural
imperialism.

---

[57] This is the move recommended by the political theorist John Gray, who considers
liberal theory to represent "the prejudices of an Anglo-American academic class that
lacks any political understanding of political life in our age; an age distinguished by the
collapse of the Enlightenment project on a world-historical scale." John Gray, "Against
the New Liberalism: Rawls, Dworkin, and the Emptying of Political Life," *Times Literary
Supplement*, July 3, 1992, p. 13. For a critique, see Ira Katznelson, "A Properly Defended
Liberalism: On John Gray and the Filling of Political Life," *Social Research* 61 (Fall
1994).

[58] Martha Nussbaum notes, "I have observed the frequency with which attacks on
reason (and also on Enlightenment universalism) have been used to discredit feminist
attacks on local traditions that subordinate them. These experiences have confirmed
me in my conviction that feminism needs to be able to avail itself of robust notions of
reason and objectivity." In "Feminism and Philosophy: An Exchange," *New York Review
of Books*, April 6, 1995, p. 48.

Berlin's quest for a liberal pluralism centers on the distinction between pluralism and relativism. Pluralism, he writes, "denies that there is one, and only one, true morality or aesthetics or theology, and allows equally objective alternative values or systems of value," while relativism is "a doctrine according to which the judgement of a man or a group, since it is the expression of a statement of a taste, or emotional attitude or outlook, is simply what it is, with no objective correlates which determines its truth or falsehood." The first, he insists, does not entail the second. Hence it is possible to see the world through the eyes of other cultures and thus escape "the ideological prisons of class or nation or doctrine" while remaining free to denounce brutal and unjust practices in other cultures. "I repeat, pluralism—the incommensurability and, at times, incompatibility of objective ends—is *not* relativism; nor, *a fortiori*, subjectivism, nor the allegedly unbridgeable differences of emotional attitude on which some modern positivist, emotivists, existentialists, nationalists and, indeed, relativistic sociologists and anthropologists found their accounts."[59]

Your work and Berlin's stake out the attractive offer of a nonrelativist pluralism that I, too, embrace. Yet the marriage of liberalism and pluralism, like that of liberalism and socialism, as already noted, is difficult. The range of moral dissonance and group diversity liberalism regards is unclear. The achievement of a genuine neutrality among values and ways of life based on a sharp distinction between the public and private spheres cannot be fully realized. Liberalism's universalism and individualism make it hard to find a place inside the doctrine for the recognition of groups, including cultural and national groups, as legitimate rights-bearing units of citizenship. Liberalism finds it very difficult to transact with people whose self-understandings and moral commitments reject liberal principles. In a world full of views and practices liberals disdain, it is no simple matter for liberalism to discover nonparochial criteria for

---

[59] Berlin, "Alleged Relativism," pp. 87, 80, 87.

making judgments in the precarious space between relativism and cultural imperialism.[60]

Most liberals who wish to advance this project usually turn to John Stuart Mill, especially to his vigorous defense of a diversity of ethics and ideas in *On Liberty*. In *The Church and the Left* you characteristically deployed Mill more than any other Western theorist to define your own liberal and pluralist commitments. "To give any fair play to the nature of each," you cite, "it is essential that different persons should be allowed to live different lives."[61] Likewise, Kymlicka strongly defends liberalism's current capacities as a normative political philosophy by claiming his arguments connect "with the political morality of modern liberals from J. S. Mill," rather than with "seventeenth-century liberalism."[62] This, I hope to show, gets things backward.

IV

In spite of his support for slavery and England's imperial program,[63] Locke, not Mill, sets liberalism on the course you and Kymlicka value. Locke, himself a dissenter who fled England, made an unprecedented case for toleration at a time of enormous religious strife. Critics have adduced more than a few reasons for setting his arguments aside. Locke appears not to value diversity as such, either as a good in itself or as a path to individual self-development. Rather, he argues that intolerance is irrational and ineffective.[64] His writing possesses a peculiarly

[60] I recognize that by referring to liberalism in the singular, I run just the risks of essentialism and decontextualization I caution against in my discussion below. Though there is no single liberalism, there is a liberal tradition with central tendencies that interact with local, particular circumstances.

[61] Michnik cites and discusses Mill in *The Church and the Left*, pp. 143–44.

[62] Kymlicka, *Liberalism, Community and Culture*, p. 10.

[63] For discussions, see James Farr, "So Vile and Miserable an Estate: The Problem of Slavery in Locke's Political Thought," *Political Theory* 14 (1986); and Wayne Glausser, "Three Approaches to Locke and the Slave Trade," *Journal of the History of Ideas* 51 (July–September 1990).

[64] For this line of argument, see Sheldon Wolin, *The Presence of the Past: Essays on the*

Christian character (he announces his subject at the start as "the mutual Toleration of Christians")[65] and applies religious toleration solely to a limited set of people (not to atheists or those whose religious beliefs challenge the legitimate rule of the state, nor to Jews, who can be repressed or repatriated on economic or political grounds, nor, it appears, even to Catholics, who are suspect because of their allegiance to a foreign power). These restrictions, detractors insist, are symptomatic of how exclusions are embedded in liberalism's theoretical core.[66] Locke's work also is considered so tightly bound to the historical context of the Reformation and so imbricated with nonconformist theology that it has little to say to us today in more secular times.[67] Religious toleration itself, moreover, is said to provide a poor model for securing other kinds of difference (in which Locke, in any event, was not interested).[68]

Although John Stuart Mill also combined a universalistic doctrine with exclusionary practices, he is thought to cast his arguments in secular terms far more congenial to the late twentieth century. Unlike Locke, Mill placed diversity at the center of his argument for toleration as an instrument in the search for truth and as an essential feature of the growth and experience of individuals.[69] Like Burckhardt and Tocqueville, he prized a

---

State and the Constitution (Baltimore: Johns Hopkins University Press, 1993); and Jeremy Waldron, "Locke: Toleration and the Rationality of Persecution," in Mendus, ed., *Justifying Toleration*.

[65] Locke, *A Letter Concerning Toleration*, p. 23.

[66] See Uday Mehta, "Liberal Strategies of Exclusion," *Politics and Society* 18 (December 1990).

[67] John Dunn, "What Is Living and What Is Dead in the Philosophy of John Locke," ms., cited in Mendus, *Toleration and the Limits of Liberalism*, p. 24; Alan Ryan, *Locke* (Oxford: Oxford University Press, 1984), p. 59.

[68] McClure, "Difference, Diversity and the Limits of Toleration."

[69] For discussions, see Wendy Donner, *The Liberal Self: John Stuart Mill's Moral and Political Philosophy* (Ithaca: Cornell University Press, 1991); John Gray, *Mill on Liberty: A Defence* (London: Routledge and Kegan Paul, 1983); Alan Ryan, *The Philosophy of John Stuart Mill* (London: Macmillan, 1988); C. L. Ten, *Mill on Liberty* (Oxford: Clarendon Press, 1980); and Dennis F. Thompson, *John Stuart Mill and Representative Government* (Princeton: Princeton University Press, 1976).

diversity of individual views and values as part of dynamic theories of personality and history.[70]

This conventional rank-ordering of Locke and Mill constitutes a serious error. Mill's discussion of toleration—mixing claims on behalf of individual self-development, recipes for truth-discovery within a given culture, and bigoted denunciations of non-European peoples—is more racist and firmly fixed in conventional imperialist assumptions than Locke's. Mill's work also is more individualist, more ethnocentric, and more disingenuous in that it appeals to universal values without practicing or extending them.

Mill restricts pluralism in *On Liberty* to opinion within a given relatively homogeneous culture by qualified individuals. Appalled by the dismaying tendencies to conformity caused, he thought, by the extension of democracy, Mill mounted a defense "of genius, and the necessity of allowing it to unfold itself freely both in thought and in practice" under the adverse affairs of an England "now all collective" where "individuals are lost in the crowd." To be sure, Mill writes not only that there should be "different opinions," but "different experiments of living"; nonetheless, he immediately underscores the imperatives of individual choice: "The worth of different modes of life should be proved practically, when any one thinks fit to try them. It is desirable, in short, that in things which do not primarily concern others, individuality should assert itself." As far as I can tell, there is only one place in *On Liberty* where Mill comes close to an appreciation of what might be called a genuine multiculturalism rather than an appreciation of options within a single culture. In his famous debunking of China (where "the despotism of Custom is complete"), he asks, "What is it that has hitherto preserved Europe from this lot?" and he returns the answer, "their remarkable diversity of character and culture . . .

---

[70] For a comparative discussion of their views of diversity, see Alan S. Kahan, *Aristocratic Liberalism* (New York: Oxford University Press, 1992), pp. 104–106.

[and] plurality of paths." Here he stresses not only that "individuals, classes, nations, have been extremely unlike one another," but that "each has in time endured to receive the good which the others have offered."

Though this discussion strains in the direction of an appreciation of cultural pluralism and hints at its possibilities within a determinate liberal framework, it is intended only as an adjunct to Mill's assertion "of individuality as one of the elements of well-being," which, after all, is the title of the section in which this discussion can be found. Moreover, within the same paragraph, Mill directly indicates that his central concern is with the diminution of diversity within English culture. "Different ranks, different neighbourhoods, different trades and professions lived in what might be called different worlds" have become, "at present, to a great degree . . . the same," forming "so great a mass of influences hostile to Individuality."[71]

In order to legitimate his theoretical claim on behalf of the protection of minority cultures, Kymlicka shows that Mill's individualism is not simply presocial or abstract but that he values individual liberty as providing means for the development of human character and for the intersubjective discovery of truth. Unlike Bentham, who cared about "the freedom to pursue existing ends, which were taken as pre-theoretically given,"

for Mill the conditions under which people acquired their ends were important: it mattered whether their education and cultural socialization opened up or closed off the pos-

---

[71] Mill, *On Liberty*, pp. 72, 81–89. European diversity looks rather different from the outside. The St. Kitts novelist Caryl Phillips observed of his Oxford experience, "A large part of finding out who I was, and what I was doing here, would inevitably mean having to understand the Europeans. I could not believe that the British really were any different from the French, or the Spanish from the Swedish. All these different nationalities were to be found in college, plus many others. They all seemed to share a common and mutually inclusive, but culturally exclusive culture. Reorienting myself in Britain seemed spurious; the problem was a European one, as exemplified by the shared, twisted, intertwined histories of the European countries." Caryl Phillips, *The European Tribe* (New York: Farrar, Straus & Giroux, 1987), p. 9.

sibility of revising their ends. He believed this was important because people not only want to act on their choices,
they also want to get those choices right.[72]

Kymlicka persuasively insists that *On Liberty* demonstrates that
the common communitarian, socialist, and feminist view that
liberalism is excessively atomistic understates liberalism's capacities to treat individuals as situated and embedded in social
roles, networks, and relationships. But his reading also is mis-
leading. It implies that Mill sought to deploy his embedded individualism in the service of a thoroughgoing cultural pluralism. For this, there simply is no textual evidence, only wishful
thinking.

Mill placed the majority of humankind outside liberty's
sphere. Immediately upon announcing his harm principle,[73]
the centerpiece of *On Liberty*, Mill added, "It is, perhaps, hardly
necessary to say that this doctrine is meant to apply only to
human beings in the maturity of their faculties"; hence "we may
leave out of consideration those backward states of society in
which the race itself may be considered in its nonage." Whereas
"in all nations with whom we need here concern ourselves"
compulsion is to be resisted, "despotism is a legitimate mode of
government in dealing with barbarians, provided the end be
their improvement, and the means justified by actually effect-
ing that end."[74]

On Liberty's defense of colonialism and identification of the
task of European colonizers as that of elevating backward people and societies managed the double feat of simultaneously
making liberalism universally applicable yet distinctively European. By pursuing this course, Bhikhu Parekh has observed,
Mill made liberalism "missionary, ethnocentric and narrow, dis-

---

[72] Kymlicka, *Liberalism, Community, and Culture*, p. 19.

[73] "The sole end for which humankind are warranted, individually or collectively, in
interfering with the liberty of action of any of their number, is self-protection." John
Stuart Mill, *On Liberty*, ed. John Gray and G. W. Smith (London and New York: Routledge, 1991), p. 30.

[74] Ibid., p. 31.

missing non-liberal ways of life and thought as primitive and in need of the liberal civilizing mission." His obsessive antitraditionalism, rather than celebrating difference, achieved the opposite by underscoring the values of "autonomy, choice, individuality, liberty, rationality, and progress" as if their meaning and content can take only one acceptable form because they are either beyond history or are the preserve of only one civilization. Millian liberalism thus became "the other of its other and gave itself an impoverished identity."[75]

Locke's writings, to be sure, also are characterized by a contradiction between an expansive philosophical anthropology in which all are born free and equal and the application of a classificatory scheme based on the possession, or nonpossession, of reason as the basis for political inclusion. In developing such a view of the world, Locke drew on existing conventions, distinguishing between well-bred gentlemen and servants as well as between aboriginal peoples and Western Christians. These distinctions, Uday Mehta incisively discerns,

> refer to a constellation of social practices riddled with a hierarchical and exclusionary density. They draw on and encourage conceptions of human beings that are far from abstract and universal and in which the anthropological minimum is buried under a thick set of social inscriptions and signals. They chart a terrain full of social credentials . . . the natural individual equipped with universal capacities must negotiate before these capacities assume the form necessary for political inclusion.[76]

These bases of exclusion do "circumscribe and order the particular form that the universalistic foundations of Lockian liberalism assume," and, as Mehta vigorously argues in his discussion of British colonialism in India, they promote a form that "historically has left an exclusionary imprint in the concrete

---

[75] Bhikhu Parekh, "Superior People: The Narrowness of Liberalism from Mills to Rawls," *Times Literary Supplement*, February 25, 1994, pp. 11, 12.
[76] Mehta, "Liberal Strategies of Exclusion," p. 438.

instantiation of liberal practices."[77] But note that Locke's grounds for exclusion are conventional and historically situated. Under particular norm-governed circumstances they can, and do, exclude; but these disbarments are not inherent or necessary to the doctrine itself. "It was only towards the end of the 'age of Enlightenment' that a scientific racism came to secure the distinctions between different groups of human beings," Peter Hulme observes. "For Locke, as for Descartes before him—the monogenetic tradition of Christian thought guaranteed the essential unity of the human species, even unto the uttermost part of the earth."[78] Mill's particularism is far more insidious:

> Where Locke speaks of the identity of our faculties and the commonality of our birth, Mill speaks of the differences of people's cultures, social development, and races. Locke responds to the charge that his state of nature is a historical fiction by referring to "the inconveniences of that condition and the love, and want of Society no sooner brought any number of them [men] together, but they presently united and incorporated, if they designed to continue together," and that therefore the historical absence of such a state is to be understood by reference to the immediacy of its provenance. Civil government is, as he says, "everywhere antecedent to records." In contrast, Mill makes representative government contingent on a precisely articulated and specific developmental trajectory. Far from being antecedent to records, it requires records of dense and exacting specifications.[79]

From the perspective of pluralism, Mill's liberalism is deficient in two additional respects. Not only was he virtually silent

---

[77] Ibid., pp. 438–39.

[78] Hulme, "The Spontaneous Hand," p. 33. He did note that Locke's distinction between those in possession of reason and those without "still contained within it a powerful set of consequences: the penalty for the failure to see reason could be severe."

[79] Mehta, "Liberal Strategies of Exclusion," p. 446.

about religion, but as a strong antiliberal partisan of tradition, Mill was dogmatically secularist, hence less tolerant than is ordinarily allowed. By dividing the world between the rational and the prejudiced, with religion cast outside reason, Mill provided a strong, partisan moral theory. "*On Liberty*," Maurice Cowling has written, "contrary to common opinion was not so much a plea for individual freedom, as a means of ensuring that Christianity would be superseded by the form of liberal, rationalistic, utilitarianism which went by the name of Religion of Humanity. . . . Mill's object was not to free men, but to convert them to a peculiarly exclusive, peculiarly insinuating moral doctrine."[80] Further, the reasons Mill adduces in favor of toleration concern the indispensability of diversity to the discovery of truth, implying a teleological process that will reveal "truth" as a singular correct object. Diversity thus provides situational means to a sole ultimate homogeneous end.

On Liberty does provide a fierce defense of individual freedom of opinion and expression as required for individual growth and the reasoned pursuit of truth. No wonder you are drawn to it. But Mill's text simply is no good as the footing for a liberalism comfortable with human plurality. Locke, by contrast, whose work appears narrowly circumscribed to religion, indifferent to the range of diversity, and less concerned with the right to be different or with official neutrality than with prudential reasons for toleration, nonetheless provides a vastly superior approach.

If Mill wrote with a secure aristocratic remove, Locke's *Letter* was penned with an acute sense of urgency during a period of legal terror against religious dissenters. In 1683, the year Locke fled to the United Provinces (only to return in 1688), Algernon Sidney and Lord Russell were executed after the Rye House plot to seize the king failed; and in 1685, when Locke wrote the text, over one hundred dissenters were executed in reprisal

---

[80] Maurice Cowling, *Mill and Liberalism* (Cambridge: Cambridge University Press, 1963), p. xiii.

following the Monmouth Rebellion.[81] The same year, France's Edict of Nantes granting a large measure of religious freedom to Protestants was revoked. Locke wrote not only to affirm religious pluralism but to search for a formula for social peace.

His text is permeated by the smell of fear. Calling intolerance a leading source of war, Locke argued that the existence of state churches cultivates strife but that an equally treated plurality of religious sects could undergird public peace by enhancing and diffusing the stake members of civil society have in social and political arrangements. Institutional monism equals war; institutional pluralism conduces peace.

For Locke, intolerance in the specific case of religion hence is not so much wrong as irrational because it promotes violence. The Clarendon Codes, the series of four laws passed between 1661 and 1665 to strengthen the position of the Church of England and suppress dissent after the restoration of Charles II, Locke observed, had ushered in a period of covert religious practice, the flouting of the law, widespread imprisonment, and instances of martyrdom. "The Code," James Tully notes, "created a permanent underclass, oppressed and denied access to public life and to publication, who struggled for toleration."[82] Locke enlisted in this cause because he saw that a policy of uniformity caused, rather than responded to, civil unrest.

Locke did not bet on the elaboration of a doctrine of rights or on a strict level of state neutrality, both of which were beyond practical grasp at a time of fundamental religious disagreement, but on a set of claims about the obligation of rulers not to be intolerant for circumspection's sake. Rulers have to respect the zone of belief because it exceeds their legiti-

[81] James Scott, Duke of Monmouth, landed in Dorset and was proclaimed king, but forces loyal to the Catholic James II routed his insurgent force. Monmouth was beheaded. For a discussion, see Christopher Hill, *The Century of Revolution, 1603–1714* (New York: Norton, 1961), p. 197.

[82] James Tully, "Locke," in J. H. Burns, ed., *The Cambridge History of Political Thought, 1450–1700* (Cambridge: Cambridge University Press, 1991), p. 646. The Clarendon Codes provide a pivot for Richard Tuck's comparison, "Hobbes and Locke on Toleration," in Mary G. Dietz, ed., *Thomas Hobbes and Political Theory* (Lawrence: University of Kansas Press, 1990).

mate brief, fosters conflict, and, at best, produces inauthentic compliance.

It is fashionable not only for liberalism's critics but for its own theorists to downplay the relevance and incisiveness of Locke's *Letter*. Thus, to note a leading example, Jeremy Waldron faults Locke's emphasis on procedures and process rather than on systematic principles. Locke's doctrinal reticence, he believes, fails to credit the possibilities that belief can be coerced or that coerced belief can be sincere. Without better doctrine, Waldron claims, Locke makes liberal claims to religious freedom vulnerable to effective statist impositions.[83] But how, Locke might have responded, can better doctrine on its own rejoin to power? The great strengths of *A Letter Concerning Toleration* rest on Locke's decision not to ground his pluralism in abstract deductive reasoning but to rely on a strikingly modern deployment of political, sociological, and psychological understandings.

Three building blocks are especially important for Locke's discussion of toleration: the differentiation of human life into "separate and distinct" spheres;[84] his delineation of an institutional arena located in the overlapping zone between the state and civil society akin to Jurgen Habermas's notion of the public sphere;[85] and a view of human personality as syncretic and multiple.

As a realist, Locke developed his political thought on the basis of mapping the pattern of differentiation between the state and civil society increasingly characteristic of the postfeudal world. He treated this institutional distinction as providing the basis for a "social sphere which was self-enforcing rather

---

[83] Waldron, "Locke: Toleration."

[84] Locke, *A Letter Concerning Toleration*, p. 33. For discussions, see Robert P. Kraynak, "John Locke: From Absolutism to Toleration," *American Political Science Review* 74 (March 1980); and Selina S. Chen, "John Locke's Political Arguments for Toleration: A Toleration for Our Times?" Paper presented at the Annual Meeting of the American Political Science Association, August 31–September 3, 1995.

[85] Jurgen Habermas, *The Structural Transformation of the Public Sphere* (Cambridge: MIT Press, 1989); for a discussion, see Jean L. Cohen and Andrew Arato, *Civil Society and Political Theory* (Cambridge: MIT Press, 1992), chap. 5.

than dependent upon external, sovereign coercion,"[86] and he built his case for religious toleration on the existence and significance of this dualism: "I esteem it above all things necessary to distinguish exactly the Business of Civil Government from that of Religion, and to settle the just Bounds that lie between the one and the other," cautioning, "If this not be done, there can be no end put to the Controversies that will be always arising, between those that have, or at least pretend to have, on the one side, a Concernment for the Interests of Mens Souls, and on the other side, a Care of the Commonwealth."[87]

But for Locke, these were not hermetically sealed arenas. The boundaries dividing them, especially in periods of uncertainty and conflict, he thought, are permeable and negotiable. During the seventeenth century, it was impossible to place life's activities neatly in the zone either of the public or of the private. As Ingrid Creppell acutely argues, Locke identified an overlapping arena she calls a public privacy. God, Locke insisted, though a matter of private belief, had to be worshipped in a public way before a community of witnesses. Unlike the public in the unified Christendom of the medieval world, religion now was marked by the heterogeneity of belief. Locke thus combined the public expression of private faith in a public sphere characterized by an unprecedented plurality. Hence his notion of toleration protected more than private values. As Creppell asserts, Locke's position

> pointed crucially to a "space" in which presentation of one's religious identity in public was protected from interference or coercion by others and by the state. . . . This juridical space of protection (a cold, formal state of affairs) was much more than that because it involved expression/display, on the one hand, and recognition/awareness on the other (a "hot" substantive state of affairs). This created

---

[86] Ingrid Creppell, "Locke on Toleration: The Transformation of Constraint," paper presented at the annual meeting of the American Political Science Association, September 1–4, 1994, p. 14.

[87] Locke, *A Letter Concerning Toleration*, p. 26.

a type of community that was neither purely formal nor purely confessional. It was indeed a community insofar as it involved expression and recognition, but the heterogeneity at its core also left a distance between members, requiring a guarantee from the state of protection of its members. This space or community I have called a public privacy: it emerged as a buffer zone between the purely private (intimate family) and the purely public (law and coercion). In it, persons acknowledged a type of involvement without demanding total exclusivity and intimacy.[88]

If Mill treated diversity as a condition of self-development, Locke supported his overlapping dualisms of church and state and private and public with an even more thoroughgoing psychological pluralism. He viewed human nature as variable and multiple and understood human identity to be constructed from a congery of various differences. As Creppell observes, by "focusing on the divergent modes of a person's existence, Locke underscored that within one person multiple points of view and multiple experiences were possible." His portrait of the multiple self treats toleration as essential to a person's internal plurality and development "by providing the person with alternative points of view or focuses of identification. Distinctions of this nature may lead persons to see themselves as having multiple allegiances and a number of sources of meaning and motivation in their lives."[89]

In a sharp critique both of Locke and of the treatment of group and ethical plurality by liberalism more generally, Kirstie McClure has argued that religious toleration provides an insufficient basis for a more broad-gauged appreciation of difference. She mounts three arguments. First, she rightly understands (as both you and Cardinal Wyszynski have, from opposite sides of the question) that Locke's toleration entails a reduction in the dimensions of religious belief from a unified organizing principle to private opinion. Locke's *Letter*, of

---

[88] Creppell, "Locke on Toleration," p. 18.   [89] Ibid., p. 19.

course, was thoroughly Protestant in arguing that Christian doctrine supports the proposition that individuals must be free to discover their own path to salvation. The result of these moves, McClure claims, is a reduction both to the scope of religion and in moral and cultural dissonance. Second, she also correctly sees that this form of toleration, from the outset, was designed to go hand in hand with the validation of a standard of harm that leaves it to the state to adjudicate degrees of permissible difference. "The boundary of toleration," McClure writes, is "civilly defined by the criterion of harm; that is, by the empirical determination of whether particular acts and practices are demonstrably injurious to the safety and security of the state or to the civil interests of its citizens." Third, she believes that Locke's stark split between public and private might work for religious belief but not for other forms of difference like those of gender and race which necessarily possess a public component.[90]

If McClure's first two objections are accurate, they are virtues for Locke, and for liberalism more generally, especially under democratic conditions. What is attractive about Locke's bounded religious pluralism is an epistemological uncertainty entirely uncharacteristic of Mill. For Locke, the right to worship as we wish and to be free from state compulsion in this area is mandated by our inability to know the single right truth. Would McClure wish to counsel otherwise? Moreover, can we do without a state-centered sanction of harm?

Her third complaint, her most basic, is wrong precisely to the extent that Creppell's reading of the consecutory mutual constitution of public and private in Locke is correct, as I think it is. The separation of spheres does not require the absence either of robust relations or of transactions. Race, gender, sexual preference, and other bases for human heterogeneity do not appear either in the public or private domains exclusively but in both and in their overlapping intersection. Contra McClure,

---

[90] McClure, "Difference, Diversity, and the Limits of Toleration," pp. 380–81.

they do not differ from religion; hence Lockean toleration is not a highly localized subject. Rather, its very particularity establishes a broad and effective way of thinking about difference within a liberal frame without requiring, centuries later, an encumbrance with the imperial assumptions Locke thought part of the natural order of things.

V

In an important departure for a tradition that has had precious little to say about moral and group pluralism since *On Liberty*, a growing number of Anglo-American liberal theorists has been turning, especially since 1989, to the problem of difference. Just as the social liberals of the turn of the century took seriously the egalitarian assessment of liberalism, this group of thinkers has sought to address traditionalist, communitarian, and feminist critiques and the manifest global resurgence of nationalism and ethnic chauvinism shading into xenophobia by turning to issues posed by human dissimilarity. They recognize that with the exception of a very small number of countries (such as Iceland and the two Koreas), the world no longer consists of hermetically sealed cultural units.[91] In this approach, liberalism keeps its universalist Enlightenment commitments but becomes more suited to "the historical and social circumstances of a democratic society"[92] by devising a secure place for the recognition of difference inside liberalism's doctrinal edifice without privileging any specific dominant way of life. As we have seen in the cases of Locke and Mill, most of the great thinkers in the liberal tradition have done quite the opposite; Locke's defense of toleration depends on a Protestant view of salvation, and Mill's defense of diversity is based on a Periclean

[91] Kymlicka begins his most recent book by noting, "Most countries today are culturally diverse. According to recent estimates, the world's 184 independent states contain over 600 living language groups, and 5,000 ethnic groups. In very few countries can citizens be said to share the same language or belong to the same ethnonational group." Kymlicka, *Multicultural Citizenship*, p. 1.

[92] Rawls, *Political Liberalism*, p. 154.

"conception of human excellence." What might be called the new liberal pluralism, one sympathetic interpreter has written, tries instead "to free the defense of diverse experiments of living from the outlook of one such experiment."[93]

This body of work, most notably in lectures by Rawls and in ambitious efforts by Kymlicka,[94] paradoxically extends the liberal tradition's core notion of toleration beyond religion and opinion by contracting liberalism's sphere of justice and morality. This orientation seeks a firm basis for political liberalism as a minimal moral conception specifying the rights and duties of citizens in abstraction from any specific cultural or moral set of commitments, whether theological, national, or communal; or, indeed, liberal, as in the case of the kind of thoroughgoing individualism that has put liberalism at odds with various forms of tradition and community. In a discussion quite close to yours in *The Church and the Left*, Charles Larmore argues that a commitment to core liberal political values such as equal respect for all members of the polity need not imply that these values

> must pervade the whole of social life. Private associations cannot violate the rights of citizens. Yet they can continue to organize their internal, extrapolitical affairs according to "illiberal" principles—principles which deny their members equal rights and require them to defer to traditionally constituted authority. The Catholic Church, for example, is a legal institution in our society, but it does not handle its ecclesiastical affairs on the basis of toleration. It may not burn heretics, for that is contrary to their rights as citizens, but it may still excommunicate them.[95]

[93] Joshua Cohen, "A More Democratic Liberalism," *Michigan Law Review*, 92 (May 1994): 1543–44.

[94] Rawls, *Political Liberalism*; Kymlicka, *Liberalism, Community and Culture*; Kymlicka, *Multicultural Citizenship*.

[95] Charles Larmore, "Political Liberalism," *Political Theory* 18 (August 1990): 350. Locke, it might be recalled, did believe it permissible for the Church, like any private association, to expel members, but he insisted that care be taken not to injure the person's body or estate affecting that person's standing in other realms.

In his new work, Rawls identifies "the problem of political liberalism" in terms of the kind of question Locke asked in his *Letter on Toleration*: "How is it possible," Rawls has written,

> that there may exist over time a stable and just society of free and equal citizens profoundly divided by reasonable religious, philosophical, and moral doctrines? This is a problem of political justice, not a problem about the highest good. . . . What are the fair terms of social cooperation between citizens characterized as free and equal yet divided by profound doctrinal conflict? What is the structure and content of the requisite political conception, if, indeed, such a conception is even possible? . . . What is new about this clash is that it introduces into people's conceptions of their good a transcendent element not admitting of compromise. This element forces either mortal conflict moderated only by circumstance and exhaustion, or equal liberty of conscience and freedom of thought. Except on the basis of these last, firmly founded and publicly recognized, no reasonable political conception of justice is possible. *Political liberalism starts by taking to heart the absolute depth of that irreconcilable latent conflict.*[96]

No longer, as in his *Theory of Justice,* are ethical principles seen to reflect a shared morality or the reduction of people to individualist abstractions with broadly common motivations. Instead, Rawls's focus now is on the conditions required for a decent public life in recognition of human complexity, variety, and possibility. No longer is there a gathering of undifferentiated, abstract persons in search of common ground behind a veil of ignorance. No longer are principles of justice advanced as matters of morality shared by all, but as codes that make a public political life possible based on an "overlapping consensus" drawn from vastly different commitments and identities that are not compatible. This is an approach grounded not in

---

[96] Rawls, *Political Liberalism*, pp. xxv–xxvi; emphasis added.

the flattening of difference but in the mutual accommodation of difference within a common public frame. A person's features, which Rawls once thought irrelevant to the formation of conceptions of the good—such as ethnicity, gender, race, and moral outlook—now are made central to the genesis and content of political argument. Liberalism still requires consensus, but it is far more limited, now located in a zone where different moral and cultural views can overlap to support political rules that permit the reproduction of these values and ways of life. In this way, "Rawls wishes to free the democratic ideal of a shared arena of public deliberation among equal citizens from dependence on the particular ethical outlook of any subset of the public."[97]

By this route, Rawls has turned to the key issues about liberal politics and diversity you posed in *The Church and the Left*, raising for discussion some of the same difficulties addressed in your text. If the plurality of ethical views and groups is to define a public sphere where an overlapping consensus obtains, which views are to be admitted and how are entry rules to be defined? Must people modify their deeply held identities and preferences to qualify? Can views be reasonable in the now much disputed private sphere but not reasonable when inserted in the public? After all, your fellow activist and friend Father Tischner criticized your distinction between a dangerous and a good Church based on his fear that your liberalism entails so much of a reduction to the character of Catholic belief and practice that it amounts to an assault on Church prerogatives.[98]

If John Gray's fiery dismissal vastly overstates the "almost fathomless shallowness"[99] of Rawls's attempt to find a modus vivendi for different moral views and cultural practices within a liberal framework, the contrast between Rawls's and Locke's

---

[97] Joshua Cohen, "A More Democratic Liberalism," p. 1544.

[98] Jozef Tischner, *Marxism and Christianity: The Quarrel and the Dialogue in Poland* (Washington, D.C.: Georgetown University Press, 1987). For an elaboration of their points of agreement and disagreement, see Adam Michnik, Jozef Tischner, and Jacek Zakowski, *Miedzy: Panem a Plebanem* (Krakow: Znak, 1995).

[99] Gray, "Against the New Liberalism," p. 13.

portrayals of dissonance and conflict nonetheless is striking. Rawls specifies a broadly consensual public arena without much clamor. He does identify a civil society of diverse groups and commitments but one separating ways of life by distinctive social groupings who appear to interact and conflict rather little. Unlike Locke's multiple individuals who oscillate between values, positions, identities, and possibilities, Rawls's actors are fixed in given social and cultural locations. Moreover, his assumption about hermetically sealed zones of politics and private morality, very much like that of Locke, seems far more like a hopeless fantasy than your grounded portrait of Poland which was criticized in just such terms by Antoni Slonimski. Rawls's actors continue to be decidedly and exclusively rationalist. Though he is concerned about human propensities for nonrational solidarities and destructiveness (these, I should hasten to add, are not reducible one to the other), fear never makes an appearance. But what is to happen when fraternity turns into chauvinism or when solidarity begets a Hobbesian war? Rawls still would like to keep moral and group conflict outside the public realm and admit it only when capable of contributing to an overlapping consensus. Would that social reality were so tidy![100]

Rawls, of course, is not alone among liberal theorists in trying to construct a liberal pluralism. Kymlicka, for example, has sought to do more than show how it is possible for people with different cultures and codes to share a polity. He has been concerned to demonstrate, first, that liberalism is as capable as communitarianism in valuing the social nature of human life, and, second, that liberal principles oblige the protection of minority cultures from encroachment by the dominant culture. Since most of the world's countries are to some significant degree genuinely multicultural, liberalism's cherished values of toleration, choice, and equal respect can have meaning only to

---

[100] Rawls's text also oscillates, but only partially recognizes the fluctuation, between abstract and concrete discussions of difference. For a critique along these lines, see Perry Anderson, "On John Rawls," *Dissent* 41 (Winter 1994).

the extent minority cultures are granted conditions within
which they can thrive or at least not disappear or be assimilated
unwillingly. Accordingly, he has sought to incorporate within
liberal political and moral theory a textured account of the relationship between individual persons and the cultures and communities with which they are engaged and encumbered. Drawing on an autonomy-based view of liberalism, Kymlicka deploys
a combination of arguments based on equality, the rectification
of historical wrongs, and the intrinsic value of cultural diversity
to show how some sorts of collective rights are compatible with
liberal principles. Likewise, both Joseph Raz and Yael Tamir
extrapolate cultural pluralism from liberalism's historically
constitutive commitments, finding no grounds for distinguishing between the right of individuals to equal regard and respect
for their cultural self-determination, including their shared histories, traditions, discourses, and activities.[101]

Read together, these various efforts admirably seek to transcend the dominant slack universalism of the liberal tradition
while staying inside the most valuable of its Enlightenment
values to seek bulwarks against the disasters a collapse of the
Enlightenment project would portend. In this, they seek to escape what they correctly see as the ethnocentric traps of communitarian and republican emphases on solidarity and on collective self-governance in pursuit of the common good by all
citizens, an alternative that places a high value on the seemingly
attractive claims of strong citizenship, public as well as private
mutuality, and shared traditions. Alas, ever since Athens, this
approach has exhibited tendencies even more powerful than
those found inside the liberal tradition toward exclusion and
the repression of difference.[102] In the American setting, Rogers
Smith cautions, "any honest assessment of [republicanism] as

---

[101] Joseph Raz, "National Self-Determination," *The Journal of Philosophy* 87 (September 1990); Raz, "Multiculturalism: A Liberal Perspective," *Dissent* 41 (Winter 1994);
and Yael Tamir, *Liberal Nationalism* (Princeton: Princeton University Press, 1993).

[102] For an appreciation of the potential tyranny of society by a communitarian critic
of liberalism, see Charles Taylor, "Modes of Civil Society," *Public Culture* 3 (Fall 1990).

an actual American communal tradition must recognize that
in legal and political debate it has usually and quite naturally
served to assist the repressive side of American ethnocen-
trism."[103] As an alternative to liberalism, communitarianism
tends to be vague, romantic, anachronistic.[104] "The communitarian critics want us to live in Salem," Amy Gutmann com-
ments, "but not to believe in witches."[105]

Yet in spite of their considerable attractiveness, the recent
efforts to identify a liberal pluralism by Rawls and fellow liberal
theorists are marked by more than a few serious problems. By
and large, they lack an institutional component. The rationality
of their public sphere is far too pat. Their portrayal of difference tends to be rather too orderly and sanitized, downplaying
the remarkable interlacings and amalgamations of human life,
the rich varieties of cultural traditions, positions, and relationships, and ever-present possibilities for ugliness and unspeak-
able brutality exercised in the name of difference. They further
understate liberalism's repressive legacies in grappling with cultural collisions and its exclusions of interstitial and marginal
peoples in practice and in doctrine; they underestimate that
the lure and power of identity come from the contested layer-
ing of numerous differences and local commitments that mix
the reasoned, the nonrational, and the irrational in uncertain
measure; and they fail to see that rationality itself is not a fixed
universal attribute even when limited to the public life of citizens and the state.

Also see the seminal work on the relationship between the invention of "freedom" and
slavery by Orlando Patterson, *Freedom, vol. I: Freedom in the Making of Western Culture* (New
York: Basic Books, 1991).

[103] Rogers M. Smith, "The 'American Creed' and American Identity: The Limits of
Liberal Citizenship in the United States," *Western Political Quarterly* 41, 2 (1988).

[104] For arguments along these lines, see H. N. Hirsch, "The Thernody of Liberalism:
Constitutional Liberty and the Renewal of Community," *Political Theory* 14 (August
1986); and Simon Caney, "Liberalism and Communitarianism: A Misconceived Debate," *Political Theory* 40 (June 1992).

[105] Amy Gutmann, "Communitarian Critics of Liberalism," *Philosophy and Public Affairs* 14 (Summer 1985): 319.

But, above all, these attempts to expand the notion of justice as fairness to cultural groups are unpersuasive in their insistence that liberalism's principle of neutrality be extended to preclude multicultural conflicts from entering the public arena. When this sanitized requirement is applied to actual circumstances—say, to communal conflicts in India, Romania, or Bulgaria, to disputes about immigration and the character of universities in the United States, or to the killing fields of former Yugoslavia—it proves either impossible or unnecessary. Further, the very notion of universal citizenship in circumstances of cultural conflict inevitably evidences a lack of neutrality in settings of unequal group numbers, legitimacy, capacity, and power.

In each respect, Kymlicka's work pushes the analytical liberal tradition harder and further than the others; yet in so doing, he also helps clarify the limits of mainly abstract, deductive liberal theory. He stresses the importance of institutions and discusses group self-governance and parliamentary representation for national minorities (which he defines as "distinct and potentially self-governing societies incorporated into a larger state");[106] but this institutional turn proves to cover very few cases of cultural heterogeneity. He actually values cultural difference as a means to enrich human choice but also seeks to constrain it so tightly within liberal values as to discount and subdue diversity. While insisting that "cultural membership gives rise to legitimate claims," he stipulates that individuals make and remake their identities, question their culture's practices, and possess the option to withdraw from its embrace. "Liberal values," he insists, "require both individual freedom of choice and a secure cultural context from which individuals can make their choices."[107]

This stance attractively brings his project very close to yours in *The Church and the Left*, yet in so doing it also highlights some

---

[106] Kymlicka, *Multicultural Citizenship*, p. 19.

[107] Kymlicka, *Liberalism, Community and Culture*, pp. 55, 4, 169.

of the more difficult issues concerning toleration and social recognition. Kymlicka presents cultures as constituting enclosed and discrete ways of life, insisting that cultures remain something like separable islands.[108] But in so doing he underplays the mutual constitution of cultural contact and the tendency for all cultures to change and develop in interaction with others. He further downplays the internal heterogeneity of cultures, thus inviting a conflation of the potentially separate arenas of group and moral pluralism. People may share a language, a tradition, a history, and memories without necessarily sharing a single moral code. Likewise, ethical views may bind together people of very different cultures; Polish Catholics and African-American Baptists may come to abhor abortion equally. Further, Kymlicka inadequately confronts the problem posed for liberalism when relatively enclosed cultures sanction or practice deeply illiberal activities such as preventing young girls from achieving a high level of education.

Kymlicka appears to insist that for minority cultures to be eligible to make collective claims in a liberal political order they must disavow the fundamentalist claim "that the best community is one in which all but their preferred religious, sexual, or aesthetic practices are outlawed" and they must refrain from imposing a tyranny of the majority inside their own cultures. "Any liberal argument for the legitimacy of measures for the protection of minority cultures," he concludes, "has built-in limits. Each person should be able to use and interpret her cultural experiences in her own chosen way."[109] Minority rights and the enhancement of cultural diversity, he insists, are conditional on the existence of freedom within minority groups and their acceptance of the norm of personal autonomy.[110] In effect, Kymlicka constructs a virtually unachievable situation. Most cultures or subcultures do not self-govern by liberal rules,

[108] Kymlicka, *Multicultural Citizenship*, pp. 102–103.
[109] Kymlicka, *Liberalism, Community and Culture*, pp. 171, 197, 198.
[110] Kymlicka, *Multicultural Citizenship*, pp. 152ff.

nor do they internalize liberal values highlighting the virtue of individual choice. To the contrary, they usually seek to impose religious belief and authority, particular moral codes and practices, and they implement more than a few forms of discrimination. Do these realities make them ineligible to participate in Kymlicka's liberalism? Sensitive to the charge that his requirements make liberalism itself sectarian, Kymlicka distinguishes between the insistence on and the imposition of a norm. Liberals, he argues, should deploy a theory of minority rights consistent with liberal values, but they should not seek to impose it coercively in practice except under exceptional circumstances. This formulation exposes the limits of political theory disconnected from history and sociology. Either the theory does not amount to much in the end (why worry about liberal standards if they are not enforceable?); or, alternatively, if such standards are to be consistently carried through (against Kymlicka's preferences), they threaten to become instruments of repressive imposition.

If the requirement of conformity to liberal norms proves either too strong or unenforceable, Kymlicka's other operational idea, his insistence on the right of an individual to exit from his or her group, is too weak. It leaves untouched group practices lacking in respect for human persons, presumes that the right to exit will confer a reciprocal right to enter, and fails to confront the social reality that in the majority of the globe's circumstances the decision to exit from one's cultural community virtually guarantees a deracinated and dangerous form of social death.

Notwithstanding these various problems, the work of Rawls, Kymlicka, and other liberal theorists seeking to make sense of conflicts of value and culture challenges us to fashion doctrines, policies, and institutions that can discover a balance between robust and tamed difference; that can identify a distinction between cultures about which a relativist morality is appropriate and discrete practices where more general standards must apply; that can discern distinct dimensions of difference (from diversity through incompatibility to incommensurability); and that can discriminate between the rights of cultures and the rights of individuals within cultures.[111]

VI

A revealing exchange between Tony Judt and Yael Tamir helps account for the limitations of recent liberal theory in dealing with cultural heterogeneity.[112] It also reminds us of the insufficiently exploited potential of Locke's prudential and realist *Letter* and of why Isaiah Berlin's approach to the mating of liberalism and pluralism is both closer to Locke than the work of such social contract theorists as Rawls and considerably more appealing (so much so, that theorists with very different convictions often wish to claim him as their own).

Tamir's defense of the possibility of a liberal nationalism is couched in the Rawlsian terms of *A Theory of Justice.* "The purpose of the Rawlsian thought experiment," she writes,

> is not to structure world order from the beginning, but to find the most just and desirable way to rule our world in light of a given set of shared values. The parties, then, must be aware of basic facts about this world that are relevant to their moral judgment. The role of the veil of ignorance is to conceal from the parties only those facts that are morally irrelevant and can bias their judgment as self-interested individuals. According to my theory the abstract fact that individuals are members of nations is morally relevant.[113]

The role of his, and her, kind of political theory, she continues, unlike the work of historians and social scientists, "is not to give 'plausible accounts of our world' as it is, but as it should

---

[111] Lukes, *Moral Conflict and Politics*, p. 9.

[112] The exchange appears in the letters column of the *New York Review of Books,* June 23, 1994. It was provoked by Tony Judt, "The New Old Nationalism," *New York Review of Books,* May 26, 1994.

[113] Yael Tamir, "Letter," June 23, 1994, p. 64.

be." The constitution of theory as if "from nowhere"[114] constitutes rigorous and nonparticularistic interventions in a given
social and political reality, often with subversive intent (as with
Rawls on inequality). For Judt, by contrast, *political* theory must
aim at guiding judgments and prompting acton; thus it requires particularity as well as sociologically and politically plausible stories about the world. From this perspective, he asserts,
it hardly makes any sense to treat national membership as an
abstract proposition. It is, rather, "a very particular, contingent,
partial, and variable historical condition."[115]

Most contemporary liberal theorists who address cultural
and group pluralism undertake a program like Tamir's whose
hypothetical constructions of desirable social orders gain
power and clarity from the approach's decision to lift the level
of abstraction to secure the rigor that philosophy can offer. But
these advantages are achieved at the cost of the shortcomings I,
and Judt, have identified; so much so, that this work risks dismissal as being beside the point in our disordered, disarranged
world. Yet the historical and sociological temptation promoted
as an alternative by Judt threatens to leave our attempts to
discover decent ways of living unguided by useful theory or
standards.

More promising is the type of engaged political argument
Locke produced, which oscillates between contextual-historical
and theoretical contention and is tempered by an appreciation
for complexity, contradiction, and moral ambiguity.[116] These
are the traits that also make Isaiah Berlin's semisystematic polit-

---

[114] Thomas Nagel, *The View from Nowhere* (New York: Oxford University Press, 1986).

[115] Tony Judt, "Reply," *New York Review of Books*, June 23, 1994, p. 64. For a more
systematic elaboration of this view of the value of engaged social criticism as opposed to
what he called the "path of invention," see Michael Walzer, "Three Paths in Moral
Philosophy," in Walzer, *Interpretation and Social Criticism* (Cambridge: Harvard University Press, 1987).

[116] As Richard Ashcraft points out, not only in his *Toleration* but throughout his writings on politics, "Locke believed that political theorizing was an exercise in practical
reasoning. He took political actions to be guided by beliefs grounded upon probable
evidence constrained by a few fundamental tenets of a theoligally structured morality." Richard Ashcraft, "Locke's Political Philosophy," in Vere Chappell, ed., *The Cambridge Companion to Locke* (Cambridge: Cambridge University Press, 1994), p. 226.

ical theory so inviting and important. Above all, he has aimed to place within liberalism a rich pluralism of values and forms of life whether they appear inside a given culture or between traditions. For Berlin, conceptual issues—whether concerned with liberty, pluralism, the Kantian concept of autonomy, or the implications of his attraction to a Humean skepticism—always are entwined with history, sociology, and literature. When asked, "Do you consider your work a philosophical investigation or a historical one?," Berlin replied, "How can I distinguish? . . . Philosophy comes from the collision of ideas which create problems. The ideas come from life. Life changes, so do the ideas, so do the collisions. . . . Philosophy is not like inorganic chemistry."[117]

As an immigrant from Riga, an Englishman, and a committed Jew, Berlin has pressed an orientation combining a fierce sense of duty to the central humanist values of the Enlightenment[118] with a passionate defense of particularity. He insists that a strong plural liberalism must discover historically specific ideas and patterns of negotiation in order to make it possible to live with the conflicts and ineradicable tensions inherent in this dual set of affirmations.[119] Like Locke's, Berlin's cosmopolitanism is inscribed with local commitments; and his liberalism insists on acts of institutional creativity to construct context-sensitive fields of play within which competing values can contend with provisional outcomes substituting for a war of all against all.

Between virtually every line in his prose is Berlin's ambiva-

[117] Ramin Jahanbegloo, "Philosophy and Life: An Interview," *New York Review of Books*, May 28, 1992, pp. 49–50.

[118] John Gray thinks Berlin to be an anti-Enlightenment figure, but this is plain silly. See John Gray, *Isaiah Berlin* (London: Harper Collins, 1994); and the stinging review by Steven Lukes, "Pluralism Is Not Enough," *Times Literary Supplement*, February 10, 1995. I return below to Berlin's sympathetic treatment of anti-Enlightenment thinkers, the basis of Gray's peculiar and implausible reading.

[119] See Edna and Avishai Margalit, eds., *Isaiah Berlin: A Celebration* (London: Hogarth, 1991); Claude J. Galipeau, *Isaiah Berlin's Liberalism* (Oxford: Clarendon Press, 1994); and Roger Hausheer, "Berlin and the Emergence of Liberal Pluralism," in *European Liberty: Four Essays on the Occasion of the* 25th *Anniversary of the Erasmus Prize Foundation* (The Hague: M. Nijhoff Publishers, 1983).

lent appreciation of the history of the engagement of Jews with the Enlightenment and the liberal tradition.[120] If the Enlightenment softened the animus of European societies toward their Jews, it was deeply hostile to Judaism. "The notion that Judaism was a tenacious, as well as ancient, superstition, a device of priests to promote their own power, which, in some measure, still held modern minds in thrall, so thoroughly permeated Enlightenment thought that it may, without exaggeration, be described as one of its fundamental principles."[121] The personal anti-Semitism of an Erasmus or a Voltaire is less significant than the constitutive anti-Judaism of Enlightenment ideas that treated the religion and way of life of traditional Jews as ossified custom emblematic of the primitive and superstitious provincialism Enlightenment reason was designed to overcome.[122] Jews, most *philosophes* thought, composed a fanatical, ignorant sect. As a consequence, they refused to credit (as even medieval Christendom had) the communal autonomy and internal self-development of the Jews or permit them to define their own ontology and system of rationality outside the Enlightenment's universalist framework.

As Ernest Gellner has observed, the emerging societies of the modern West were "not only due to be more rational than the *ancien regime* . . . [they were] also destined to be more mobile, *open*. (Karl Popper's famous phrase, whatever important functions it also performs, contains an implicit justification of the abandonment of minority communities.) This being so, the new order absolutely needed a *shared* cultural idiom, rather than a multiplicity of in-group jargons. It was only natural that

[120] The discussion that follows draws on Birnbaum and Katznelson, "Emancipation and the Liberal Offer."

[121] Jonathan I. Israel, *European Jewry in the Age of Mercantilism, 1550–1750*, rev. ed. (Oxford: Clarendon Press, 1989), p. 232.

[122] By contrast, both Spinoza and Marx treated Judaism as a metaphor for liberalism. "Both Judaism and liberalism, they thought, are concerned only with men's actions, not with their opinions; both Judaism and liberalism, they thought, promote legalistic and materialistic recognition of individual self-interest." Joel Schwartz, "Liberalism and the Jewish Connection: A Study of Spinoza and the Young Marx," *Political Theory* 13 (February 1985): 58–59.

this idiom should be that of the majority group, especially if it *already* contained a powerful literature of Enlightenment."[123]

Politically emancipated European Jews discovered they faced a no-win situation. They found they neither could assimilate as individuals nor maintain a robust collective identity. When Jews in central and western Europe took advantage of the economic roles that opened to them with the decline of guilds, the importance of finance in periods of war, and the rapid increase in trade of various distances, Enlightenment ideas and values profoundly affected the hierarchies, institutions, and social integration of their communities. Life-styles liberalized. Rabbinic authority weakened. Religious observance, and respect for Jewish tradition, declined. "The prevailing characteristic of the western European Jewish mind from the second quarter of the [seventeenth] century onwards was one of increasing rejection of its own intellectual culture and tradition."[124] This collective erosion of the oligarchical and solidaristic structure of Jewish communities that had occupied well-defined locations in the medieval Christian world was accompanied now by individual exit options, the most extreme of which was conversion. Jews now possessed exit visas by virtue of their changed collective condition, but their access to entry tickets as liberal individuals hardly was assured.[125]

One of the paradoxes of the post-Enlightenment world and the liberal political offer it extended was that Jews were asked, in effect, to divest themselves of their particularities in the name of universal human values; but having done so, the price of their acceptance was an embrace of specific national cultures they found themselves within, frequently by chance. Yet from the perspective of these cultures, Jews were inauthentic partici-

---

[123] Ernest Gellner, *Culture, Identity, and Politics* (Cambridge: Cambridge University Press, 1987), p. 78.

[124] Israel, *European Jewry*, p. 257.

[125] Zygmunt Bauman, "Exit Visas and Entry Tickets: Paradoxes of Jewish Assimilation," *Telos* 77 (Fall 1988). For a nuanced discussion of the mutual engagement of Jews and Enlightenment values and opportunities, also see Hannah Arendt, *Rahel Vernhagen: The Life of a Jewish Woman* (New York: Harcourt Brace Jovanovich, 1974).

pants. The more they sought to assimilate, the more they appeared as a definable subgroup whose zest for inclusion
marked them as different. "Jews," Alan Ryan observes, "were
now not merely fellow nationals practicing a different religion
but unreliable semi-strangers in whatever nation they hap-
pened to inhabit." For "once nationality became the vital social
cement, the Jewish position was more than less awkward."[126] In
the past, Jews had been able to tradeoff humiliation and social
inferiority for long stretches of relatively unhindered communal existences. Now, community identification, resources, and
mobilization became a hindrance to incorporation into modernity. Further, even though Jews were granted the right to exit
the world of the ghetto as a group, their "entry tickets" required
them to come in as individuals, yet "in the eyes of the majority
which had emancipated them, they remained members of the
accursed emancipated minority. They continued to carry the
stigma of their membership for everyone to see. . . . Once
granted full citizenship rights, Jewishness became a badge of
shame. By Mendelssohn's advice, like the family dirty laundry,
it was something one wisely kept at home."[127] In sum, inside the
liberal order growing numbers of Jews found themselves suspended, as it were, in the no-person's land between the once
secure confinement of compact spatial communities in a hostile environment and the status of unanchored and terribly vulnerable liberal citizens. They gave up the implicit knowledge
that comes from the possession of a language and a culture
without gaining secure alternatives.

The provisional standing of Jews in putatively liberal political
orders became increasingly manifest especially in the big, cos-
mopolitan cities like Frankfurt, Berlin, Budapest, Vienna, and

---

[126] Alan Ryan, "Letting Them Live," *London Review of Books*, August 4, 1988, p. 6.

[127] Bauman, "Exit Visas," p. 51. Thus when Jews opted for such newly opened professions as medicine and law they did so as individuals; but the collective outcome was a
redefinition of these occupational niches as distinctively Jewish. Even Freud needed his
Jung to legitimate and extend the reach of psychoanalysis. Josef Hayim Yerushalmi,
Freud's Moses: Judaism Terminable and Interminable (New Haven: Yale University Press,
1991).

Warsaw to which large numbers of Jews migrated in search of incorporation. There, they discovered unparalleled opportunities and choices. By 1900, Budapest's Jews composed a quarter of the city's population (though only 5 percent of Hungary's) and half of its voters because of schooling and financial requirements for the franchise. In Vienna, where fewer than two hundred Jewish families had been tolerated before 1848, Jews grew to 10 percent of the population by the First World War, and they achieved a commanding presence in the arts, banking, and commerce. But in neither city did they reestablish a distinctively Jewish culture. Liberalism had seduced these urban Jews without providing the quid pro quo of the reciprocation of full admission. Yet, in full understanding that all the alternatives were worse, they remained the region's last liberals (as well as the last patriots of the Hapsburg dynasty) long after the desertion of the German Austrians; and, into the 1930s, the last social democrats.[128] Jews, Helmut Gruber ruely has observed, were betrayed, even reviled, by the various modern liberal, pan-German, socialist, and Communist political movements they had been pivotal in establishing.[129] In the crunch, even the friends of the Jews displayed a very limited sense of moral obligation, one characterized less by indifference than by ambivalence.[130]

---

[128] See Istvan Déak, "Fun City," *New York Review of Books*, March 16, 1989; Peter Pulzer, "A City of Blood," *London Review of Books*, November 9, 1989; and Michael Ignatieff, "The Rise and Fall of Vienna's Jews," *New York Review of Books*, June 19, 1989. After the inauguration of universal suffrage in Austro-Hungary in 1905, the anti-Semitic Christian Social party outpolled the socialists, and Austrian Social Democracy itself became a federation of national parties. For a discussion of Jews and the crisis of German liberalism, see James J. Sheean, "Different, Ignoble, and Alien," *Times Literary Supplement*, July 31, 1992.

[129] Helmut Gruber, "Red Vienna and the 'Jewish Question,'" *Leo Baeck Institute Yearbook* 38 (1993).

[130] For a provocative argument along these lines, see Tony Kushner, *The Holocaust and the Liberal Imagination: A Social and Cultural History* (Oxford: Blackwell, 1994). A small bit of anecdotal evidence. When William Shirer, the chronicler of Nazism, published his reflections on "midcentury," he observed that he had lived through "a time of unparalleled violence, revolution, war, bloodshed, tyranny, confusion, and strife. My own generation had known little else. It had lived from early youth entirely in an Age of Conflict, as the historians were beginning to call it. Even in the intervals between the

Based on his appreciation of the corrosive claims of the Enlightenment on the Jews, who at once became more (by inclusion) and less (by the price exacted for incorporation), Berlin
has been deeply empathetic toward those who claim rationalism and liberalism have made them victims by undercutting
the bases of their valued particularity. For this reason, he coun-
sels understanding of Counter-Enlightenment thinking he
scorns.[131] Like your own search for an engagement with the
Catholic Church, but unlike most other liberals, Berlin has
been prepared to take the plaints of antiliberal writers and traditions seriously.

His fascination with the enemies of Enlightenment reason is
double-edged. As his studies of de Maistre and Hamman show,
Berlin fears the potential of their violent, dogmatic, boldly irrational, romantic antimodernism, but he appreciates their realism and heterodoxy. Berlin writes that Maistre

> was an original thinker, swimming against the current of
> his time, determined to explode the most sacrosanct plati-
> tudes and pious formulas of his liberal contemporaries.
> They stressed the power of reason; he pointed out, per-
> haps too gleefully, the persistence and extent of irrational
> instinct, the power of faith, the force of blind tradition,
> the willful ignorance about their human material of the
> progressives—the idealistic social scientists, the bold po-
> litical and economic planners, the passionate believers
> in technocracy. . . . His realism takes violent, rabid, ob-

wars and the revolutions and the harrowing crises, one felt one was living in, as the
poets and the psychologists said, an Age of Anxiety, with the threat of a new war, a new
revolution, a new bomb, another aggression, another crisis frightening the frenzied
mind and exacerbating nerves already frayed." But his book of over three hundred
pages was silent about the catastrophe of Europe's Jews as it reviewed the history and
circumstances of France, Austria, Germany, Britain, and the United States. Not a word.
William Shirer, *Midcentury Journey: The Western World through Its Years of Conflict* (New
York: Farrar, Strauss and Young, 1952), p. 4.

[131] This vein is especially apparent in Isaiah Berlin, *The Magus of the North: J. G. Hamman and the Origins of Modern Irrationalism* (London: John Murray, 1993).

sessed, savagely limited forms, but it is realism neverthe-less.[132]

When Maistre's words became flesh in fascism they produced an "inestimable cost in human suffering," but, Berlin observes, they also "vindicated [his] depth and brilliance."[133] The abuse of reason fosters tyranny, Berlin shows, but he credits those who resist reason not only with a more powerful appreciation of the range of human propensities than most liberals wish to see but with an understanding that liberal reason has entailed huge sacrifices of cultural difference. For these reasons, he has auda-ciously grafted onto liberalism the entire range of pluralisms "of the Enlightenment's severest critics, the Vicos, the Herders and the Hammans."[134] In short, like Locke, Berlin knows we are neighbors in a storehouse of power and unreason; that in patrolling against extreme and pathological deployments of cultural assertion we must acquire a taste for realism, a re-flective appreciation for liberalism's limits, and regard for the sentiments of its enemies.

Berlin's project of a plural liberalism seeks a balanced com-mitment between the ideals of rationality and rights under-stood in an intrinsic and irreducible Kantian sense to apply universally irrespective of cultural or geographical variations and a more than grudging recognition of the communal, reli-gious, ethnic and national ties that are vital to the human im-pulses of belonging, recognition, and self-definition.[135] Berlin's considerable contribution is to insist that the positions repre-sented by Tamir and Judt are insufficient. The elaboration of systems of rights and principles of justice as tasks of abstract

[132] Isaiah Berlin, "Joseph de Maistre and the Origins of Fascism," in Berlin, *Crooked Timber*, pp. 166–67.

[133] Ibid., p. 174.

[134] Mark Lilla, "The Trouble with the Enlightenment," *London Review of Books*, Janu-ary 6, 1994, p. 12.

[135] For a critique of Marxism's philosophical anthropology for overlooking these motives and feelings, see G. A. Cohen, "Reconsidering Historical Materialism," *Nomos* 26 (1983).

rather than as practical reason gains power only when deployed inside the messiness of history; the focus on history, cultural difference, and group variety, in turn, prolapses into an abnegation of judgment if we confuse pluralism with relativism and insist that liberal matters of rights and justice merely express one among many equally valid life forms. There is no proper resolution of these matters, only a permanent tension, Berlin suggests. Clearly, from this perspective, a collaborative division of labor in ways of working is called for. While it makes no sense to insist that Tamir learn to be a historian of specific countries and cultures, or Judt a philosopher, it would be sensible to pressgang both to a project of mutual intelligibility wedded to a powerful liberal set of commitments.

VII

A cautionary tale. One of Kymlicka's symbolic choices unwittingly reveals the pitfalls inherent in the application of timeless, abstract theory to specific circumstances and reveals liberalism's threat to minority cultures under conditions of unequal power. The cover of *Multicultural Citizenship* is illustrated by the painting "The Peaceable Kingdom" by Edward Hicks, probably painted in 1834. Kymlicka explains:

> It illustrates the signing of a treaty in 1682 between a group of Quakers and three local Indian tribes, the Lenni Lenape, Susquehannock, and Shawnee, allowing for the establishment of a Quaker community in Pennsylvania. (The Quakers were one of the few groups to honour their treaty commitments.) Hicks, a devout Quaker, viewed this treaty as the beginning of the "peaceable kingdom" prophesied in Isaiah, in which love will replace hostility and competition both amongst humans and in the natural world (e.g., "the lion will lie down with the lamb"). I chose this painting because it portrays and celebrates a form of multiculturalism that we often ignore . . . the situation of indig-

enous peoples and other non-immigrant "national minorities" whose homeland has been incorporated into the boundaries of a larger state, through conquest, colonization, or federation.[136]

Actually there are fifty surviving versions of Hicks's painting of "A Peaceable Kingdom." What they depict in radiant, utopian terms is the treaty of friendship signed between the Lenni Lenape, the Delaware Indians, and Penn in 1683 beneath a large elm tree in the Indian village of Shakamaxon, soon located inside the city boundaries of Philadelphia. Certainly the fabulous quality of Hicks's paintings reflected Penn's desire to establish a relationship with the Indians based on harmony and regard.

In fact, the situation in Pennsylvania proved significantly more complicated than Kymlicka, or the emblematic painting he selected, allowed. To be sure, William Penn did attempt to found a European colony as a free home for the Society of Friends without harm to the Indians. Yet even this attempt could not escape the realities of America's house of power. For it was in Pennsylvania that an experiment in religious freedom—liberalism's most cherished aim—clashed with deeper forms of cultural contact. Kymlicka wished the case to illustrate liberalism's multicultural capacities, but what it teaches is the limits of good intentions in the face of vast asymmetries of power and the limits of political theory insufficiently attuned to history and social reality.

As it turned out, the Quaker colony produced an unmitigated disaster for the Lenni Lenape.[137] Not for a lack of cultural respect, however. Penn, who studied the tribe, thought them superior to Europeans in some respects; they were more hospitable, more deeply sagacious, more averse to war. He approached the tribe with an offer to settle with their "love and

---

[136] Kymlicka, *Multicultural Citizenship*, p. vii.

[137] This discussion draws on the brilliant chapter on "Cultural Relationship as 'Holy Experiment': The English in Pennsylvania," in Bitterli, *Cultures in Conflict*, pp. 109–32.

consent." Like Las Casas, Penn considered the Indians to be proto-Christians who belonged to the Christian community even before being baptized. When Penn concluded agreements with the Lenni Lenape, he took care to treat them as equal agents according to the English legal codes of the day and made sure to explain the implications of the agreements he signed with them.

Soon, however, this benign cultural contact proved to be a collision. As the numbers of immigrants searching for religious freedom outstripped Penn's original expectations, pressures grew on the Indians to cede more land by agreement. Some of the individuals with whom the Quakers made agreements lacked the authority of their clan to do so. More seriously, "the Indians, unacquainted with European notions of property and accustomed to frequent changes of residence, could never fully accept that these land transfer agreements were final."[138]

The Quakers, moreover, soon lost control of Pennsylvania to settlers from other denominations. After two decades of conflict, Penn conceded a new constitution for the state, the Charter of Privileges, "probably the most liberal to be found in any English possession across the Atlantic."[139] Land transfer agreements soon accelerated under the pressure for forced expulsions. Deception now marked their character. In the famous "Walking Purchase" of 1737, the Lenni Lenape agreed under duress to give up as much territory as a person could walk in a day and a half, assuming a distance of about thirty miles. Instead, the white settlers sent three trained runners who covered more than twice that ground. By 1754, the Lenni Lenape were allied with the French in the French and Indian War. Today, what remains of the tribe (some nine thousand people) live on reservations in Ontario and Oklahoma.

This was no happy multiculturalism. The outcome was inherent in the initial terms of contact and contract. The deal struck

[138] Ibid., p. 122.
[139] Ibid., p. 126.

under the elm tree was at odds with the Lenni Lenape's conception of property and their seminomadic style of life; and the commodities they were offered in exchange for their land made them ever more dependent on white civilization. Even under Penn's benign guardianship, the Indians were denied social integration or the chance to maintain their traditional way of life.

This sobering history reminds us that if we are to make sense of the relationship of liberalism and cultural pluralism, the defining issue must remain that of toleration; but not toleration considered abstractly inside assumptions of homogeneity in the manner of Mill, but within the world's actually existing storehouse of power and unreason characterized by a wide array of divisions between ethnic groups and categories based on status and ascriptive characteristics. In specific settings marked by such differences, where often there is little comity or common ground, who and what is to be tolerated, how might toleration be promoted and secured, and how should limits to toleration be defined, set, and enforced to reduce risks of harm and induce a fair peace?

Adapting Partha Chatterjee's approach to these issues in contemporary India, I would characterize a multicultural situation in settings of differential power as tolerant when it meets two conditions: first, that groups can secure recognition for "the right not to offer a reason for being different . . . provided it explains itself adequately in its own chosen forum. In other words, toleration here would be premised on autonomy and respect for persons, but it would be sensitive to the varying political salience of the institutional contexts in which reasons are debated";[140] second, that institutional and legal conditions exist for the protection of this right even, perhaps especially, in circumstances where vastly unequal distributions of power threaten to make a mockery of liberal procedures and protections no matter how genuine the goodwill of the dominant party. What

[140] Chatterjee, "Secularism and Toleration," p. 1774.

such an orientation achieves is the introduction and recognition of an irresolvable tension between what might be called an external and internal perspective into the heart of liberal theories of toleration. Ordinarily, liberal theorists treat the question of minority rights from the logical and normative perspective of their own doctrine, but the approach of Chatterjee simultaneously requires an internalist, actor-centered, perspective that leaves it to members of cultural groups, in effect, to participate in defining satisfactory conditions of toleration. Pushed hard, such a group-centered orientation based on claims not to be obliged to justify local norms and behavior challenges majoritarian norms and rejects the hegemony of prevailing definitions for the terms of public discourse as groups resist submission to efforts under the rubric of a state's sovereign capacity to impose singular conceptions of reason and citizenship.

Can such claims to stand aside without requiring justification be acknowledged, a skeptical liberal might ask, without lapsing into a relativism bereft of standards? Under what conditions can groups asserting the right not to offer reasons expect this prerogative to be respected by others? In confronting these issues, the conundrum for liberalism is exquisitely difficult. Its ability to find grounds to respect cultural diversity sits uneasily with the unitary rationalism of its philosophical anthroplogy of free and equal persons. Such a framework incorporating all of humankind is vital to the possibility of making judgments about permissible behavior on the assumption that humanity shares common traits of condition, morality, and reason; that is, "that there are certain moral propositions that are true for all people in all human societies, and therefore, people in one society have a legitimate right to declare that a particular political or social form in another culture is immoral."[141] Surely we cannot do entirely without universal standards of justice. Could slavery, for example, ever be admissible under the claim of not having to give reasons?

---

[141] Eli Sagan, "Cultural Diversity and Moral Relativism," ms., spring 1993.

I think the metaphor of neighborliness introduced into discussions of toleration by Susan Mendus helps provide a useful
orienting point of departure in confronting such questions.
Clearly, under conditions of cultural diversity and unequal
power, communitarian conceptualizations of society's units as
friends who share assumptions and ways of life are not just inapt
but potentially coercive; yet the individualism characteristic of
the liberalism of John Stuart Mill likewise either is largely beside the point or provides a justification for cultural contraction
and group hegemony. The alternative Mendus proposes is that
we learn to think about groups as transacting neighbors who
inhabit partially common and partially separate spaces. Neighborliness implies more by way of mutual obligation and civility
than relations between individuals strategically pursuing preferences and interests, but it requires far less conformity than is
implied by the language of community. Ordinarily, neighbors
do not owe each other reasons, but this pattern of abnegation
is far from absolute. Customarily, neighbors police themselves
and are expected to sanction those in their ken who act in
ways that threaten the breakdown of contingent consent. Yet
when we hear screams emanating from the home of a neighbor
or witness the mugging of one neighbor by another, we are
obliged to call the police.[142] In such circumstances, liberal doctrine insists that punishment not be collective, directed against
the group from which the offending persons come.[143]

At issue, it seems to me, is the daunting question of how
neighborly relations of toleration are to be defined and institutionalized in ways broadly consistent with both liberal ideas and
the internalist perspectives of cultural groups in specific historical settings. Put differently, at issue is how we might fill
the space located between liberalism's rather undemanding

[142] Mendus, "Strangers and Brothers."

[143] There is a practical dimension to this restriction. As Fearon and Laitin argue,
such collective forms of social control tend to produce spiraling intergroup violence.
James D. Fearon and David D. Laitin, "Explaining Interethnic Cooperation," paper
presented at the Annual Meeting of the American Political Science Association, August
31–September 3, 1995.

insistence on an individual's right to exit from a given group or culture and its stringent stipulation that groups must self-govern by liberal standards.

Based on the assumption that norms are not free floating but are shaped by institutions, what I think we are after is the elaboration of institutional arrangements and settings, which necessarily will vary from place to place, likely to elicit neighborly relations on the basis of what Margaret Levi calls contingent consent (that is, consent less situational than that implied when actors are treated as economistic rational maximizers pursuing instrumental self-interests but less uniform, fixed, and definite than when actors belong to single cultures characterized by unselfish shared norms).[144] In circumstances of cultural pluralism, institutions matter because they can shape and cultivate norms of neighborliness, adjudicate conflicts in particular contexts and situations, and induce actors to share standards for self-governance and for their involvement in the public realm. Rather than spend our time in the quest to parse and refine liberal doctrine, we should invest more creativity aimed at developing institutional rules, sites, and arrangements to induce contingent consent and provide locations for the play of a conflictual but peaceful politics of identity and difference.

To do so means taking institutional and political pluralism seriously in conjunction with the pluralism of values and cultures. The very idea of pluralism, to which you, Adam, have been so attracted, in fact has a complex lineage in the American pragmatist tradition which, if attended, suggests just this joining of elements. In the late nineteenth century, William James and his American pragmatist circle invented pluralism (the term itself was first codifed by John Dewey in a 1901 dic-

[144] Margaret Levi, "Are There Limits to Rationality?" *Archives Europeenes de Sociologie* 32, 1 (1991). She argues here that social norms are not usefully contrasted with instrumental rationality or with self-interest; instead, she sees rationality as a methodological presupposition into which norms enter as goals and conditions. I have also profited from the discussion of contingent consent in Bo Rothstein, "Just Institutions Matter: The Moral Logic of the Universal Welfare State," ms., 1992.

tionary of philosophy and psychology) as an approach to deal
with the period's massive immigration of potential strangers
and as an element for the elaboration of a public philosophy
appropriate to the new social structures of industrial capitalism.[145] Informed by this legacy, Harold Laski and other thinkers
in early twentieth-century England, including G.D.H. Cole and
John Neville Figgis, developed a model of political organization
focused on the self-organization of civil society that transcended both a liberalism of atomic individualism and an over-
reliance on the state (thus anticipating key themes in the East
European opposition movements).[146] In the United States,
Arthur Bentley, who also was influenced by James, published
his *Process of Government* in 1908 (a landmark in American political science that later helped spawn the midcentury focus
on the pluralism of interest groups), arguing that interest
groups are specialized collectivities at the center of political life
that share basic features with other, nonpolitical, examples of
social interaction and link civil society to the formal institutions of government.[147] Soon thereafter, Horace Kallen, perhaps the first to use the term cultural pluralism, argued that
liberalism must do more than merely tolerate diversity but
must actively learn to pursue it, at least to the point of inducing

[145] I rely here on Olivier Zunz, "The Genesis of American Pluralism," *The Tocqueville Review* 9 (Winter 1987/88). For a reminder that pluralism and liberalism do not necessarily make automatic partners, see George Crowder, "Pluralism and Liberalism," *Politi-
cal Studies* 42 (June 1994). The text is followed by a reply by Isaiah Berlin and Bernard
Williams.

[146] For relevant writings and discussions, see John Neville Figgis, *Churches in the Modern State* (London: Longmans, Green, 1913); Paul Q. Hirst, ed., *The Pluralist Theory of the
State: Selected Writings of G.D.H. Cole, J. N. Figgis, and H. J. Laski* (London: Routledge,
1989); Henry David Magid, *English Political Pluralism: The Problem of Freedom and Organization* (New York: Columbia University Press, 1941); Bernard Zylstra, *From Pluralism to
Collectivism: The Development of Harold Laski's Political Thought* (Assen, The Netherlands:
Van Gorcum and Company, 1968); and David Nicholls, *Three Varieties of Pluralism* (London: Macmillan, 1974).

[147] Arthur F. Bentley, *The Process of Government* (Chicago: University of Chicago Press,
1908). Bentley's ideas were codified, elaborated, and placed at the center of the disci-
pline by David B. Truman, *The Governmental Process: Political Interests and Public Opinion*
(New York: Alfred A. Knopf, 1951).

cultural groups to maintain a thick voluntary institutional life as a counterweight to the society's powerful tendencies toward assimilation.[148]

These three strands in post-Jamesean pluralism (civil society, interest group, and cultural pluralism) potentially entwine to form a supple braid connecting collectivities of various kinds in civil society to the state. When these three pluralisms are taken together, they help identify a zone akin to that of Locke's public privacy by furnishing institutional vehicles for group particularity to enter the public arena as voluntary interest groups. In this manner, groups can become political neighbors who are not expected to repress their competing cultural or ethical preferences or contain them wholly in the zone of the private. In turn, the subsumption of nationality, religion, and ethnicity into the interest group form entails the thinning out of cultural intensity required for the play of liberal democracy in which there can be no permanent or ultimate winners.

It is the promise as much as the practice of this multidimensional pluralism that you find so appealing in what you call the spacious homeland of the United States. You rightly find admirable the coexistence of a liberal view of citizenship with the recognition that it is legitimate for members of groups to decide how they wish to manage their identities described by such hyphenated terms as Polish-American or Jewish-American. "An ethnic American," Michael Walzer notes, "is someone who can, in principle, live his spiritual life as he chooses, on either side of the hyphen. In this sense, American citizenship is indeed anonymous, for it doesn't require a full commitment to American (or to any other) nationality."[149] You ruefully remarked in your New School lecture that "I believe there will never be a European nation of the kind of you have in America."

You understood that the attractive joining of cultural and

---

[148] Horace Kallen, *Culture and Democracy in the United States* (New York: Boni & Liveright, 1924).

[149] Michael Walzer, "What Does It Mean to Be an American?" *Social Research* 57 (Fall 1990): 611.

political pluralism is premised on complex conditions hard to replicate elsewhere; but it is worth remembering that the pluralist vision is a limited one here as well. American history is replete with sagas of ethnic repression and revival and with recurring quests for loyalty and homogeneity. Further, because they lack any official or compulsory character, cultural groups in America have a precarious existence, always fighting and frequently failing to hold off the general culture's powerful lures of assimilation. But most important, American pluralism and its English cousin have lacked an appreciation for differential power. The largest "minority" in the United States may be designated as African-American, an ethnic and cultural marker like those of other hyphenated groups. But their place in American history and society has been defined far more by racialized coercion than by consent. Indeed, American citizenship has been marked by vastly different patterns of incorporation and group resources even for the mass of the nonblack population, the descendants of voluntary immigrants.[150]

For this reason I long have been attracted to yet another variety of pluralism that treats the segmentation of "plural society" into two or more ethnic, cultural, or racial groups in terms of differential distributions of money and wealth, status, and political power. Written mainly by anthropologists working in postcolonial Third World countries, the plural society tradition has been attuned to liberalism's shortcomings and the play of difference under conditions of structured inequality. Writing about places composed of two or more cultural units with distinctive institutions, these scholars have focused on settings where order and justice depend far more on the practices of common political institutions and the terms of linkage each group secures to them than on shared values and consensual commitments. Plural societies, they have understood, are not all or nothing propositions, but their conditions vary according

[150] For a more general discussion along these lines stressing class differentials in experiences of citizenship, see M. L. Harrison, "Citizenship, Consumption and Rights: A Comment on B. S. Turner's Theory of Citizenship," *Sociology* 25 (May 1991).

to the institutional relations groups forge with each other and with the polity they share in common. What matters are the *terms* of group political participation and incorporation, whether they are differential or equivalent, the type of justice they embody, and the kind of consent they produce.[151]

The overlapping issues of ethnic, national, racial, linguistic, and cultural difference too often are treated as if they are all essentially the same, but from an institutionalist and pluralist perspective it is important to sort out different types of situations and the range of institutional and legal responses appropriate to each. Currently, there appear to be four types of especially explosive situations:[152] hierarchies where social class coincides with ethnic or racial membership and where ruling minorities exercise political and military power over subjected majorities; target minorities that stand in the way of states, especially new states, being able to achieve the appearance of being a "nation" with internal and external legitimacy, hence they invest heavily in the production of artifacts of identity as official languages and official histories; regionally concentrated minorities usually distinguishable on a linguistic basis who either once were part of some different state or had a history of autonomy; and culturally interspersed populations who, under normal conditions, tend to live in reasonable multicultural harmony but, once tensions arise, see themselves as surrounded by one another and hence tend to react violently in what they perceive as self-defense.

In each of these settings, institutions matter at least as much as ideology and ideas. As bundles of intersubjective, connected, and persistent norms, and as formal rules and organizations, institutions shape human interaction, limit and define the scope of choice, and confer social and political identities out of

[151] I discuss this literature in Ira Katznelson, "Comparative Studies of Race and Ethnicity: Plural Analysis and Beyond," *Comparative Politics* 5 (October 1972).

[152] I draw here on Ira Katznelson and Aristide Zolberg, "Nationality and Diversity," remarks presented at the Democracy Seminar Network meeting, Stupava, Bratislava, May 1994.

the welter of possibilities through language, incentives, and sanctions. Institutions shape the capabilities and preferences of actors to which they confer a social quality; and they define a hierarchy of issues from those that are taken for granted as background conditions, those that persist unadjudicated, and those that are the legitimate subjects of conflict and political assertion. Liberalism's successes thus depend not only on the ways it takes cultural conflict seriously but on the details of its institutional topology.

VIII

But what of the question of Europe and Eurocentrism? Is a liberal orientation to pluralism hopelessly mired in the history of colonial domination and incapable of grappling with the post-colonial situation?

In the here and now, Isaiah Berlin reminds us, we must reckon not only with the "brutal and destructive side of modern nationalism . . . in a world torn by its excesses," but also with the way passionate particularities express "the inflamed desire of the insufficiently regarded to count for something among the cultures of the world. . . . It must be recognised for what it is—a worldwide response to a profound and natural need on the part of newly liberated slaves—'the decolonised'—a phenomenon unpredicted in the Europe centered society of the nineteenth century."[153]

At a time when increasingly robust exchanges of information, goods, and people have become the norm even for the most isolated regions of the globe, all the world again have become Jews, but this time the emancipated ones of postemancipation Europe. Freed from the shackles of their political disabilities, they can choose among cultural loyalty, exit, or voice.[154] Whichever they select, their cultures no longer can

---

[153] Berlin, *Crooked Timber*, p. 261.

[154] Albert Hirschman, *Exit, Voice and Loyalty* (Cambridge: Harvard University Press, 1970).

remain the same, as if they are isolated atolls. The range of options is vastly greater than it ever has been; perhaps also the dangers both of xenophilia and xenophobia. But there is no turning back to a simpler world of cultural hierarchies and cultural essentialism.

Ironically, the decolonized, post-Communist (and postapartheid) world more than ever is a European, and Europeanized, one. In the conclusion to his *Wretched of the Earth*, Frantz Fanon implored, "Let us decide not to imitate Europe; let us combine our muscles and our brains in a new direction. . . . Let us not pay tribute to Europe by creating States, institutions, and societies which draw their inspiration from her."[155] The problem with this sentiment is its utopianism and misapprehension. Nowhere did, or could, the anticolonial project divorce itself entirely from Europe, its ideas, and forms (where it has tried, as in Cambodia, only catastrophe has followed). Moreover, as Todorov has put it, "Europe"

> is not a simple thing; it has practiced universalism and relativism, humanism and nationalism, dialogue and war, tolerance and violence. In choosing one of the terms of these alternatives over the other, one is not choosing the Third World over Europe, but one European tradition over another. . . . Once again, colonialism and its ideology win a dark victory over their adversaries, since the latter have decided to worship the same demons as the former. . . . The racist, nationalist, or relativist arguments that appear throughout anticolonial discourse do not make decolonization any less necessary, any more than Christian and humanist arguments justified the colonial cause.[156]

Decolonization itself was marked from the start by "Europe" because the nationalist leadership was drawn virtually everywhere from a tiny proto-elite with educational access to the col-

[155] Frantz Fanon, *The Wretched of the Earth* (New York: Grove Press, 1968), pp. 313, 315.
[156] Todorov, *The Morals of History*, p. 58.

onizer's world. Given leave to exit their traditional milieu, they were not granted entry for full membership in British, Dutch, or French society; but nor were they wholly outside of it in spite of recurring efforts by the colonizers to draw the lines between us and them very sharply.

Thus, in 1878, the Vernacular Press Act drew a distinction between the English-language and native press in India in an effort to stamp out sedition. More generally, this was part of a larger attempt, in the manner of John Stuart Mill, under Liberal party auspices to demarcate more clearly a proper civil society of citizens from the colonized as subjects. When Indian nationalists recoiled from this exclusion, their ultimately successful struggles came to be marked by the categories and ideas of the colonial power. If the British thought the Indians incapable of acquiring the values of the Enlightenment, the nationalists differed less with these values than with their noninclusion. They tended to embrace the Enlightenment's endowments. Yet they could not simply be modern or liberal in general. Rather, in what became quite a typical pattern, nationalist elites forged particular links with local and traditional cultures in order to mobilize a popular base; but in so doing, they also transformed and Europeanized it by incorporating the masses into Western categories and structures.[157]

In Indonesia, for example, May 20 is marked each year as the Day of National Awakening to commemorate the founding in 1908 of Budi Utomo, a nationalist organization created by Javanese in their late teens who were studying at the Western-type medical school in Batavia, the coastal colonial capital of the Netherlands Indies. Budi Utomo's leader, an East Javanese

[157] I draw here on Chatterjee, *Nationalist Thought and the Colonial World*; and Partha Chatterjee, *The Nation and Its Fragments* (Princeton: Princeton University Press, 1993). He stresses the centrality of race as a marker between those eligible and those outside civil society. For a discussion of whether and how gender inequalities were essential to imperial authority and colonial racism, see Ann Stoler, "Making Empire Respectable: The Politics of Race and Sexual Morality in 20th-Century Colonial Cultures," *American Ethnologist* 16 (November 1989); and Stoler, "Sexual Affronts and Racial Frontiers: European Identities and the Cultural Politics of Exclusion in Colonial Southeast Asia," *Comparative Studies in Society and History* (July 1992).

named Soetomo, late in life wrote *Kenang-Kenangan* (Memories), an autobiography that treats the author's separation and
connection with his ancestry. It underscores the nationalist
elite's inventive project of cultural reclamation in spite of their
inability to return to the thick enclosure of Javanese culture.
There was no turning back; nor was there a rupture between
past and present. Instead, Soetomo attempted to construct a
new kind of tradition: "a way of making connections in separation." His solution lay in forging of a new identity: not Javanese
(or Dutch) but Indonesian. Soetomo was challenged, Benedict
Anderson has written, "to proceed into the colonial Western
world without imitation; at a deeper level, how to imitate one's
forbears without imitating them, but not to abandon Javanese
tradition when one no longer lived imbedded in it."[158] This I
believe to be the basis of any meaningful cultural and group
pluralism under current conditions.

Such combinations of local cultures and the full range European values, ideologies, and institutional forms today define
the globe's diversity. Though a particularly privileged example
of this imbrication, the story Kwame Anthony Appiah tells of his
father's burial in Ghana is exemplary of both the mutual relations and tensions that define the plural identities we must
learn to value yet bring under control. Professor Appiah, a philosopher who teaches Afro-American studies at Harvard, was
born in Kumasi to a West Country English mother and a Pan-
Africanist, Ghanaian nationalist, Methodist, British-trained bar-
rister father, the brother of the Asante king. Writing about his
father's funeral, he notes that the elder Appiah had managed
these multiple identities; but in death, their incommensurable
claims about how his father should be celebrated and buried
demanded adjudication. The choices were not abstract or re-
mote, but local and particular, distinguishing Asante from
modern Ghana and both from English legacies:

---

[158] Benedict R. O'G. Anderson, *Language and Power: Exploring Political Cultures in
Indonesia* (Ithaca: Cornell University Press, 1990), pp. 253, 267.

Throughout the service, lawyers in their court robes stood guard at the head and the foot of the coffin, taking five-minute turns to honor their colleague. If I turned to my left and scanned to the right, I could see the *abusua*, first; then the royal party; then the priests of all the various denominations; then, behind the head of the chairman of the PNDC on the wall, the plaque in memory of my father's father, who had also served this church. Further to the right were the serried ranks of the legal profession in their robes. On my immediate left was my uncle T.D.; behind me my sisters, my Nigerian in-laws and friends, my friends from America. And to my right, somber and dignified in her black scarf, was my mother. All the identities my father cared for were embodied about us: lawyer, Asante man, Ghanaian, African, internationalist; statesman and churchman; family man, father, and head of his *abusua*; friend; husband. Only something so particular as a single life—as my father's life, encapsulated in the complex pattern of social and personal relations around his coffin—could capture the multiplicity of our lives in a postcolonial world.[159]

Because our world is postcolonial and trans-European, liberalism no longer possesses the singular authority that once drew on the distinction between "Europe" and the rest of the globe. Nor, in turn, can the remainder of the world escape from Europe or from the liberal political ideology it so assertively has sought to deploy, especially after 1989. But as the endless travails of Sarajevo or votes for Le Pen also signify, neither can Europe elude the snares of fierce and defensive particularity.

What Berlin understands, as I believe you have, is that under current conditions choices that once seemed clear are both despicable and irrelevant. The question of "Europe" and opposition to it has been altered in form and opportunity. Liberty,

---

[159] Kwame Anthony Appiah, *In My Father's House: Africa in the Philosophy of Culture* (New York: Oxford University Press, 1992), pp. 192, 191.

Mill and other liberals of his time believed, is the ethical product of an advancing, superior European civilization. This remains an important strand of cultural and political discourse in
the West. Alternatively, critics of liberalism's beliefs and practices often embrace a radical relativism: "values count only in
and for the context in which they were born; Western values are
bad because they are Western (all pretense to universality is a
bluff)."[160] These are dreadful alternatives.

Like Locke, Berlin teaches two critical lessons. First, the varieties of tribal identities and self-conceptions that order and
confer meaning on people's lives, for which they sometimes are
prepared to murder or are willing to die, are constructs beyond
reason. They are neither premodern atavistic survivals nor commitments with a given, fixed character. They cannot be wished
or coerced out of existence. Nor should they, for they are the
stuff of beauty and nobility as well as danger. Second, the management of identities to increase their ability to flourish while
diminishing their menace requires the prudent application of
reasonable doctrines and institutions on a case-by-case basis
geared to particular circumstances.

The key questions confronting us in grasping and managing
differences concern not whether but which Europe to favor:
Europa Christiana, colonial Europe, liberal Europe, Nazi Europe, nationalist Europe, integrated Europe? That of the
Herder who could describe other cultures without ethnocen-
tricity or of the Herder who rejected the unity of the human
race? The Europe of extraordinary cruelty or the Europe with
"the capacity to step outside its exclusivity, to question itself, to
see itself through the eyes of others"?[161] Fanon, not atypically,
utterly renounced the West; "When the native hears a speech
about Western culture, he pulls out his knife—or at least makes
sure it is within reach."[162] But in so doing, his Afrocentricity
mocked the worst aspects of Eurocentricity: its exclusiveness,

---

[160] Todorov, *The Morals of History*, p. 58.
[161] Kolakowski, *Modernity on Endless Trial*, p. 18.
[162] Fanon, *Wretched of the Earth*, p. 43.

essentialism, racism, and search for a common and singular civilizational core.[163]

In any event, there is no escape from mutual constitution. The processes that once defined early modern Europe—growing institutional and cultural similarity; the differentiation of the state, economy, and civil society; the breakup of enclosed, holistic, monopolistic systems of belief (whether religious or secular or a mix of both); the creation of knowledge elites; and increasingly extensive and volatile patterns of cultural contact under conditions of unequal power—now are defining features for the entire globe.[164]

Liberalism first was created in such circumstances as a set of regulative ideas with which to protect heterogeneity and cope with its perils. If it cannot learn to do so today under conditions more egalitarian but more difficult, the lions will devour the lambs.

Yours,

I K

---

[163] For a discussion, see Kwame Anthony Appiah, "Europe Upside Down: Fallacies of the New Afrocentrism," *Times Literary Supplement,* February 23, 1993. "The proper response to Eurocentrism," he writes, "is surely not a reactive Afrocentrism, but a new understanding that humanizes all of us by learning to think beyond race" (p. 25).

[164] It is important not to overstate current trends. The world, after all, was "genuinely global" a century ago after the invention of the telegraph and long-distance transportation integrated North America, Europe, and its overseas colonies. Nonetheless, the accelerated pace of communications, economic interdependence, and population movements have created conditions for a qualitative change. Eric Hobsbawm, *The Age of Empire, 1875–1914* (New York: Pantheon, 1987), pp. 13–15. There is a thoughtful discussion in Sidney Tarrow, "Fishnets, Internets and Catnets: Globalization and Social Movements," paper prepared for the Conference on Structure, Identity, and Power, Amsterdam, June 1995.

INDEX

ABOUT THE AUTHOR

IRA KATZNELSON is Ruggles Professor of Political Science and History at Columbia University. He is the author of *City Trenches: Urban Politics and the Patterning of Class in the United States.* With Mark Kesselman, he is the coauthor of *The Politics of Power: A Critical Introduction to American Government,* and, with Margaret Weir, *Schooling for All: Class, Race, and the Decline of the Democratic Ideal.* He and Aristide R. Zolberg are the coeditors of *Working-Class Formation: Nineteenth-Century Patterns in Western Europe and the United States* (Princeton), and with Pierre Birnbaum, he is the coeditor of *Paths of Emancipation: Jews, States, and Citizenship.*